Now is not the time for flowers

STACEY HEALE

Now is not the time for flowers

**What No One Tells You About Life,
Love and Loss**

BLINK

bringing you closer

First published in the UK in 2025 by Blink Publishing
An imprint of Bonnier Books UK
5th Floor, HYLO, 103–105 Bunhill Row,
London, EC1Y 8LZ

Owned by Bonnier Books
Sveavägen 56, Stockholm, Sweden

Hardback – 9781785120251
Paperback – 9781785120299
Ebook – 9781785120275
Audiobook – 9781785120282

A CIP catalogue of this book is available from the British Library.

Designed by Envy Design Ltd
Printed and bound in Great Britain by Clays Ltd, Elcograf S.p.A

1 3 5 7 9 10 8 6 4 2

MIX
Paper | Supporting
responsible forestry
FSC® C018072

www.bonnierbooks.co.uk

*To Greg – for showing me what brave
creativity looks like.*

*For Dalí and Bay – to show you bravery, creativity,
messiness and love all look very similar.*

Contents

Author's Note

Writing about your own life is a strange thing. To distil hurricanes down to a mere breeze can feel disingenuous; how can we ever encapsulate the entirety of huge moments? Ultimately we can't, but it's important we try. It's why we need the writers, poets, artists, content creators and actors to create spaces in which we can discuss the complicated business of being human. We are a species of storytellers, an act used not just to entertain but to reassure us that we are not alone; that we have between us far more in common than which divides us.

I am only too aware of the difficulties in writing about the dead. I may as well have booby-trapped the path myself with snakes and grenades. The snapshots I offer here are only that – images taken through my particular lens. Each are my own thoughts, memories, opinions and experiences from this moment in time. If I were to write about the same topics in ten years, I'm sure this would be a very different book.

These words are a flare from my rowboat out on the rocky seas. Their sender is not looking for rescue, but only to add some light in a dark sky. I hope you can see the lights if you're lost out at sea too.

Prologue:
Soulmates Are Bullshit

'Soulmates are bullshit.'

That's my opening gambit to tonight's late-night conversation. These conversations run like clockwork; you could set an alarm by their timing. The day is over, Greg and I are in bed. I've quickly glanced at a book only to realise I'm too tired to take anything in, so I turn my light off while Greg settles into a weighty tome on the life of da Vinci or the philosophy of Kierkegaard for a few hours. This is the point in the day where lightbulbs come on in my head and life begins to make sense. However, this is when Greg is done with all communication and wants to lose himself in words. I want Big Chats in bed; he wants to forget the world exists and read. Fifteen years together has not led me to accept this, a fact Greg finds bewildering. It's a shame he chooses to read heavyweight authors when he has his own bright spark philosopher who springs to life every night lying right beside him. He hasn't commented on my bold statement, so I repeat it, a bit louder for impact.

'SOULMATES ARE BULLSHIT.'

Greg sighs, immediately worn out by our differing circadian rhythms. He bites, definitely not something he always does.

'And why do you think that?' he says, keeping his eyes firmly on the book. This is all I need to begin a quickly improvised lecture on my big thoughts for the night. Here we go.

'Soulmates feel like a trap, like a cult we are brainwashed into as children, especially girls. The idea that there is One Special Person for you that is your destiny waiting to be fulfilled is an insidious way to train us into a small life. There are so many obvious problems with it as an idea. What are the chances in a world of nearly eight billion, at this particular point in time, of your particular sexuality and age range? If you believe in this outsider maths, you must believe that everything is destined and preordained for you, and to think you have no agency over your life and decisions is just terrifying.'

Silence. I'm not deterred, I know how to play the long game.

'Also, at what point are you meant to decide *who* your soulmate is? Surely it would need to be on your dying day, so you've experienced every relationship you're ever going to have. If I think back to my first boyfriend, when I was sixteen, I absolutely believed he was my soulmate because I was feeling romantic love for the first time, and it was overwhelming. Only time, experience and heartbreak lead you to think this may have been a bit hasty and naïve so you shouldn't have said to him that you would give up going to

2

study at London College of Fashion, your long-held dream, just because he wanted you to stay in your hometown so he could work for his dad's business, selling office furniture.'

More silence. This might be because I am yet to take a breath.

'Also, what does this mean for every other relationship you have? I absolutely believed in the love between me and my boyfriend in my early twenties. We didn't work out, but it was a great relationship that I still draw on for examples of how to love. You were with your first girlfriend for eleven years. Do those relationships lose their worth because they didn't lead to marriage or children? Is your soulmate just the relationship you have for the longest or that you happen to be in when you die?'

'I don't know.'

I ignore the passive tone that probably indicates that Greg is actually still reading and plough on.

'I'm not sure if anyone gets married or has children thinking they intend to break up, but if half of all marriages do end, is that their quota of soulmates gone? They may have believed they were with their soulmate but then their husband runs off with someone from work – what does *that* mean to the idea?'

Greg sighs again. 'This is just so many questions, so late at night.'

I've broken him down, possibly by force instead of general interest, but I'm in.

'People *should* question this.' I continue: 'I think the whole thing is totally unrealistic. I can see why people would want to buy into it, the whole soulmates marketing team has you believe that all hard work and compromise will be irrelevant because, one day, you will find someone for whom you will have to do nothing and will get endless, unconditional love in return. It's marketed as the ultimate romantic gesture but it's so limiting and controlling. It's just like in *Dawson's Creek*, when Dawson kept Joey on an emotional leash by constantly saying, "But you're my soulmate." That was marketed at teenagers, and I absolutely fell for it. I never want our girls to believe that they need to have only one all-singing, all-dancing, destined-by-a-deity relationship instead of being open to love and the way life ebbs and flows.'

Greg puts his book down – the holy grail of these late-night conversations – and is now obviously thinking about the topic. I'm on a roll so I don't give him a chance to verbalise any response.

'Oh yeah, and what if your soulmate is DEAD?' I raise my voice for effect. 'They've been killed in a freak accident, so you never meet them. Or what if the person you believe is your soulmate dies when you're with them? Do you just have to accept that you've had your go at happiness and get on with being alone till you die and accept there is no more love out in the world for you?'

Greg takes the opportunity to speak in the tiny pause I take for breath. 'So, you don't believe in soulmates at all?' he asks.

'I absolutely do believe in soulmates. I know that I have deep meaningful connections with you, with our children, with friends, my family and our dog, but in terms of romantic soulmates, I believe there are many, many people in the world you can fall in love with and have a happy life. Anything else feels too much like the film *Sliding Doors* for me; you want to move to Spain but no, you can't, because what if your soulmate has been planted in your hometown and you miss them by moving away? I think a much more romantic dialogue is to keep choosing that person every day, on every good, bad and boring day, without a golden ribbon tied around your wrists keeping you together by some kind of magic.' I pause because I'm now aware I don't even know what Greg believes and this conversation could be a terrible decision. 'So . . . what do you think?'

'No, I don't believe in soulmates,' Greg says. 'I believe we choose people to love every day and we carry on choosing that person, I suppose, until we don't or we die. Or they die. I imagine life is like a *Choose Your Own Adventure* book from the eighties – you get loads of different stories to try out; it's just when you choose one, it means that you *don't* choose others. I suppose if someone dies then you haven't chosen to end the story; it's been ended for you.' A pause. 'What would you want me to do if you died? Would you want me to be with someone else?'

'OF COURSE,' I almost shout. 'Please do take this as unwavering conformation that I want you to be with someone else if I died, and the sooner the better. I wouldn't want you moping around, thinking to yourself, Oh, Stace has just died, I must respect her legacy. Absolutely not, just get on with it. Bring a girlfriend to the funeral if you want. I have no problem with that now and nor will I have when I'm dead and zipping around the universe.'

'Wow, so romantic!' Greg smiles to himself in the soft light. 'Good to know I have your approval.'

I'm silently congratulating myself on initiating such a good topic, one Greg cannot turn down as he's now fully geared up for a Big Chat.

'I know exactly what would happen if I died,' he continues. 'You would be straight in with Doctor Max, living the high life and taking his kids on holiday to the Maldives with his hefty doctor's pay packet.'

Doctor Max is the fictional character we created to joke about men that I might leave Greg for. The character was formulated during a pregnancy doctor's appointment where I spotted an attractive, dark-haired GP in the waiting room and mentioned to Greg, with a wink, that I hoped he was who I was seeing. He reminded me I was waiting to be seen for severe haemorrhoids and would I really want such a sexy doctor poking around between my legs? A point well made and, thankfully, it was a young female nurse who inspected my rectum being pushed out by a large baby but so began the legend of Dr Max.

'Absolutely. I will need a strong shoulder to cry on and a large credit card to support my widow drinking and shopping habits. He will need to deal with the fact that I still love my dead husband though. That might be weird for him.'

'I'm sure he will be mature enough to cope with it. I think you'll have a very happy life together; just maybe wait till after the funeral . . . it might be awkward with my family.'

'Fine, fine, just so you know, though, you don't have to wait. If The French Artist slinks along into your life, please snap her up immediately. As long as she's nice to the girls. Actually, it's none of my business. I'll be long gone, do what you like.' The French Artist is Greg's equivalent of Dr Max, who we joke about him leaving me for. She is very chic, has an apartment in Paris where she sleeps all night and paints all day. Her name is probably Persephone.

Greg has given me as much as he can for the night and is

picking up his book again to signal that the conversation is over and official reading time has begun again.

'That's good to know,' he says. 'This won't be happening for a long time so I'm sure we have time to talk about it more – when it's not late at night and I want to read and not delve into the workings of all human relationships. Goodnight. I love you.'

'Of course we have time. All the time in the world. Sweet dreams. I really do love you, my non soulmate.'

* * *

Just as fictional as Dr Max and The French Artist was the idea that any of this would come to pass. Yet, just three days later, Greg became a writhing silhouette in the dark of our bedroom. There was no late-night tussle of a conversation; just pain and paramedics in the space where we had talked. They feel around his abdomen, a volcano of agony, and he is taken away, away from the safety of our bed and us. Three days later, the world swings wildly on its axis and the consistency of air changes to honey.

Three days later, Greg is told he will die and we will have to put our soulmate theory to the test.

Introduction:
We Don't Know What
We Don't Know

'What would happen if one woman told the truth about her life? The world would split open.'
MURIEL RUKEYSER

Summer 1996

On a bright April lunchbreak in our last year at school, me and my best friends, Beth and Anna, are skipping our usual routine of pasties and chocolate bars bought from the local shop to eat at Beth's house. We should be on prefect duty, guarding the main entrance for stray kids wanting to eat lunch in the corridors instead of outside on the designated benches. As Head Girl, I chose this particular area for us because it's easily the best spot in the school: a radiator for the winter months, an unrestricted view of the playground to spark juicy gossip topics and a huge ledge to dramatically lean on while we moan about how we hate school and can't wait for college because, now we are sixteen, this is all just so *childish*.

This new adult feeling, mixed with the authority of the

9

Head Girl badge on my tie, means I believe I can do whatever I want now. I don't think I'm a great fit for the job of Head Girl and it was obvious from the gasps and whispers when it was announced that many people, mostly teachers, felt the same. When walking to the front of the hall in front of the whole school to accept my position, I silently clocked the multiple eyes looking me up and down with a mixture of confusion and horror. Their new model pupil wears no proper uniform to speak of – maybe a small nod to the school colours of black and white but all items are heavily embroidered and adorned with badges of the Cure and Joy Division, accessorised with bright cherry-red hair and matching Dr Martens decorated with painted daisies and tie-dye laces threaded with multi-coloured beads. My nails are painted black and I have three sets too many of earrings, most acquired on a school French exchange program. I had been singled out on the coach to be told categorically *not* to get any piercings during our day out in Nice, which I did straight away. On the same day, I pretended to pierce my own nose with a magnetic stud in a supermarket in front of our horrified French hosts and made them cry in the cheese aisle.

The confused expressions at my new role are well founded, not only down to aesthetics but because I have never shown any interest in the academic version of a child's pageant crown. No one can understand why I want the role; it isn't to put in my immediately defunct Record of Achievement or to rub shoulders with the teachers. My reason is simple – to stop Amy Wilson from becoming Head Girl. Amy could plausibly have been created by AI as the perfect candidate for the title – she is smart, loved by teachers, never in trouble and, importantly, relishes telling people what to do.

She wants the role so badly, having talked about it endlessly since we were eleven. It is ingrained in the fabric of our year group and assumed by pupils and teachers alike it is a done deal. As someone who believes they know everything, Amy is the last person on earth I want telling me what to do and I'm not the only one. As a sacrificial lamb, I decided to run for Head Girl to take one for the team and informed everyone if they voted for me, I would let them do whatever they wanted. I could not give one fuck about duty or rules, as displayed by leaving my prefect post to sit in Beth's kitchen and gossip freely about the hot topic of the day – the pregnancy and abortion rumours about a girl in our year.

'So, do you think it's true?' Beth asks as she pulls out the plates for our toast.

'I don't know. I don't really know her very well,' I reply, while spinning on a stool, 'but she would be stupid to have gotten pregnant so close to our exams.'

'If it is true,' Anna adds, 'then that is A LOT to go into your GCSEs thinking about, I'm worried enough already.'

'Why wouldn't you just use protection? I don't understand,' I exclaim in indignation, adding, 'I don't think I could have an abortion. Just imagine it, it's your baby, your own child. I wouldn't want to be a pregnant teenager or a teenage mum. I want to be at least thirty when I have a baby, but I just couldn't get rid of my own baby.'

After dissecting the life choices of the girl we barely know, we walk back to an afternoon of revision for our looming GCSE exams, confident in ourselves and our knowledge of the world. We are smart young women, destined for academic success and Big Things, which definitely do not include becoming pregnant at sixteen.

It is only three weeks later when I find myself standing in my kitchen, holding a positive pregnancy test in front of my boyfriend and both our mums. It is only five weeks after our lunch debate that, without hesitation, I have an abortion – four days before my first GCSE exam.

At the tender age of sixteen, being a pregnant Head Girl and having a termination was my first real moment of understanding a profound truth about life: you don't know until you know. It had been so simple to rant over toast about what an acquaintance should do about her hypothetical pregnancy, but when it came to my very real one my opinions changed entirely. There was no way I could have a baby – I knew this stone-cold fact as soon as I saw the blue lines appear. My boyfriend was my first; we had only started having sex two months earlier. He was two years older than me, but this meant nothing in terms of maturity. On the day I had the abortion, I let the general anaesthetic wear off on my parents' sofa with a hot water bottle on my womb and received a phone call from him to say he had been stopped in his car for driving while firing a fire extinguisher out of the window at pedestrians. I may have been little more than a child myself, but I knew he was not the sort of person I wanted to have children with.

I realised I knew little about what I was capable of, what I was not capable of and, crucially, what a situation I had never experienced would feel like until I was in it myself. We have a natural attachment to certainty; there is safety in feeling sure you know how the world will unfold at a certain time. As we become adults, there is a transition brought about by difficult things happening that breaks this hypnotic view of the world and its mechanics, but still, do we ever grow out of it?

My life expanded to become the usual mix of hard stuff, brilliant things and run-of-the-mill normality. I lived a traditional life in many ways. I followed the clear checkpoints girls and women are guided towards: a partner (preferably The One); a house (preferably a beautiful one you own, maybe with high ceilings and sash windows); children (preferably nice ones that don't smash up Tesco Express while you're in the queue) and the newer addition the old-school fairy tales didn't include – career (preferably well paid where you love every moment). When the pace of life increased, running in time with the thump of my biological clock, grabbing for the next rung on the ladder in my career, it was hard to listen to the voice in my own head. Above the noise I had created around me, I couldn't hear the girl screaming, 'But how do I want this to look?'

I eventually had my first baby seventeen years later at the age of thirty-three. The birth of my two daughters Dalí and Bay, born two years apart almost to the day, signalled another season of my life when I realised we have no idea about anything until we have lived it ourselves. Becoming a mother was huge but there has been no bigger or more monumental event in my life than my husband Greg being diagnosed with terminal cancer on Bay's first birthday and eventually dying five years later. There has also never been a time I've felt more out of my depth, confused, gaslit or generally shocked at how I felt and dealt with a situation. I was thirty-six years old, with a baby, a toddler and a partner who was going to die very soon. This was not what I had planned, and I had no idea how to deal with any of it.

I started in the way any good academic would; I devoured books about cancer, dying and any other hard thing like

I was a ravenous animal in a bleak winter. I wanted to ingest the thoughts and insights of those who had lived through the same thing, my appetite insatiable for understanding what was happening to us and how this was going to feel in the future – what is it *really* like to watch someone die? What do I need to do to cope? How does a relationship withstand the pressure when Death is on the horizon? This question was particularly pertinent, the year before Greg's diagnosis being the most difficult we had endured in ten years together and leading to a temporary split between us.

In the same year cancer entered our lives, the book *When Breath Becomes Air* by Paul Kalanithi was released. An immediate hit, it documented the thoracic surgeon Kalanithi's thoughts and feelings after he was diagnosed with incurable lung cancer and became the patient he had dedicated his life to helping. Despite everyone in the world reading the book at the beginning of 2016, it never appealed to me; with two babies under three, I was too busy reading parenting articles on my phone through the night. I didn't want to spend any time in that world, until it became my own permanent abode. As soon as Greg was diagnosed, I read the book as part of my secret library, hiding the stories with dark, bleak endings within the covers of happier novels so as not to give the impression to Greg or anyone else I didn't believe what they did – that Greg could somehow beat this. Hoping for the best but preparing for the worst was how I coped in these bleak months.

In the prologue to the book, Kalanithi writes about the imminent breakdown of his marriage with his wife Lucy just before his terminal prognosis. They are both leading doctors in their fields – he a neurosurgeon, Lucy in internal medicine

– but the pressure of both careers leads to confusion as to how they can continue together, a situation I'm sure many couples find themselves in after a certain amount of time together.

I read these lines with bated breath, my mouth open to take in each word like a chocolate delicacy. But the words are painful to swallow, as I witness the pain and distress of the rusty cogs of their long-term romantic relationship grinding together. He is finally diagnosed with the lung cancer he believed he had and, at that moment, nothing else mattered to them. All their arguments, sleeping on sofas and thoughts of leaving evaporated. I understood this explicitly as it's exactly how I felt. When you are told the worst news, the world melts in front of your eyes like a Salvador Dalí painting and all that is left is love. I understood their intense desire to never leave, to be there until the end, with statistics telling me the end for Greg would be in about two years, and with only a 5 per cent chance of him still being alive in five.

For Paul and Lucy, the prologue of the book details how strong they became as a couple after the diagnosis, how they became an indestructible team to take on an invisible beast together. Their crumbling marriage is not mentioned again until the epilogue, written by Lucy after Paul died. She jokes about how the secret to a successful marriage is a terminal diagnosis and how its deep impact fortified their relationship.

I finished reading what is a luminous masterpiece but, personally, I was crestfallen; not for them, of course – I was genuinely thrilled they found the space and means to find a way back to each other in their walk up to the edge of the world. Lucy's ending words are a soothing balm about love in its most shiny presentation and how it can lift you up in the darkest moments to see light over the hill in the distance.

But I wanted to know how the *really* hard stuff played out; how they moved from a distant and difficult patch in their relationship to an impenetrable bond until Death needed to use his scythe to prise them apart. I was going through exactly what they had but it didn't look like this. The more I read about other couples in our situation, the more I saw the same cookie-cutter narratives again and again – the hero's journey, the brave and stoic patient, the tolerant and strong carer. Each person has an epiphany that transcends the everyday normalcy of their relationship, which usually consists of texts mostly focusing on who is going to pick up some milk and late-night debates on who was the best member of the Beatles.

No, I was sad for myself, so much so I threw the book of a dead man across my room in anger. I wanted to shout into the pages, 'So, you never had any problems ever again?'. Ultimately, these personal details about their relationship were just that – theirs to choose what they shared and what they didn't. We hold great attachment to the idea of 'not sharing your dirty laundry in public', especially when it comes to details of relationships, health, sex, money or parenting. Nevertheless, I was still angry at not finding my own story written on these pages. Where was the nuance of long-term relationships and examples of how these ships creak and moan against the turbulence of life? Does death and grief mean we can never talk about the realities of our lives again?

I was not angry with Paul and Lucy Kalanithi or their beautiful book; I was furious at the realisation we don't talk about the details behind the hard, complex stuff that happens in our lives. This led me to ask the difficult question of why that is and ultimately why I wanted to write this book.

In writing, it is considered better to 'write from the scar, not the wound'. This may be true sometimes but, ultimately, I wildly disagree with the sentiment. We need to hear stories told close to the bomb site as we emerge from the rubble. We need the roving reporters on the ground to tell us what the next few steps will entail. We have heard the stories with ten-year perspectives, when the edges have softened and colours have faded; when the once red-raw wounds have healed into icy white scars and the passage of time has tinted everything with a rose-pink hue. There is gold in the wreckage beneath our bloodied feet as we drag ourselves away, in the clarity mixed up with the mess before you have figured anything out, before you can understand and fit everything into a neat box.

There are some essential pieces of information that would be useful to know in advance at key moments in a woman's life: that the blood of your first period is often dark brown and will look like you've shit yourself; that doggy-style sex leads to vaginal flatulence; that what goes up, must 'cum' down; that having a puppy is very similar to having a newborn baby; that you will probably hate your partner after your baby is born. I grew up with the tattered pages of the sex scene in Judy Blume's *Forever* and *More* magazine's 'Position of the Month' acting as a children's Kama Sutra. These were the nearest insights into understanding what sex was *really* like, to bridge the awkward videos shown at school and the weird illustrations in the *Growing Up* book my mum gave me.

I wish I had known more detail; that desperation could masquerade as love when having sex with a boy so he wouldn't go with any other girls on the holiday he was about to leave for. I wish I had known before the months of living without sleep and only porridge to eat that receiving a double first-class honours degree would be irrelevant to anyone bar your family because no one will ever ask you your grade. I wish someone had sat me down in my fashion lecturer job to explain there would never be a day my to-do list would be finished, only added to, so stop killing myself by trying.

There is validation and connection when we give voice to those feelings of loneliness and isolation that come from living in the spaces we don't talk about. The kind of spaces or feelings that often exist in broad strokes where detail and nuance are absent. I want to offer tangible, real-life vignettes of what those specific feelings actually look like and how they manifest themselves through our complex and flawed human brains.

We are reluctant to discuss the detailed workings of our marriages and long-term relationships because of an ingrained loyalty, that ours may not look like everyone else's on the inside and the real fear that they won't stand up to interrogation.

We don't like to discuss our parenting because the pressure to be perfect is overwhelming and the guilt of not doing it right is crippling.

We don't want to discuss our desires, whether they be sexual or ambitious, for fear of being branded too much, too greedy or aggressive.

We don't want to discuss illness because so much of it is undignified and unsettling.

We are afraid of what can happen to us and those we love.

We can't talk about grief because of its messy nature and how uncomfortable it makes us feel.

We don't dare discuss Death because it is a terrifying, abstract, unknowable monster on the horizon that we want to ignore for as long as we can.

We don't want to discuss how our identities can be fragile and change over time. We are afraid that closer inspection will shatter our ideas of who we are.

We are reluctant to discuss our growth for its power to elevate us and possibly move us away from a life and people we love. We fear appearing egotistical and want to appear small to support others to feel bigger.

We 'think' we are communicating and in contact with others because of social media. It feels like we 'talk' all the time – we connect online, we put our feelings into 280 characters, we will boil down the emotions of a lifetime, thousands of hours of big feelings, weird emotions, off-topic revelations into something that is digestible and pleasant. We 'like' a post, sending a heart emoji when someone talks about a problem with their child or their recent diagnosis, and it can feel the same as a hug. We can genuinely feel we are up to date with those we haven't seen for twenty-five years because we see their lives on our phones. It can feel as if you intimately know someone because you've just watched a five-minute video of them deciding which tiles to choose for their bathroom renovation. We are with them on the journey, weighing up the options and silently thinking, *I think the grey will make it all a bit dark.* Yet it is impossible to boil down huge personal moments like grief, post-natal depression or the complexities of love into an itemised list to fit into 280 characters or a single image. Social media is not the vehicle for intricacy or delicacy.

You could argue that we talk about issues now that

have previously been taboo – we know more about issues relating to race, LGBTQI+ communities, baby loss, infertility, menopause, grief, abuse and mental health than ever before. The internet and social media have helped to educate those who have no experience of them and offer a space for those who have but with such a small space for dissection, we need to distil our experiences down into soundbites and bullet points to access our ever-decreasing attention spans. Our hot takes need to be snappy, inoffensive, linear, cohesive and ultimately positive. Easy to digest tick lists like '10 things to say to a mother after baby loss' or '5 signs you might have depression' have their place, and can often cut through the relentless avalanche of information we consume, but such reliance on a diluted interpretation is a disservice to the richness and nuance of all those complex experiences. There is also the fact that most communication happens in public, with others able to comment and judge, acting as immediate censorship. The real conversations often happen in the DMs, where there are only two pairs of eyes. This is where I have been told the most surprising secrets, urgent confessions and elaborate lies.

There are other sacred spaces where these stories can be told in detail: in the toilets of nightclubs, in WhatsApp group chats, in a therapist's office, in the pages of a book. In these spaces, we tell the most personal stories of our lives – of how we wish our mum had died instead of our dad, how we wish we had never had children, how much we love porn. To not have access to these spaces and stories holds collateral damage for us all; it keeps us isolated and believing that our complicated problems and feelings are just ours, instead of those shared with many. Women who tell stories from when things go wrong are often categorised as mad, chaotic, unstable and unreliable despite telling an honest and vulnerable truth about their lives. We are rewarded and cheered for becoming more palatable. We need to understand how storytelling is our weapon against small lives and the ultimate tool for connection.

To tell the explicit truths of lives is critical; to refrain from doing so keeps us lonely and isolated. Women are shamed for their emotional natures and their desire to talk so much, so we've shut down these avenues between us. Who is this silence serving? It most certainly isn't women or their children. We are left alone in our neurosis and worries while our kids see us carrying on regardless, ingesting that the way forward is to keep quiet. To be honest is to show care, for ourselves and others. There is integrity in truth; it is freeing even when it's painful and hard. Sometimes it can land like a blow to the head, but its ripples are in no way as far-reaching as secrets. Everything unsaid can sit inside your veins like poison.

This doesn't mean everyone needs to know everything, far from it. Some thoughts and feelings I've had are confined to the text messages between me and my best friends or the office of my therapist. I've had some thoughts that no one will ever know. There are specific things Greg never wanted me to talk about, which I never have and never will. I also see things through the lens of my children as they become older regarding ideas of consent and exposure of their personal experiences. We have lived through the most illuminating stories that could shine a light on how childhood grief manifests itself, but they are not my stories to tell.

This is not a guidebook. In fact, 'there isn't a guidebook for this' is a phrase repeatedly thrown around, mostly during situations you think there *would* be a manual for by now, because as humans we have all been in the same boat again and again for millennia – parenthood, love, pregnancy, heartbreak, illness, grief, death, birth. What *have* we learnt from the billions of people before us? The book *The Hitchhiker's Guide to the Galaxy* centres on the joke that the answer to the ultimate question of life, the universe and everything is 42, an arbitrary number picked by author Douglas Adams. It taps into our collective desire to have some kind of definitive, rock-solid answer to explain all of *this* but, as Adam's farcical response suggests, it is just as ludicrous to ask the question as it is to think there is an answer.

We know there is no ultimate guide for life because of the shared issue with *all* our lives – there is no one way to live it. Even before you filter every experience and thought through your own childhood, family dynamics, privilege, socio-economic situation, race, sexuality, gender, religion, support network and everything you've ever consumed and learnt. Each person experiencing the same situation will process, disseminate, act upon and evaluate their life differently.

Even with no clear destination in mind, we still try to make connections and understand the complexities of other people's lives that often make no sense at all. We may want to assign deep, symbolic significance to things because then our deepest need as humans will be resolved; that of safety and belonging. There are few things more terrifying than realising that you have no clue what you're doing. Luckily, we can balance this existential dread in the realisation that we *all* feel like we are about to fall off a cliff edge at some point in our treacherous yet beautiful lives.

Love

Ted Hughes and Sylvia Plath

I am about to tell my dying husband my lifetime dream is going to come true.

After an unexpected phone call earlier today, the current tar-black atmosphere is suddenly dispersed with the luminosity of possibility and excitement, feelings I have long forgotten. I'm sat alone in my quiet, empty house, drinking in my surroundings. The silence is deafening and feels like a held breath; this space is usually punctuated with the loud singing and screaming of two young girls accompanied by multiple sources of music playing in different rooms, mixing nineties grunge with sixties and modern pop in a torturous audio soup. There is usually a TV on that no one is watching, and our blind toy poodle Milk accompanies the racket by barking into the ether at nothing in the garden. Usually, I am leant up against a counter in the kitchen, a spot well worn, as I chat to my husband Greg about politics, family and rating our favourite Britpop albums. This used to be the soundtrack of my home up until very recently, but now it is silent.

Everything in this room now looks like a film set, with props brought in to give the impression of a 'typical family home': the ill-advised baby-pink velvet sofa covered in milk stains and felt tip; the framed picture of my husband and me smiling at a terrible dinner we had been at years ago. Moments before the picture was taken, I had moaned I would get some kind of food poisoning from the meat left out under the hot lights of the carvery. 'I didn't even know carveries still existed,' I had whispered to Greg. Did that dinner even happen? We look so young in the photo; he has bright blond hair because he is a singer in a band and that's what bands did in the early noughties. I'm wearing a 1960s-print dress and long orange earrings. This must be fake because I would never have bought those earrings, surely? I don't remember throwing up either. Maybe the meat was OK.

All I hear is silence and yet all these items are shouting stories at me. Every scuffed skirting board, every book, every plate here has at least twenty stories attached to it, some kind of in-joke and moment in time that anchors us to this place, together. We had been in this room when we found out I was pregnant with our first baby. We had sat on the floor and cried in a ball, meshed together in grief when my husband's grandad died. We had sat by the window on our second date, watching *Under Milk Wood* on a laptop and eating frozen burgers in Greg's house, that would one day become 'our house', barely furnished except for a sofa donated by his ex-girlfriend's parents and an underwatered plant wilting in the corner. I didn't find out how the film ended because we were too busy kissing and falling into a new world that was just ours.

That beginning of us was dizzy-making and so full of hope and potential. Every moment was a gasp at what we would feel next and how it would unfurl. We now know how this will end, the story of us. This time, there is no fizzy kiss, no dazzling thrill to cling onto, when falling in love makes six hours dissolve in a minute. Time has ripped through the fabric of us, all fifteen years gone in a second, and now there are only moments left. There is still so much to say even though we have barely left each other's side for our entire relationship. So much I want to highlight and underline multiple times with a marker pen in the transcript of our relationship. How do you decide what to say when you have only a few chances left? I decide to tell him about the phone call.

Greg has left the hospice and moved back into his parents' house. I gently knock on the door of his childhood bedroom and tiptoe in. There's something about illness that makes you want to whisper and move slowly, even more so when Death is hiding in the shadowed corner, as if a loud noise or fast movement might spur him on and bring the end quicker. The light is surprisingly bright despite the drawn curtains, the September sun keeping summer's dream alive. The air is heavy with reverence, almost like walking into a church, but here the iconography on the walls is not of saints or deities. The walls of this church have been decorated by our daughters, who claimed this room at their grandparents' house as their own years ago and have crudely taped posters of Ariana Grande and Little Mix above the bed at jaunty angles. There is a poster that screams the words 'GOOD VIBEZ ONLY' in fluorescent colours, transforming the bed into an even more surreal altar.

As I step into the room, I press record on my phone. I've been secretly recording my short conversations with Greg for weeks, mostly chatting about the most banal topics, but I need proof that it was real, that *we* were real. I need to know that he really knew this before he never knew anything about me again. Greg opens his eyes ever so slightly and quietly whispers a greeting in an indistinguishable sound. His voice has changed completely, another brand-new fact to add to the many I am learning every day about Death and the body's process in slowly breaking down. Greg's voice has always been one of my favourite things about him; his speaking voice had always been boyish and tripped off his tongue as if he was telling the best secret on earth. His singing voice balanced an angelic falsetto with a yappy growl and was often mistaken for a female vocal. Now there is barely a whisper, just a low rasp.

'Here he is!' I almost shout as I enter, the adrenaline running through my body acting as a megaphone for words that need to be delicately whispered, the desperation for levity overriding any protocol of dealing with Death. I start a breezy yet long-winded conversation about how big the fan is that I've ordered for his room – a £600 panic purchase in the middle of the night at the thought of Greg dying in unbearable heat. I may not be able to stop Death and his rapid approach, but I *can* make sure the whole event has optimum air conditioning. I ramble on with loud nerves – that I don't know where it will go in such a small room, that it has a remote control and, WOW, can you believe it can detect formaldehyde? Such utterly boring and inconsequential details for the living, let alone for the actively dying.

I ask him how he's feeling – a stupid question but still one that we all seem to ask him from moment to moment, as if waiting for the response to be, 'I'm about to die.'

'I'm not sure,' Greg whispers as I perch on the end of the bed. 'The things I'm craving, I'm not sure they're making me feel good.'

'Like cream soda?' I ask.

Greg has barely eaten anything since moving from the hospice to his parents' house and it shows; he is emaciated in the way everyone conjures up when they think about cancer, how its poisonous tendrils ravage the body of its flesh. We have all seen these images on TV adverts for cancer charities, the ones I used to look away from because I didn't want to think about it, but now it's all I can see. We are living in the hidden moments, when people begin taking close-up photographs of lovingly held hands, cropping out the limbs and faces so as to not show or have to remember the gaunt and jaundiced figures of their loved ones at the very end.

Greg is having cravings that remind me of mine during pregnancy; my insatiable desires had been for intense flavours to overwhelm my taste buds, specifically salt and chilli, but Greg craves the taste of nostalgia in blue slushies and Coke floats from his childhood holidays spent with extended family on the Isle of Wight. Downstairs, an extra fridge has been donated by kind friends to Greg's parents so they can stock the ingredients for specialist drinks to be made at a moment's notice. Greg's brother Aaron is nominated to drive around the city on his moped to find anywhere serving blue slushies at any hour of the day. This is a well-oiled ship despite the fact it's sinking.

Greg whispers something indistinguishable back, leaving a silence, so I take my moment to tell him about the phone call. It feels like a Big Deal, like asking someone to marry you or the anticipation of revealing you're pregnant. I don't even know if this is the right thing to do. Is this selfish? Does he want to know this on his death bed? I have to take the chance because I will regret it for the rest of my life if I don't, so I lie down next to him on his single bed and hold his slight hand, with Ariana looking down on us from above as if she is an angel. Luckily, I can tell you word for word what was said because I have the recording, otherwise my trauma response would have cleanly wiped this moment from my memory.

'I have something to tell you . . . no one else knows . . .

I only want you to know . . . just me and you . . . (pause to cry). I spoke to a publisher earlier . . . they really like my writing and . . . they want me to write a book.' A long pause because there is no more oxygen left and the room is spinning.

Greg smiles slowly with closed eyes.

'That's fantastic news . . . that's fantastic news . . . that's fantastic news . . . f-fantastic . . . fan news, Stace.' He stop/ starts squeezing my hand like Morse code.

'It's all so bittersweet though . . . (much crying) . . . I just so wanted to tell you . . . I just wanted you to be proud of me . . . (sobbing) . . . I love telling you things that will make you proud of me and . . .'

There are no more words except the truth I don't want to say out loud. Even though we are here, in this child's bed with morphine dripping between us, I don't want to admit that we are at the end, with our toes hanging over the edge of the world where Greg is about to disappear into the universe forever. I don't want to admit this is probably the last conversation we will ever have.

The timing of the phone call is strange, arriving at the most inopportune moment, but in many ways it fits perfectly into the weird and dreamlike world of watching someone you love die. In the incomprehensible situation of Greg dying of bowel cancer at forty-four when we have small children, it seems almost reasonable that I would suddenly receive a call to be offered the chance to write a book, when the tsunami wave has finally reached us after five years of watching it creep closer from the shoreline and now towers above our heads, about to hit.

Greg is always my loudest cheerleader and believes in me when I don't believe in myself. He encourages me to ignore the obtuse and often vicious voice in my head that whispers, 'I am an imposter'. He is a creative in every sense of the word. Greg is a singer, songwriter, guitarist, artist, poet – even when he played football as a kid, he was exceptional and was destined for Big Things until a knee injury changed his trajectory. I've always described him as 'disgustingly talented' because how many innate talents does one person need? But in fact, I glow with pride at his creativity and humble way of excelling in everything he tries. I'm never jealous but I often wish I could project myself out into the world like he does. Greg is the person who tells me again and again – you ARE a writer, you ARE an artist, you ARE a curator, and leaves no space for conversation to the contrary.

I will never get to have this again, to feel the warmth of his pride in me, but I have this right now – the chance to tell Greg I am going to live my dream of becoming an author. I had always wanted to write; as a child, I wrote and illustrated long stories of imaginary creatures who lived in the woods. As a young teenager, I created dreamy scenarios about older boys I secretly swooned over at school. As an adult, I didn't think I had any stories to tell or anything important to say – not enough to fill the pages of a book. Now I have something to write but I wish with all my heart I didn't.

'I feel like I'm taking your creativity baton,' I whisper into his ear. 'I'm just finishing what you started.'

'Just make sure . . . you write a brave . . . brave book . . . otherwise what's . . . what's the point?' Greg smiles with his eyes closed as he drifts back into sleep. Somehow, he manages to say his final coherent sentence without pause.

'I always preferred Sylvia Plath to Ted Hughes anyway.'

How to reluctantly find a rockstar boyfriend

I didn't want a boyfriend. I most certainly did not want one who was the lead singer of a band. My teenage self would have thought this was a dreamboat situation but, at twenty-six, it sounded like the worst idea ever. Earlier that year, I had come out of a quite nice but ultimately confusing eighteen-month relationship, the kind where they buy you first editions of your favourite childhood books but never stop letting you know how terrible they think your clothes and jewellery are. The type of relationship where your boyfriend will, instead of going on holiday with you, go on a stag weekend to Prague with a group of men that includes your ex-boyfriend and, on their return, you learn they had jointly oiled up a gyrating woman in a private lap dance. It was a mid-twenties relationship where you start thinking you want something more serious but realise what you have is not it. I eventually stopped going to his student-style digs with its dirty carpets and torn posters of the Beatles, stopped sleeping on his futon, bought a car and ended it. Then I drove straight into the most terrible, harrowing relationship I've ever encountered, even though its entire rise and fall lasted only two months. This one was the kind of relationship you fall into because your self-esteem is non-existent, and the initial love-bombing hides the fact they are vicious and mentally unwell. The kind where you need to keep a trail of emails as proof for the police and cry under the stairs at work because you're scared for your safety. It ended and I absolutely did not want another boyfriend for a million years.

That was my firm mindset when I went for lunch on a hot summer's day with my old friend, Aaron. We were sixteen when we met at college and became tight friends, despite being a strange pairing – me with bright pink hair and a fake fur coat; Aaron with a skinhead, Burberry checks and Reebok Classics. Our friendship didn't make much sense, our groups never overlapping, but we revelled in the mismatch. During lessons, we shared Walkman earphones, one in each of our ears to listen to sad music and make inappropriate jokes. Aaron left college before our final exams and we lost contact. It was nearly ten years later in a different city when I was offered a last-minute ticket to see a band whose keyboard player's face I recognised as his. After the gig, we spent hours talking at each other, every sentence rushed to fill in the years. I said a quick hello to his brother, the shy lead singer of the band I'd heard of but never met before, who was sat in the corner and writing something on the wall of the dressing room with a marker pen.

D . . . E . . .

He looked up at me. 'It's bad luck to write your band name on a dressing room wall, it means you won't play there again,' he said quietly as he finished his graffiti with the name De La Soul instead of his own band name – Delays.

His voice was so delicate, like baby's breath but with a hint of jelly to it. It reminded me of Rick Moranis' character in *Ghostbusters* ('Oh Dana, it's you!') or the scrappy yelp of Dogtanian from the 1980s kids' cartoon *Dogtanian and the Three Muskehounds*. Earlier in the evening I had stood open-mouthed in the crowd when he sang the opening song, as he sounded like an angel, not a scruffy urchin type so common in indie bands of the time. In fact, if I were to describe him, I would say everything about him was beautiful.

'Are you superstitious, then?' I asked.

'Of course. Aren't you?' he replied.

I didn't know how to answer so didn't and went home.

The chance reunion with Aaron meant we became as tight as ever again, sending stupid messages in the night and meeting for coffee when we could, when his band weren't touring the world and becoming famous. I watched on in awe as Delays' popularity all over the world grew, standing on the sidelines with my pom-poms.

Two years on, Aaron and I sat drinking Coke floats in the sun, talking about music and fashion over lunch. He mentioned his brother Greg, the shy lead singer, had just split up with his long-term girlfriend of eleven years. I almost choked when he suggested we should consider meeting up as two newly single people. I was set on being single for a long time and couldn't think of anything worse than going out with a rock star who was on tour all the time.

Everyone in our city knew who Greg was despite no one really knowing him at all; the local singer with an unusual falsetto voice who wore silver trousers and eyeliner, known for being a hermit despite being in the charts. Even though I knew it would be a bad idea, I allowed myself a moment of fantasy; after all, Greg was out-of-this-world dreamy, like a character in a film you would cry over as a teenage girl. In the interviews I had seen over the years, he was shy and quietly funny, obviously the leader of the band with a measured confidence but happy to let his brother take the limelight. I had always been struck by his beauty and obvious love of literature and film, his extensive knowledge spilling out organically into every interview. When I first heard Delays' music, his falsetto range gave his already ethereal aura an angelic quality that I was drawn to.

I was very wary of meeting Greg, despite having a crush on him from afar; because of Aaron being in the band, I proudly had a poster of Delays on my bedroom wall when I was a student, so, weirdly, I'd already spent a lot of time gazing at Greg as my life unfolded in my early twenties. Everyone knows you should never meet dream boy material, let alone go on a date with them. Also, it was obvious without meeting we were cut from very different cloth. I was known as a party girl, the type who would carry a toothbrush in her bag for whoever's floor I would stay on after a night out while he was known for never going out and for reading Proust. The prospect of dating someone just coming out of an eleven-year relationship didn't appeal either; at twenty-nine, they may as well have been married for fifty years. It was all a terrible idea for so many reasons, but I still let Aaron type Greg's number into my phone.

A few days later, I was sat on the doorstep of my friend Beth's house, waiting for her notoriously late arrival. I was bored, mindlessly flicking through messages on my phone and saw Greg's phone number. I paused, trying not to act in my usual impulsive way, but I texted him anyway, knowing he would never remember the girl questioning his graffiti in the dressing room in the Midlands years before. It was a strong move. I imagined how all the fans of his band would love to do this. Did this make me a groupie?

ME: *How did people used to communicate with strangers before phones?!*

Casual, easy breezy, wry humour. No kiss on the end. A question so looking for a reply but still non-committal. Use of exclamation mark so he knows I'm being funny but also, URGH, exclamation marks are too wacky. Does it read like a joke or a riddle? Oh fuck. I'm acknowledging I'm a stranger, which shows I'm self-aware but also that I'm possibly a stalker or psychopath. Do I sound like a murderer?

Beth arrived and we drank tea and gossiped about people we knew. Hours passed. My phone beeped.

GREG GILBERT (DELAYS): *Probably smoke signals between the villages.*

His reply produced a teenage thrill of electricity through me. This was a disaster. No. No. No. This is not what I wanted. Months later, I found out Greg had been furious with Aaron for giving his number to someone he didn't know and was horrified when I messaged him, but curiosity won out at who was this stranger who would send such a bizarre question out of the blue.

The messages kept going back and forth like coy love notes sent across a classroom. Greg's words were smart, endearing and funny. I addictively wanted to hear the next thing he thought. After six weeks of texts and anticipation, we decided to meet in person, the weight of potential heavy in the air between us.

I don't know if you could call it a blind date but it felt like one. The only other blind date I had been on was at seventeen, with a boy who smiled like Wallace from *Wallace & Gromit.* We went to the cinema to see the bizarre date choice *Con Air*, during which I nervously rambled non-stop through the whole film. I had just passed my driving test and had taken my mum's car for the first time. On the way home, I was stopped by the police for hazardous driving and asked to take a breathalyser and walk in a straight line while Wallace watched on in the passenger seat. He tried to kiss me as I dropped him at his house, but I pulled back abruptly, hitting my head on the window and exploding in nervous hysteria at the thought of kissing his huge Wallace mouth. I also knocked a wing mirror off my mum's car on the way home, the cherry on top of a disastrous evening.

To see Greg sitting by the harbour waiting for me was like a champagne cork popping in my heart. It was a bright sunny evening on the south coast. He wore a T-shirt with a lobster print and drank tea even though it was summer. I was expecting a character full of philosophy and brooding but, instead, I found the most golden boy with every throwaway pop culture reference under the sun, impressions of his family and a soft high-pitched laugh that made me dizzy. The evening kept spinning until one of my work colleagues popped the bubble, appearing from nowhere drunk and giddy, wanting to chat and ask who Greg was. At exactly the same moment, a girl working at the bar had printed a picture of Greg in the office and had come over to ask him to sign it. We looked at each other and smiled, creating an immediate secret code between us that others could never infiltrate.

We sat through *Pirates of the Caribbean 4*, an awful film I ignored entirely because I was hypnotised by Greg's leg next to mine. His hands were those of an artist, delicate and long, used with confident moves. We didn't hold hands during the film, but I fantasised about what it would feel like, his skin touching mine. When we left it was still warm, and as we walked through the car park of the cinema, he pointed out the star constellations starting to appear above us and gently touched my fingers with his. I pulled him towards me and, as we kissed for the first time, our teeth hit because we were both smiling so much.

Ex-boyfriend dreams a go-go

When Greg and I first started dating, we went to the closing night of a legendary local nightclub, The Nexus – along with apparently every other person from the music scene in our city, including three of my ex-boyfriends I noticed the moment we walked in. This number didn't include people there I'd had sex with; nothing proves the incestuous nature of a small city more than a reunion. I felt travel sick from being transported back and forth to different ages of my life in one scan of the room, like Ebenezer Scrooge in high heels. It was surreal to chat over a beer with one ex about his family's new dog, one about his new diet and fitness regime and fully ignoring the other, to then leave with Greg as the Ghost of Christmas Present.

'I wonder if I've just experienced what it's like to be at your own funeral,' I asked Greg on the way home, although I doubted any of these ghosts from my past would even attend.

I never experienced anything as weird as that night again, but I dream about my ex-boyfriends a lot. As in, *all* of the time. It is my brain's stress dream of choice. Again and again, I'm either drawn back in time to be in relationships of the past or thrust into a future with them. I wake up most mornings feeling so confused – what do these men want? What are they trying to tell me? Yes, of course I've Googled what all this might mean – what on earth was the internet invented for if not this type of pressing question? Theories range from having unresolved feelings (nope) to recognising you're ready to move on with your life and devote yourself to new relationships (already happened). Whatever the reason, it's unnerving to start the day with the taste of a past life still lingering on your tongue.

They all make an appearance but with differing regularity; my subconscious seems to have no preference if they were one of the nice or not-so-nice ones. This makes it sound like there are dozens of men all eager to punctuate my psyche but there are only five ex-boyfriends. Five men on rotation in my dreamscape who I ricochet from hating, to having sex with, marrying, to my brain's favourite go-to, wondering how on earth I am back with them and desperately wanting to leave.

There is someone else I have dreamt of for years – easily once a week – a boy from my past who was never an official boyfriend but still appears night after night, representing something I can't quite put my finger on. When I spent a lot of time with him in my early twenties, we danced around each other and lived out scenes of a music video: dancing in a club, drinking at house parties where the police were called, having food fights in restaurants. On the day after Greg and I announced his diagnosis publicly, he phoned to tell me his girlfriend had just been diagnosed with a brain tumour. (My brain: if everyone else is dead, maybe we will get together in the future.)

I may not want to relive the past or have these men wheeled out every night by my cryptic subconscious, but still, I am generally very happy these people have existed in my life. Because something wasn't 'forever' doesn't automatically mean it was bad or didn't offer something important, whether that be a lesson to learn or just *fun*. Imagine that! Something being 'just for fun' is not a road many women are encouraged to walk down. That said, I generally ignored that idea to follow a more traditional path of hunting down all the emotionally unavailable men in town, offering up my self-esteem as a sacrificial lamb.

There was a lot wrong in many of those relationships, but they can't only be judged harshly; they were also full to the brim with exciting times, new experiences and pivotal moments. It's important to remember not *all* of my relationship with Greg was worth eulogising either; there were times significantly more painful and destructive than I had experienced beforehand *because* of the depth of our relationship. The boyfriend who asked loudly in a shoe shop, 'Why can't you just wear trainers like everyone else?' could never hurt me in such ways because he didn't have the same access to my heart.

As I turn off the light for another night of dreams, I wonder if this is what people mean in a near-death experience when they say 'my life flashed before my eyes'. I have an idea of who and what would make the cut, but now I'm thinking my subconscious will pull out some wild card obsolete supporting cast members to make a cameo appearance. I really hope it's not the boy who said he hated my shoes. I'll be annoyed if he is my last thought on earth.

Ex-girlfriend on the phone

A few days after Greg died, I unlocked his phone to make sure I could retrieve his photos of the girls. I'd had many thoughts about the ethics of looking through his personal belongings. I wouldn't do it while he was alive so why should I now? But still . . . this little black box housed the most important time machine, the only breadcrumbs I could offer my children to any kind of path to their dad.

The last file opened appeared on the screen. It was from SJ, Greg's ex-girlfriend. The image showed her looking directly into the camera, her big eyes glistening with tears. At first, I thought it was a photograph but realised it was a video. I didn't know if I should watch this personal message. You could fill hours with a philosophical debate about whether it was ethical but I watched it – of course I did. As the last message open on the screen, I wanted to see what Greg saw, what he felt before he was too weak to even hold his phone.

The two-minute video was a very definite goodbye. SJ looked straight into the camera to connect with Greg's eyes while they could still see her. This intimate moment was never meant for me, but I couldn't look away from the beauty of seeing the love she had for him and how fondly she remembered their relationship. I felt a soft excitement in being a late voyeur to another side of Greg, to hear stories I had never heard about times they had shared.

The video finished with a shaky, final goodbye, a tight embrace through a screen. It was a full stop, not a comma, but with no touch, no walking in the opposite direction. Only a button to press 'send' and a hollow space where your heart was. Is this how people felt in the pandemic, saying goodbye to loved ones through screens? There is no air here, nothing to grab onto, except love.

I hope Greg was able to watch and feel that love from SJ on his deathbed, for all the love he had given and received over the course of his life to reverberate through his aching bones. To witness this beautiful goodbye was a lesson that love can never be a possession to hold and keep for ourselves; it's a transient energy living within its own rules, not set by us. Ultimately, his love never belonged just to me; it was shared between all the other soulmates he had met along the way, romantic and platonic. This division of love doesn't take anything away from our relationship; we had our own flavour only we could taste and never explain to anyone else.

As I stood giving Greg's eulogy at his funeral, I saw SJ sat in the congregation, her face coming into focus between a mass of eyes. For a second, everything paused as we smiled at each other. To see her, in among the hundreds there, showed me we are all built from so many different stories, all adding to the rich textures that make us who we are. I loved Greg because of how the love he received had shaped him and, in the future, I hope someone else will love me because they see the impact Greg's love has made on who I am.

After the service, I left the crematorium building as a choking ball of adrenaline, holding the hands of Dalí and Bay and gasping for fresh air. I had never experienced anything remotely like Greg's funeral; the collective energy was palpable and, for most of it, I sat open-mouthed with my head tilted backwards, trying to let the energy I felt growing within me escape. We were the first ones outside, about to lead the meet and greet for the congregation. As I opened the doors, I was shocked to see the person waiting outside: Joe, my childhood sweetheart, one of the good ones and an old friend of Greg's (I told you small cities are incestuous). I couldn't have thought of anyone more appropriate to be standing there in that moment, the universe showing me that love weaves itself through our lives in the most mysterious of ways.

Space ghosts

'Fuck off' was my immediate and very genuine answer when Greg asked me to marry him.

It was 3 a.m., the fourth feed of the night for three-month-old Dalí, and I was so delirious with exhaustion I could barely read the words on my phone asking Google 'how to get your baby to sleep more'. The shuffling around had woken Greg up and he started to chat to me about who knows what because I was essentially asleep and broken but one word stuck out as if a horn had been blown in my ear – 'wifey'.

I'd never heard Greg say this word before and he giggled as he said it. 'I'm not your wife,' I mumbled. 'Don't fuck with an exhausted new mother in her night-feed routine.'

'Would you like to be?' Greg tentatively asked. I paused, trying to weigh up how to interpret this question in my sleepy fog.

'Is this an actual marriage proposal?' I asked.

'Umm . . . yes?' he replied.

'Fuck off,' I said with my eyes still closed.

'Is that your actual answer to a marriage proposal?' Greg asked with a smile.

'Have you *met* me?' I questioned. 'Do you think this is how I would want to be proposed to? When I'm asleep and without even saying the actual words, just asking me if I would like it? You've lost your mind, boy.'

Over the next few weeks, Greg relished telling everyone I had turned down his marriage proposal and watching the look of horror on people's faces, using it like a kid setting up a prank to get another child into trouble. I stood my sleep-deprived ground.

'It wasn't a real proposal and I didn't say no,' I told everyone. 'I told him to fuck off and that's very different.'

A few months later, in bed with the lights off and the baby asleep in her cot next to us, Greg and I were talking about what happens after you die. The conversation spanned all the options: reincarnation, heaven and hell, becoming a ghost, absolute nothingness and oblivion.

'What would you like to happen when you die? Which would you choose?' I asked.

There was silence in the dark. Greg was either giving the question some proper consideration or asleep.

'Anything with you in it,' he suddenly concluded. 'I don't want nothingness because that's boring, I wouldn't get to see you. Not reincarnation because we might be put into dogs on opposite sides of the world. Not heaven and hell because, honestly, who knows where *you* are going . . . so I suppose I would have to pick becoming a ghost. We could be space ghosts together, zipping around the universe for eternity. If *Most Haunted* is still being made then, maybe we could go to the set and freak them out. To say you were the one who killed Derek Acorah would be a great space ghost story.'

Silence.

'I would love to marry you,' I whispered, and meant it.

A ghost's wedding

I never imagined I would marry someone who was going to die. But we are *all* dying, right? We are all just slowly moving towards death from the day we are born. This vague, pseudo-spiritual nonsense is what people love to say when confronted with a terminal illness in someone else. The kind of statement used to dilute the enormity of the moment, as if we are all in this whole 'being dead soon' thing together. There is the most profound difference between acknowledging the very abstract notion that you and everyone you love will die and being able to Google the scientific statistics available rating your chances of being alive on your next birthday. You don't get to be in the same gang unless Dr Google, the seemingly perennial bearer of bad news, tells you those chances will be less than 5 per cent.

Greg constantly joked about 'our panic wedding', which I laughed nervously at, but he was correct. I was no serene fiancée or even a Bridezilla – I was fucking panicked. I was panicked because the person I loved was going to die, probably very soon, so to plan a wedding held an air of farce around it. It reminded me of the engagement between two college friends when we were seventeen. Tom bought Sarah an opal engagement ring, a fact that astounded us all in the back row of our English A-level class. Their families threw an engagement party at a local community centre, where we all arrived with our teenage confusion and gifts.

'What the fuck do you buy seventeen-year-olds who are getting married but are blatantly *not* going to get married?' I had asked Beth as we trawled the BHS homeware section for ideas. We settled on a teddy-shaped cookie jar that spoke when you lifted the lid because we were children being asked to play adult and this is what we believed we would want in our adult, married homes. We had watched as they opened the presents in front of everyone, genuinely bewildered at how happy they seemed to receive a double duvet, not to mention how any of the real adults in the room believed this wedding was actually going to happen. They wanted to get married because their teenage brains and society told them it meant they loved each other, but only three months after the bizarre party, the same under-developed cognition also told them the marriage couldn't go ahead, possibly for a reason as important as Tom couldn't get past the fact Sarah thought the latest Blur album was better than their earlier work. The duvet was ruined on purpose in anger with red wine and the opal ring was thrown into some tall grass. I asked Beth if she thought it would be rude to ask for the cookie jar back. She thought it best to let it go as collateral damage in teenage heartbreak.

Greg and I got married for two reasons and I desperately wish one of them was to be given a talking teddy cookie jar. One was an enormous, overwhelming romantic reason and the other was secretive and strategic. The big intention to be married was to tie a big bow on the memory box of our relationship. I had seen people getting married in hospital beds, with nurses as witnesses and the ill patient looking as though they may not make it through their vows, and always thought, What's the point? because isn't marriage about the future? I get it now; it may not be a statement of long-term intention but acknowledgement of the love that exists in real time. It is a marked moment that sticks a pin in the calendar with the note 'this was us and we existed'.

We also desperately needed something nice to look forward to, given our days were mostly filled with choking down existential fear. The girls started referring to the ceremony as 'our wedding', more of a day that encapsulated our entire family. It felt like our own personal Christmas Day.

The smaller, less romantic reason to get married was because anyone in a relationship without a ring will be royally fucked, legally and financially, if one of them dies, especially if you don't have a will. Sharing children and decades of cohabitation mean nothing to a society built on the pedestal of holy matrimony. Greg believed that to even talk about wills was an omen of bad luck and signified a total absence of hope; that drawing up the paperwork would somehow act as a séance for Death to appear. For years, I had both people I knew and didn't know at all ask me in whispered tones if we had our affairs in order. The answer, like that of so many people our age, was no, not at all, because this was never going to happen to us. Until it did.

The panic element of our wedding grew spores in every crevice, even the moments supposed to bring great joy. To claim 'my wedding dress nearly killed me' feels like a cheap tagline from the *Sunday Sport* where women detail stories of sex with aliens. Those are all obviously nonsense, while this is unfortunately true.

I rushed around the department store alone, trying to find anywhere that sold milk. It turns out you can buy Korean bubble tea with mango-flavoured popping pearls in the centre of a city but there is literally nowhere to buy a pint of semi-skimmed. Weaving through racks of clothes in the womenswear department trying to find the food section,

I saw a white dress hung high on a rail. It looked nothing special in the distance, but I was intrigued by the limp fabric that resembled a sad ghost who'd given up haunting.

In fact, the fabric was beautiful crepe, the kind your mum would rub with her fingers to reassure you 'that will hang nicely'. My mum wasn't with me, neither were my daughters or a gaggle of girlfriends with glasses of champagne in their hands, accustomed to when a bride goes to try her wedding dress on. I had only myself, a brightly lit busy store filled with harassed parents and a half-drunk bottle of warm water in my bag.

There was a tiny flicker of joy when I saw my reflection wearing the dress. I filmed a twirl in the mirror to show the girls and send to my mum then quickly put my jeans and T-shirt on, straight back into the search for milk.

Everyone loved the dress, my mum suggesting we went back the next day to buy it. I wanted this so badly, to share something frivolously fun between the women in my family, but also, the thought made my windpipe contract. The temporary joy of it all would break me but the girls were desperate to see the dress, so it was decided.

The dress was still there waiting for me, the wilting sad ghost which became animated when on. Walking from behind the curtain received all the *oohs* and *aahs* of fireworks night, the kind of special reactions reserved only for brides. The sales assistants understood the language of Wedding and followed the coos like breadcrumbs, spinning me round in front of the mirrors. I felt like a ballerina twirling in a children's jewellery box, with the tinkling reverie slowly winding down while the dancer must keep spinning, her dizzy head only catching a glimpse of herself in the mirror and unable to stop.

I desperately wanted to stop but now shoe suggestions were appearing ('Yes, I'll take them, no, I don't need to try them on') and specialist bras to sit invisibly under the dress are brought in. The more I added to the ensemble, the deeper I encapsulated the sad ghost, getting ready to marry her sweetheart, soon to join the dead.

There was no fanfare or toast when buying the dress and all its accompaniments, only a rush home to pack for a holiday beginning the next day. The dress hung in the wardrobe and was not given a second thought, my concerns refocused on the locations of clean underwear and the girls' swimming costumes.

It is then that my windpipe begins to close again. A good dose of an inhaler normally blows my asthma away, but it didn't work. The girls were downstairs, Greg at his parents, so I phone mine.

'I don't want (*gasp*) to worry you but (*gasp*) I can't (*gasp*) breathe,' I whispered down the phone at my dad.

None of us *were* panicked because, as we learnt when I was a kid, rule 101 of asthma was DON'T PANIC. My dad told me to phone for an ambulance as calmly as if he were telling me to call out a plumber to fix a leaking tap. It upped the ante when he changed his mind on listening to my wheezing breath and he got in his car to drive me himself.

The day starts just like Christmas morning – my whole family awake early in my childhood home with opposing music blaring from different rooms. The buzz of excitement is mixed with a drop of unspoken sadness that no one acknowledges with words, but our eye contact lingers longer than usual, our smiles slightly more restrained.

After weeks of trying to convince Bay to wear the glittery lilac dress I've bought for her, she is still adamant she's wearing the Batgirl costume she wore for Halloween the year before. I'm quietly pleased; a costume dilutes the weight of the other wedding outfits and will draw attention away from me, although I myself feel like I'm wearing my own costume, coming to a fancy-dress party as a bride. I like the idea of having a superhero at the wedding.

In my childhood bedroom, I'm floating above my body, seeing all the past ages of myself busying around in this space – getting dressed for school, studying for exams, dressing up to go out for the night, crying at heartbreak, pacing the floor trying to get a baby to go to sleep. And now I am the bride, looking at the reflection of myself in a white dress and feather cape in a mirror still adorned with stickers from the nineties. I'm an apparition, a ghost of myself living in a memory. Can you be nostalgic for the present moment?

The whole event was stripped down in its organisation, a tiny wedding fit for a mouse, so small and purposefully quiet. All decisions are chiselled down to the bone – no guests except immediate family, no speeches, no toasts, no poignant dance. Each would act as tiny shards thrown over us like glass confetti and make every step of the day more painful. What would you say in a toast for a ghost's wedding anyway? What would you buy as a gift? There will be no gifts and no guests at this wedding because the doomed couple don't need a set of new crockery or pitying looks. We can't even add the saccharine statement 'just your presence at our special day is enough' because there are no invites either.

There is one outlier in attendance: Beth – so horrified to not be part of the day, she volunteers/shoehorns herself in as videographer and her dad Geoff and his Jaguar as chauffeur. On the morning of the wedding, I'm so pleased I had given in to her very persuasive nature because she is the tonic we all need. The drive to the venue is silly and irreverent, bursting the black bubbles inside me. We become like teenagers again, giggling in the back seats and taking stupid photos of ourselves while Geoff, a tour guide of the city's old walls, gives an impromptu lecture on all the deaths that occurred in that area and methods for covering up the smell of dead bodies (in case you're wondering, oranges and lemons make the best air freshener to cover decomposing flesh).

Seeing Greg makes my heart lurch. He looks so handsome and healthy, no one would guess the amount of tumours eating his insides and, for a second, I forget myself. We walk down the aisle altogether as a family, laughing and joking, sound-tracked by 'Waiting for a Star to Fall' by Boy Meets Girl, the song that soundtracked so many of our night drives together.

My memories stop here at the altar, except flashes of thoughts and feelings.

What does a ghost think about when getting married?

When did Bay get changed out of her Batgirl costume?

Every single member of our families is wearing blue.

What face shall I make when we get to the vows about 'in sickness and in health' and 'till death do us part'? Will everyone feel awkward? How will I say those words looking at Greg and not make them too poignant?

I wonder if I will ever get married again.

What will that hypothetical future groom wear? I quite like pink shirts on men, maybe I'll ask him to wear one. Or if it's way in the future, will we all be wearing silver? Maybe we will just be holograms.

What do other brides think about during their wedding? How many think they are making a mistake? Do they hate particular people in the congregation? Are they going over all the most inappropriate things they could say in that moment?

We spend the rest of the day at our favourite hotel, The Pig, a shady place set in the heart of the New Forest, where Greg and I have come for years to celebrate, relax and ignore the sand falling through the hourglass. Everyone heads to the bar while we retreat to our room – not for marital sex but to sleep. Greg's body is fatigued by its unusual amount of physical assertion; mine is broken by the emotional toll of the whole event. I'm not sure how many other brides can say they had a power nap in the middle of their wedding day.

In the evening, we join everyone in the private dining room to eat a meal I cannot remember anything about. What did I order from the menu and what did any of us talk about? My only memory is shouting above the music, across the large table to ask Bay if she was enjoying her meal, which she gave a thumbs-up to, and the sinking feeling this will probably be the last time I am ever here.

Greg is the first to retreat to bed while the adults sit round the drawing room fire to discuss wine-soaked topics. From the window, I watch Dalí, Bay and their cousin play outside in the garden walled with jasmine and lavender, their powdery scent hitting you as you step outside. Their delight in the dark is the quintessential naïveté of a childhood summer that I drink in to soften my hardening heart. Towards midnight, I carry Bay's soft warm body to her makeshift nest on the floor of my parents' room and watch as sleep consumes her before her head hits the pillow. This is the kind of rest I crave; the absolute physical surrender of a child's late-night exhaustion and the feeling of unquestionable safety, that when you have had enough, you know you will be carried to your bed to sleep in a carefree dream. Instead, I walk back barefoot to my own room, where Greg is in a different type of sleep, a fractious, almost unconscious stupor. I wonder if the only time he will ever experience the soft ease of a childlike sleep again will be when he dies. On the night of our wedding, my only hope for the future is that this is what death will feel like.

Love is the colour of dirt

Ask anyone on the street what they believe is the most important thing in the world and all answers will probably follow a path to one place – love. It is the human experience rated above all others, the most desirable emotion in our human library. In the past, I believed love was shown by affection and grand romantic gestures. You could calculate how much someone loved you by how well thought out and unique their Christmas present to you was. We all want *real* love and believe that when we find it, it won't be hard or complicated because *true* love will flow effortlessly like a stream into the ocean.

For all our heart emojis and dreamy ideas coloured in red and pink, love rarely shows its true colours until it is pushed down into the matted brown dirt. It's here that real love reveals itself in the energy ignited as you push back the hair of a vomiting child in the middle of the night, knowing there will be no sleep anytime soon. It is in the immediacy of grabbed car keys when a friend messages to say they are scared on a date. It is in the bittersweet sting for the happiness of the one you love who loves someone else. So much of real love revolves around bearing witness to the life of others and showing up in the hardest of times. It's in these dark shadows where love plants its roots into the ground deep beneath your feet and solemnly waits for the sun. Now is not the time for flowers; it is for sitting in the mud. There was no greater time I scrabbled around in the earth than when I became Greg's carer and advocate.

In those years, I became a workhorse for love. Caring for the medical needs of someone dissolves the spirit of romantic love to reform it into something deeper, more intense as it's born in the trenches, covered in dirt and blood. The role means to offer up some essential part of yourself alongside the lighter, easier part of your love for each other; to embody a deeper space, an exquisite agony. This is what 'in sickness and in health, till death do us part' really looks like.

Very early on, I quietly decide I am going to be the best caregiver the world has ever seen, as if proof to the universe and Greg of the intensity of my love. I lean heavily on the transferable skills I can utilise for this new position. I draw on my Head Girl/oldest child/senior academic leader energy to galvanise myself and everyone around us. At this point, I have no idea how the role will pulverise me into dust.

Much like in a dream, we are cast roles in a play we never auditioned for: Greg is given the main part of 'cancer patient' and I'm given the supporting role of 'carer'. We method act our way through and adjust our own personas accordingly. My character notes tell me I am to be strong, reasoned and patient while also having the energy of a dog with a bone to advocate through the health system. Greg is referred to by others as a fighter, a warrior who will win the battle. Behind the scenes, we compare notes and realise that while our character arcs are very different, we are both cast as stoic. Stoicism is a virtue we admire in others, perhaps because we can relax our shoulders when someone else is being strong and valiant. We use words and phrases such as 'strong', 'they fought a good battle' and 'they never lost hope' to bolster ourselves in dark times. Perhaps this is why death, in literature and in cinema, is written as a heroic goodbye, laced with poignancy and Zen-like acceptance, because it's what we so desperately hope for – not just the deaths we will eventually have to endure of those we love but also for our own eventual demise.

At the first meeting with our consultant, I arrived with the confrontational energy of a bodyguard, carrying a notebook of the entire internet's contents and the non-negotiable requirement of Dr Baggins reversing Greg's terminal prognosis. As the Best Carer in the World, I thought this was a very reasonable request. Dr Baggins, who I insisted on calling by his first name Mark because I needed to feel some equality between us, was very polite towards Dr Google, who I had asked to join us for the meeting. I challenged Mark on every point he made, pitting his world-renowned credentials and research against my scrawled notes of complicated terms I didn't understand. In hindsight, he knew everything I offered up as an antidote to death was just the snake oil Dr Google had steered me towards, but he gently asked me to put each vial down while we moved through this process systematically.

Mark wore bright patterned socks, bow-ties and waistcoats and would have been very comfortable in Tolkien's Shire. There was something about his jazzy accessories that soothed me in the way Disney characters are painted on the walls of children's care homes or hospital wards; a sleight of hand, a trick to make you look at the colour while the black tries to engulf you. Over the years, I trained myself to focus intently on these patterns, just as you might look away when watching a horror film, to convince yourself this isn't real.

Silently, I transferred the enemy status from the elusive tumours inside Greg's body to the tangible person in front of me who held our lives and future in his hands. It was much easier to question a man whose CV you could peruse than the unknowable silence of biology. This anger in me was the desperation of a sad, broken human who wanted to reverse the hands of fate. Mark was with us through the roughest of terrains, always measured with his words, always wearing a cartoon tie to lead the way into hell.

The only time we didn't see Mark in person was during the pandemic. Instead, we sat at our dining room table holding hands as Mark told us over Zoom the cancer had spread to Greg's liver. To watch yourself receive terrible news in real time is a bizarre, nightmarish experience; I was transfixed by our faces on the computer screen as we were informed our treatment options were ending and wondered if I looked upset enough. I wanted to look appropriately sad yet strong as I knew Greg would be watching for my reaction, my facial expressions deciding the impact on the Richter scale.

On the screen, I saw Greg's shoulders slouch. Such an undetectable tiny movement that would go unnoticed by most, but to me it was like tectonic plates moving. I tried so hard to listen to the medical details but my attention had moved to where Mark was calling from – a light pink room with peeling butterfly stickers on the walls. Was this his daughter's bedroom? I wanted him to have a family; somehow that would make him a better doctor in my mind. His words of destruction dissolved with the kiss of subtle pink as the backdrop.

Through the years, my roles as carer and advocate morphed to include protector. Greg asked me to never tell him any details about his condition as he didn't want to know, his mental health teetering on a knife edge. He chose never to read a single word about his illness or talk to anyone with the same diagnosis. Eventually, all information bypassed Greg entirely and was given straight to me. I analysed and disseminated scan reports for everyone so I could serve a gentler blow. We didn't use the word 'progression' because it was too real. I needed to dilute the scan results down to the strength of preschool squash until people responded with 'this is great news' or 'so pleased for you' when in fact the news was terrible. I agreed to this. I actively volunteered with my hand raised high in the air to be picked for the job, throbbing with overachiever energy. Because Greg wanted to know nothing about his illness, his body, his statistics or his treatments, he never seemed to believe his life was limited. He talked of the girls becoming teenagers and how we would deal with the ensuing chaos, as I laughed outwardly while silently screaming inside.

When we spoke of taking the girls to Euro Disney during a break in treatment, it was suggested by others we could wait until Bay was older; maybe in five years' time when she would be seven and could remember it. We did not have five years; we possibly did not have five months. We didn't have any time to wait to do anything. Everything was now, and much of my time was spent weighing up the implications of not acknowledging that truth.

I could understand all of Greg's reasons for this, as much as any mind of the living can understand the physical impossibility of death. I don't know how it feels to sense the diminishing minutes of your life slipping through your fingers, but I *can* understand why you would want, or even need, to live in a suspended version of reality. What I couldn't understand or foresee was how, in time, my decision born of love for Greg became its own sickly manifestation between us.

The secretive, unbalanced dynamic of one person knowing everything, the other knowing nothing, made it impossible to be true partners and altered the axis of our relationship irrevocably. I became more carer and less wife, Greg more patient and less husband. My role expanded as I became the keeper of secrets for a wider host of people, of facts that others didn't want to look at. These bore into me like my own cancer and dug a canyon between me and everyone in the inner sanctum who wanted to live in a blissful ignorance.

Denial and hope share an address, cohabitating in an uncomfortable relationship. In the direst of situations, is it possible to have hope without denial? Perhaps it depends on what your definition of hope is. Very often in crisis we are told to 'prepare for the worst, hope for the best' – pieces of advice that stand worlds apart from each other, covering every eventuality. As the mother who would be left alone with two small children and the patient who had been given the worst news imaginable, Greg and I ended up in polar opposite directions, but as his carer and medical advocate, I needed to pretend I was very much in his camp.

I knew Greg's prognosis when no one else did. The weight of knowing when someone will die is a very particular load. It feels like walking across a high tightrope holding a priceless crystal vase. The two different dates he eventually outlived were emblazoned in my mind every time I looked at him. I had sat alone in Dr Baggins' office and willingly asked for this information. It was never forced on me but, not one to enjoy the slow ratchet of the rollercoaster up the tracks, I wanted to know when the drop would come so I could prepare.

Greg told me at different times over the years that all he needed was hope. His version of hope meant a cure for cancer. We had seen a specialist in the early days of his diagnosis, a slick private oncologist on Harley Street whose name was often mentioned on internet forums of desperate people looking for similar hope and options. His clinic resembled a high-end spa – with coffee and expensive biscuits freely available, plush upholstered furniture and, as it was Christmastime, a real spruce tree in reception so expansive its bushy pine arms touched the high Georgian ceilings. It cost £500 for Doctor Slick to glance at your scan results and offer an opinion in your swift ten-minute appointment.

'You have a lot to be hopeful about!' chimed Dr Slick, as if he was looking at an ultrasound image and announcing we were about to have a baby instead of a CT scan black with tumours. He reminded me of Dr Hibbert from *The Simpsons*, and I immediately hated him. 'We want to stay one step ahead,' he continued. 'There are advancements in treatments and drugs all the time. The idea is to live with it, not die from it.'

This last line of Dr Slick's pep talk stayed with Greg for the rest of his life. He would regularly quote it as if holding onto rosary beads and praying. On that day in London, we walked out into the busy onslaught of Christmas shoppers and felt elated. When this news isn't illuminated by festive lights, it paints a starker image in the cold light of day; you will need to outrun nature and your own biology if you want to live and hope to fucking God a scientist hits on a wonder drug to keep your particular cancer and genome sequence at bay until the elusive 'cure for cancer' eventually arrives – ignoring the fact there are over 200 different cancers, all with different treatments.

And yet, this was all we had to hold onto. Greg held onto this idea like a Wonka Golden Ticket in a roomful of sweet-toothed kids. If he was to endure poison being pumped through his veins while kissing his children goodnight, he needed this particular flavour of hope.

Hope is such an intrinsic human desire, often grounding us in a chaotic world. It can reduce our feelings of helplessness, increase our happiness and offers a way of thinking that pushes us into action. It is the essence that things will get better, to hold on because brighter times are up ahead. We have a sporting chance. But what if we *don't* have a chance? When the odds are stacked so wildly against you, at what point does hope become denial and how does that impact how you live?

Our sense of personal hope was polarised: in one corner, Greg the idealist, and in the other, me, the realist. In the search for our own reasons to get up in the morning, we found ourselves often working next to each other – in coffee shops, in bed, at our dining table. The best times between us were in this configuration. Scribbling in notebooks, sketching drawings, outlining themes. We were a weird juxtaposition; always together, creating and talking about ideas but making sure we always circled away from the truth. We were very different people to start with – introvert vs extrovert – so it should come as no real surprise when, both hit by the same trauma, we would have different coping mechanisms to deal with it. Greg retreated to process things internally, producing the most prolific and intense art of his life, while I was standing on a hilltop with a megaphone, searching for people to hold hands with.

Greg needed hope for the most basic of human needs –

survival. My role as knowledge gatekeeper meant I knew all the details he dreaded: that there had never been any hope or real, tangible chance for Greg to live without the illness that devoured him; they were unalterably linked forever. My own hopes were secret and felt as fanciful as wishing on a dandelion, with its angel hair propellers blowing gently in the wind. I was hopeful Greg would have a 'good' death, where he wouldn't suffer unduly, either physically or mentally. I hoped he would be able to come to some resolution in himself about dying. I hoped this for him but, selfishly, for me too because it would be easier to bear. I was hopeful I would be OK in the future after Greg died. I understood the seismic shift that would take place under my feet but I had my fingers crossed I could still live a good, or even *great,* life afterwards. Over time, I realised this could not be just a wistful hope for the future; I steadfastly promised myself I would not die with Greg. His untimely death would already be a great tragedy; another would be a disservice to him, myself and, ultimately, the girls. The unnerving, inescapable difference that changed everything between us was ultimately the most basic of concepts – you will die soon, I will not.

The dynamic change wasn't just between us. Greg was met with cotton wool everywhere we went, as though he were made of fine-cut crystal; not only fragile to touch but something to wonder at. The dying man who's alive! I'm reminded of being a teenager and standing in front of the huge glass box holding Damien Hirst's sculpture of a shark preserved in formaldehyde. Its title, *The Impossibility of Death through the Eyes of Someone Living,* encapsulates this feeling so well – we know we will die but we also absolutely *don't* know at the same time, the concept being just too abstract and sitting just outside of our brain's understanding: that we will just stop existing in our current form. Even though we see death around us in so many guises – in a global pandemic, in wars on the news, in the meat we eat, in the autumn leaves – there is a level of distance because it's not *our* demise. We can feel empathy and pain for those who die and those who loved them and, sometimes, *we* are those people left behind. And yet – it's not us.

I saw people talk to Greg as though they were watching a dolphin perform at SeaWorld – with reverence but an overriding sadness that they are in this situation in the first place. At a summer barbeque, an old friend clapped her hands together with joy on seeing Greg arrive and exclaimed, 'I'm so honoured to be in your presence', as if a hotdog-eating deity walked among us. I saw him wince at the othering, separating him again from the rest of us mere mortals and our unending life forces. I know what she meant though; as people didn't see so much of Greg anymore, he had become a myth or an urban legend. Like the dolphin and the shark, he was behind glass.

At sea

Only months before Greg was diagnosed with cancer, we split up. It was a brief splinter in time, but it was a definite break. We agreed I would move in with my parents with the babies for a while.

With a decade behind us, we had never discussed not being together. There was the usual back and forth of relationships, but this moment in time bore a brand-new feeling – the ribbons lacing us together being abruptly ripped apart. There were no black and white explanations of infidelity, abuse or any hidden gambling addiction revealed. In fact, the reality was far more mundane and excruciating. A betrayal would be easier to stomach because it's absolving; we could cast all vengeful cries at the guilty party. With a lack of finger pointing, there is space to understand your role in the relationship and your responsibility in its downfall. Instead of an explosive ending, there was an anticlimactic checkmate with only losers. The truth was Greg and I loved each other, so very much, but had become strangers who couldn't withstand everything life was throwing at them as a couple.

Our home had felt like an asylum for a while. Inside lived a woman who wouldn't leave its four walls as she spiralled into a maddening post-natal depression, a man with deep- rooted OCD that toyed with his mind as a growing alien twisted his bowels into excruciating knots, a newborn baby who inexplicably never stopped crying, a toddler who learnt how to worry and a young dog who mysteriously lost her sight. In trying to hold our family and our own sanity together, Greg and I had spiralled away from each without a map to find our way back.

I never did move out because it was in the middle of this storm, both lost out at sea in separate boats, that Greg was diagnosed with terminal cancer.

For me, it was this bolt of lightning that cleared the fog between us. The sight of Death's shadowy figure appearing on the horizon had a way of producing crystal-clear clarity. In those initial months, we fell in on each other, hanging on as tightly as we could as the ship went down and all parts of our familiar world dropped away. I left my job immediately, concrete in the knowledge that everything needed to be about us.

The waves settled, the initial shock subsided, and a new everyday rhythm began but, in this calm, the cracks began to resurface. The tectonic plates beneath us seemed to split in half again and we were swept away under different currents, unable to reach each other in the ways we needed to.

I was hopeful that Greg and I would be able to come together at some point before it was too late and connect in the way we used to. I had no fixed idea what this would look like – a filmic heart-to-heart felt within reach as two people who loved words, but a quick meaningful look would suffice; a look between people who know the fibres of each other and can communicate a lengthy narrative with a mere roll of their eyes. That had always been us. I hoped there would be a moment that dissolved the past five hard years and we would be lying in bed with Greg reading, me talking endlessly and the distance between us reeled in to only the few inches between the sheets.

Time inched forward, and as I confided in others about my hope for an ending fitting for the magnitude of our relationship, the pleas from friends and family to manage my expectations became hard to ignore. My friend Anna, a palliative care nurse and death doula, gently explained to me how dying doesn't come with a romantic ending and there are very few deathbed confessionals or epiphanies.

'People die as they lived, they don't suddenly change as they are dying,' she said to break my fall.

'Yes, of course. I know. I'm prepared for that,' I replied as if I understood.

In fact, I didn't believe this at all. I thought that may be the case with everyone else but not between us. I believed we would be different because how can that *not* happen? Our love had always been so huge and tangible, the agony of our dynamic only proved that further. It seemed denial was a contagious emotion, a way to shutter your heart to what it cannot bear to accept.

The distance growing between us gave momentum to the opposite directions in which we were going. It felt like different terrains: me on a sandy shoreline; Greg on a rowboat out at sea. At the beginning, we are frantically waving at each other then, gradually, we stop, not taking our eyes from each other until Greg becomes hypnotised by the movement of the waves and I begin building sandcastles.

Mistakes lit up with Christmas lights

Long-term relationships are hard. Marriage is hard. I realise these are not brand-new gems of information; we are often introduced to this concept early as children by our parents and other adults to encapsulate the intricate web of what being with the same person for decades feels like. We then go on to possibly live it ourselves and realise, yes, this thing we were sold as The Dream is exceptionally hard work.

When you are knee-deep in the long grass of family life, work, ageing parents and modern pressures, it can be easy to forget why you wanted all of this in the first place. It is in the snapshot moments where you can see a tiny chink of light, a glimmer of understanding as to why things are good in your relationship. In these moments of clarity, you can identify what oils the cogs and keeps the mechanics of day-to-day life working. It might be connecting after long days of barely having a chance to talk by watching stupid videos of people falling off skateboards on TikTok or prioritising a date night once a week. There are also the moments where it becomes glaringly obvious what is wrong with the dynamic between two people who originally came together because of love but sometimes can't work out what happened to that amid the laundry and school emails. You wonder how you arrived at silently screaming into your pillow at night with rage at the person daring to breathe next to you.

It's often only when relationships end that we find the head space and distance to take stock and survey the lay of the land we once inhabited. In a divorce, the legal contract between the two broken lovers inherently wants there to be a good and a bad guy. Until very recently, the person instigating proceedings needed to give categorical reasons for the split. We always want to be the innocent party, the one with the list of reasons to hand over to the judge for them to nod in agreement. In the relationships I've had in my life, it always became blindingly clear afterwards that, for as much as I would want to chastise others, I couldn't deny the huge issues I brought to the table.

In this space without him, I can see the mistakes I made with Greg. The regrets I have attached to them over the years are varied: some can be pinpointed to an exact moment, and some drew blood over time, but the worst came in the last years of his life. Predominantly when I tried to take control over a perfectly curated end of life for Greg.

The term 'making memories' has a lot to answer for. I had never heard this term before Greg became ill, when suddenly every waking moment was meant to be poignant and forever locked in the treasure trove of our hearts. Death on the horizon *does* offer a perspective not often gained without a gun to your head, but still, real life beckons. I still needed to wake up every morning to make the kids breakfast and see what new murder documentaries had been added to Netflix. The pressure to live a life suddenly powered by sunshine and sugar, despite the revelation of the worst news on earth, was overwhelming. There is a weight to live like this coming from others, society, social media and the hardest voice to quench – your own.

My voice on this matter was crystal clear and didn't need encouragement from external factors – Greg will have THE most incredible last days that will be unrivalled by another human. In the absence of any real control, and only a steep descent towards the edge of the cliff ahead of us, the least

I could do was turn these last years into a spectacular celebration of his life.

An event presented itself to me as if sent from heaven. In our home city, a celebrity was always asked to switch on the town centre Christmas lights but, in this particular year, a call was put out for a pillar of the community to be nominated. I immediately thought Greg was the most perfect candidate – a well-known figure in the music industry, a loyal supporter of the city, a lover of Christmas and also . . . umm, have you heard he's DYING? This was the gold medal of the Making Memories Olympics I was determined to win. I became swept up in the fantasy of the girls seeing their dad in charge of the lights, the countdown, the mulled wine, the pride and making all the memories our broken hearts could choke on.

Without telling him, I sent in a sledgehammer nomination for Greg so heavy with emotional weight, the Grinch would have wept. Do you know Greg has a daughter whose middle name is Noelle because he loves Christmas so much?! His band's first album cover is a homage to the city! And did I mention HE IS DYING and who knows if he will even live to see another Christmas WITH HIS VERY TINY CHILDREN WHO WILL BE IN THE CROWD? The full-on assault continued on social media as I pleaded for everyone who had ever met us to nominate Greg. When he finally learnt what was happening, he thought the entire idea was ludicrous and he would never be chosen over others. He foolishly underestimated me and the love everyone had for him because he won by a landslide.

When it was announced, I danced around the kitchen screaming as if I had won the lottery and patted myself on the back. Fuck you, Death, you shall be covered in twinkling lights.

The girls swirled around in circles while Greg stayed seated, a sign I took as him being overwhelmed with excitement. No – Greg was mortified and categorically did not want to do it.

The lead-up to the event was filled with excited friends and family but also angry whispers between gritted teeth back and forth between us. It became clear I hadn't asked Greg if he wanted to stand on a spot-lit stage, watched by thousands of people while he was ravaged by cancer and chemo. He didn't; in fact, he couldn't have imagined anything worse, but by then everyone was so excited, he didn't feel he could back out.

'If you don't want to do it, then don't. Just say you're not feeling well enough, no one will argue with that,' I hissed quietly as we walked through the crowds and towards the stage.

'And let everyone down? You know I can't do that,' Greg angrily shot back.

'Just try to enjoy it. Think of how brilliant it will be for the girls.'

We barely spoke for two hours afterwards.

There are so often stories in the press about dying parents at Disneyland, desperate to make memories for their children in the best way they know how – in long queues, hot weather and paying for extortionate food and novelty T-shirts in the gift shop. I remember seeing a photograph of a father, as yellow as the sun with jaundice, sat skeletal thin in a wheelchair wearing Mickey Mouse ears at Euro Disney with his three-year-old daughter. It looked like hell on earth. And there was the truth: making memories is so often not for ourselves but for others, to offer up a heightened version of reality we believe is superior.

The idea of focusing on others became a pervasive thought of mine, even up until the last few weeks of Greg's life. I often thought about everyone outside the inner sanctum, those who loved Greg and knew he was dying but had no way to let him know how much he meant to them. In their worlds, he would just disappear into thin air. Even I haven't had the level of closure I needed, so what about them? Where does that love go? Like needing to sneeze and then losing it somewhere in your body forever, leaving you restless for the release.

I took it upon myself to act as an end-of-life matchmaker and asked on social media for all those who knew Greg to send him messages of love. It felt like a winning move – they could feel they had reached out and Greg could feel all the love he had generated in his lifetime.

It became clear very quickly how much of a mistake this idea had been. Much like the public request for Christmas lights nominations, the world moved quickly to fulfil what they thought were the wishes of a dying man.

'Why am I suddenly receiving thousands of messages?' Greg asked me when he was a few weeks away from dying. 'Everyone I've ever known is saying goodbye to me. They are using the past tense, I don't understand what's going on.'

I had fucked up in the biggest way by orchestrating a flood of letters. I assumed it would be comforting to hear the positive impact he'd had on people's lives. I was wrong – it is scary, bewildering and like watching your own funeral. I never did tell him it was me.

The bed

The bed was once a place of sanctuary, of calm and delight, but a long illness will leach its way into the cotton of the sheets, into the fibres of the mattress, until it feels sodden with bleach that will catch at the back of your throat. Our bed was broken – not just metaphorically but physically as well. The wooden bed, originally bought by Greg and his ex-girlfriend when they believed they were setting up house together, had a deep split in the wooden base. The crack was so extensive, it's unclear how the bed still stood after all these years, especially under the burden of sex, jumping children, and a dog scrambling underneath to find some quiet. It's in this bed that was bought for a different relationship that we really fell in love properly, a soft fortress to create our own world and language. It's where we retreated to watch films in the winter and drink iced tea in the summer. A place where we got to know our newborn babies, comforting them after nightmares, reading stories, greeting the excited dog in the morning. It was also the place to hide from the world when things became unbearable and bleak. Maybe the number of tears cried in that spot had warped the wood, buckling under the pressure of the heavy heads resting on it.

It's unclear how the broken bed held everything in our relationship together through so much stress. It slowly became a site of everything that was wrong, a stage to play out the final acts of us. Greg spent more and more time there; I spent less and less. It became his space for recuperation after treatment but also somewhere he would retreat to avoid the realities of what was happening. A good sleep fixes most ailments, but Greg's illness robbed the bed of its ability to help him rest and restore; no early night was going to rescue his health. As he became more ill, Greg would increasingly need to sleep, whereas I would keep going until I collapsed at night with restless children at the foot of their tiny mattresses, covered in fairy blankets to wake up startled hours later, wondering where I was. There was no bed in the house for me to lay my bones for the deep rest I needed; they were all taken by others whose needs felt greater than mine. Sometimes, I would sit in the dog bed to send voice notes to my friends, tucked away out of sight, under the coats next to the washing machine. It became the only place I could sit comfortably, even though I was hiding and sending out SOS calls into the ether.

Our bed had been a vehicle for encouraging deep meaningful conversation but over time had become a place where the chasm between us felt so large, it seemed impossible to be sharing the same duvet – our toes touching but everything else so disparate and far away. Falling asleep has the same qualities as falling in love; slowly at first then all at once, so fast you don't know how it's happened. *Staying* in love is a very different act. It is a slower dance that needs steady footwork and eye contact, something you can't do if you're facing away from each other in bed in your own thoughts.

Greg and I had never been enemies, but in this intimate place we became strangers. The slow erosion of us mirrored the cancer digging its way through Greg's body, an insidious energy that crept up on us when we weren't looking. The grief of what was and would never be set up camp in our bed and slowly built a wall of pillows between us.

I didn't realise you could have multiple relationships with the same person. Over time, there are new versions of the other person to introduce yourself to. You will also need to accept the new, different versions of yourself, again and again until you don't recognise yourself. I didn't realise I would share this bed with so many different people.

Desire

The summer of Ann

One summer, many years ago, I learnt all about desire by working in a shop selling dildos, lingerie and fake rubber vaginas. Ann Summers is often thought of for the manic home parties mums threw in the nineties, where women drunk on lurid cocktails would throw money at Rampant Rabbit vibrators and penis-shaped ice-cube moulds. It is rarely celebrated as a space for women to acknowledge and explore their sexual desires.

My summer job as a visual merchandiser felt less window dresser, more anthropological observer. On the shop floor, you were overwhelmed by the open access into other people's sexual behaviours. They fell into some easily distinguishable categories.

Firstly, the boys and men. While the vast majority of stock was directed at women, there were a lot of male visitors. Boys like plates of jelly would bumble in, jiggling with laughter and grabbing hold of each other's arms in case Sex attacked them. They would activate the voices on the animal-themed jockstraps, all sniggering like Beavis and Butt-Head, only to pulsate their way out before they showed any sort of real sexual arousal.

If men came in on their own, they'd *stride* in, taking steps too big and fast for a small shop. They would hold the delicate lace of lingerie in too firm a grip and study it as if reading complicated instructions. The most common purchases would be edible underwear and chocolate paint, items destined to disappoint any woman. They DID NOT look at the sex toys because REAL MEN DO NOT USE THEM or are NOT interested in buying them for their female partners. If they bought anything, they would definitely ask for the bag to be turned inside out to hide the Ann Summers logo.

There were also the other type of men who came in by themselves, the ones we all tried to avoid dealing with. They would enter the shop slowly and touch everything on the shelves, skulking around as if they were about to steal something, only to then sidle up and ask, 'Where are the fake cunts?' It is a unique experience to demonstrate how you would use a thick slab of rubber to act as a vagina with someone you may cross the road to avoid at night. Especially when they asked, 'Do you have any without hair?'

Some men came in with their female partners glued to their sides looking terrified. These couples would be there to buy a vibrator together and were the most fascinating people of all. I liked to think about their conversations that led to the visit: was it the woman who had stated 'I'm buying a vibrator' and the man had come along to inspect what he might feel is a threat? Was it to 'spice up' their bedroom antics after a lull in activity? Through chatting to these couples, it was often the women looking for the new sexual experiences a vibrator could offer while the men were nervous about another phallic-shaped guest in the bed. These were the men I delighted in showing our range of anal beads to, explaining how satisfying they could be on their prostate gland. Their partners were always interested and open to the idea while the men looked away in embarrassment. At the tills, I always asked vibrator buyers if they would like to purchase the sex toy cleaner Buzz Fresh. It was an easy sell; the men would say yes to anything offered to them, just so they could leave as quickly as possible.

The younger girls were always interesting to speak to,

those mid-teenagers beginning their first forays into sex and desire. They acted as if the shop was not for them yet, that maybe they were some kind of deviant for wanting to explore a burgeoning side of themselves. They would often arrive in pairs, giggling at the new world opening up before them and in awe of the underwear selection so different from the M&S fare bought for them by their nans at Christmas.

Young women would come in smiling, acknowledging the staff and wanting to chat about the intricacies of their lives. They loved to tell their funny sex stories, what worked for them (mostly anything that sucked their clit) and what didn't (a vibrator shaped like a snake head accompanied by an electronic man's voice moaning, 'Oh baby, yeah' on repeat. We all agreed no women were involved in its design). These women could regard their feelings of desire with curiosity and looked to seek pleasure without the need for shame or approval.

Middle-aged women knew exactly what they wanted. They would make an immediate beeline to us for advice on the best toy for multiple orgasms and the least irritating lube for the new dryness they were experiencing. They loved to experiment with lingerie but focused on how it made them feel, not how it would look to a man.

Sadly, I don't remember any older women at all. At that time, I imagine I ingested the pervasive narrative about this group of women and pleasure – that they aren't connected. There was, and still is, so little discussed about how we feel about sex and desire as we age, as if after an undefined cut-off point in midlife, that rich and expansive side of us naturally dies off and we never think of it again.

I didn't realise a part-time summer job in retail could teach me so much about how we perceive sex and desire, how it changes as we age and the differences between men, women and personal sexuality. The sexual bravado of men is often stuck in boyhood, when they feel desire is almost comedic and something to joke about with friends instead of feelings worth communicating with a sexual partner. Girls are scared to admit they even feel desire and confuse the feelings within them as an energy to be offered up for others to receive instead of belonging *to* them to explore.

Who knew there would be so much learning from displaying cock rings on a Saturday afternoon?

Widow's fire

On the day Greg entered hospice to begin end-of-life care, I bought myself a £150 vibrator.

On face value, this is a bizarre and wholly inappropriate fact. To discuss pleasure and death in the same context might even seem callous, but I know there will be women reading this nodding their heads. If you know, you really do *know*. If you don't, thank your lucky stars and keep reading.

Terror is a very different emotion to fear or being scared. Fear is pre-emptive; to be scared is a slow burn while terror is white-hot. It is a silent scream that can stop your heart. There is a mania that accompanies pure unadulterated terror, an energy that tries to pull your soul from your body because to sit within this feeling is unbearable. It feels like being drunk on a hysterical cocktail of adrenaline and cortisol while riding a rollercoaster. You want to scratch your own skin off to let your soul escape the life of the human you've been assigned. When Greg was told he had weeks to live, I felt this electrical terror and wanted to knock myself out with a brick.

The feeling of not wanting to be alive yourself or, at the very least, not conscious or in your own body was overwhelming. It is very different from a suicidal ideation – I absolutely *wanted* to live, desperately so; I just couldn't work out *how* to live through what I was about to experience. The desire to drown in either a body of water or alcohol was unfeasible so, instead, I began to drown myself in self-pleasure and fantasy.

It's a fucked-up feeling to realise your trigger is the death of the person you would be having sex with, but the fear of death became the most powerful aphrodisiac. It was an intense and maddening reaction, most certainly a feeling which can't be explained in any rational 'stages of grief' diagram. The proximity to death, to feel its cold hand hovering above the person you love, sent my libido into the heavens. On the surface, it felt as though these blooming thoughts meant I had some deep, unresolved issues that would need immediate psychiatric advice. It was the most unexpected emotion to arise on the clifftop at the end of the world. There was nothing to *do* with this ocean of desire; there was no one to have sex *with* – my husband was very busy with the intense business of dying and, later, actually dead. I didn't know what to do so I did what anyone does in such a situation – I Googled it.

'Why am I so horny when my husband is about to die?'

In the thousands of articles written, I discovered I wasn't a monster and this bizarre emotion even has a name – widow's fire. The term is defined as to feel an intense sexual desire in the midst of a bereavement. It is considered a natural phenomenon and a well-worn path of those who have been in close proximity to death.

Sex, desire and death have a lot in common; they are all carnal, full body experiences. To witness dying makes you want to choose life, and what is more life-affirming than sex? The circle of life, round and round, death and sex and birth on a merry-go-round together for an eternity. It's why the Baby Boomers exist – an enormous generation born out of the terror of the Second World War. It's why an influx of babies appeared a year after 9/11 and the first lockdown of the COVID-19 pandemic. I had even experienced a glimmer of the feeling before – Greg and I had decided to try for a baby straight after the deaths of his grandad and one of my best friends. It felt like an impulse, a rebound from the disaster of life and a way to inject some hope and agency into a universe that felt as if we were making decisions while drunk.

Even though this is a natural phenomenon, for our death-averse society, we prefer to revere and romanticise sex for women alongside love and marriage. When a man has died and a woman wants to have sex, all the pearls in the land are clutched, enough to rip them off their cord and scatter them across the ground to trip up the widows even attempting to acknowledge this desire. No woman broken by the death of their partner is trying to be provocative or make a big statement; they are just experiencing their life and the multitudes it produces, often at odds with other feelings and what we have been conditioned to feel is acceptable or OK in the eyes of everyone around them.

High-impact situations such as war, pandemics and natural disasters may cause an increase in sexual desire but, on the flip side, high levels of mundanity can reduce it. There are so many external factors that can impact our own desire: our self-esteem, family roles, health, trust issues, balance of power, response to stress, past abuse, dynamics in relationships. The dynamics of a couple's relationship change throughout a lifetime. As I mentioned earlier, we will have multiple relationships with the same people over the course of those relationships. This evolution of love isn't reserved only for romantic connections; it will change and develop with your parents, your siblings, long-term friends and your children.

My own evolution was happening in front of my eyes. My sense of touch began to change; as many mothers will experience, I had been over-touched by children and over-exhausted as a woman trying to do everything for everyone.

Trying to dredge up a young, energetic and sexy version of myself felt impossible when she had been buried deep under years of unworn dresses and oncology notes. I felt dead inside, as if a plug had been pulled out; there was no thought of sex because all intimacy was being drawn away from pleasure and rerouted towards the intricacies of trying to stop everyone dying. I didn't know how to be sexual in a bed crawling with sadness and unspoken words, surrounded by the medicalisation of our safe place. This is the deep ravine of anticipatory grief, a space that offers little comfort even though the person is lying next to you, still alive but a part of them already gone. I imagined our bed would someday become Greg's deathbed and I didn't know what to do with that fact. The human brain isn't stupid, it works primarily to protect itself. Something closed down in me that I couldn't reignite, no matter how hard I tried. I felt like a broken doll, not given the right parts to be a real girl.

With whatever title you want to use – widow, single – the idea of sex now feels something very different to me. I feel vulnerable in a way I never have. The openness needed for sex might expose a grief I haven't been able to tap into before and I'm scared to open up those emotions in front of someone new. There can be such joy in the dissolve of yourself and absorption of another but how can I do that when there is so little left of me to give? I first need to know where I begin and end because I don't want to get lost.

Poseidon

I can't decide if the sudden entrance of a global pandemic is either an obvious follow-up or a comical farce when you are in the middle of your own personal apocalypse.

Either way, I've never been more scared than watching the news in March 2020 when Prime Minister Boris Johnson announced a lockdown for the arrival of COVID-19 and the warning of thousands of deaths. I watched the broadcast at my parents' house alongside the entire country, open-mouthed and holding onto a doorframe to stop myself falling over. Death, death, death, death everywhere. My family has already been promised death but now it is multiplied and coming for everyone else.

So, this is actually the End of the World. We are living in the films we love to devour. I tried to remember what they did to survive in *Armageddon, Deep Impact, 28 Days Later, 2012.* Survival mode means some quick mental arithmetic.

Greg will die from this new plague, that's a given. How can he not with his lungs full of tumours?

Maybe my parents will die because of their age? My dad's COPD?

My brother is in London. He's fucked. All apocalypses focus on capital cities.

I categorically cannot die. My children cannot become orphans.

I am never going to leave the house again.

I am in the high-risk category with serious chronic asthma. On the news, they are talking about Italy, how doctors are having to choose who lives or dies. In case Covid particles slip in through the brickwork of my house, I form a master plan that's thought out on my parents' bathroom floor after a panic attack. With a marker pen, I will write I have a husband with terminal cancer and two tiny children, the doctors MUST save me. I will add my mum's phone number (fuck, but what if she's already dead? Do I have space on my arm for my dad's too? Maybe a number on each arm?) so she can beg the doctors to choose me to be ventilated and my children don't lose both their parents.

Greg was due to start his next round of treatment on the morning of 23rd March, the day the lockdown started, but his consultant calls to say it's cancelled indefinitely and no one in our house should even go out for the recommended hour walk. We are told what I feared – if Greg contracts the virus, he will die. But his tumours are growing and his treatment has been stopped, so he will probably die anyway. Checkmate.

And so begins the endless months of never leaving the house, washing all food shopping with bleach on the doorstep and the slow deterioration of my sanity. I am scared, lonely and so very tired. I don't even attempt to home-school my children; it feels an unnecessary job when at least one of their parents is about to die and the world is probably ending soon. Instead, we build a gymnasium in the garden from logs and cardboard boxes and sit in the sun drinking coffee, commenting on how we didn't expect the end of the world to be so clement.

At one point, I took to my car on the drive for the only quiet place to have a therapy session on Zoom. With my iPad precariously balanced between the steering wheel and windshield, I tried to talk to my therapist about the breaking point I was at. All the while, the Wi-Fi faded in and out and the girls stood dancing on the windowsill adorned with hand-drawn rainbows to get my attention, holding packets of crisps up to the glass while mouthing, 'Can I have these?'. I had crossed the line to insanity.

Strange feelings set in alongside the cabin fever. The desire for agency is overwhelming, so I manically begin to decorate the entire house, asking friends to drop off pots of paint and brushes. If I'm going to die, it may as well be in a freshly decorated room, in a pink called Opera Sunrise. I want to obliterate the sour taste of fear so indulge in the multiple bottles of wine friends leave on the doorstep, a silent gesture of sympathy for our bleak situation. The eerie midsummer weather in winter adds to the dystopian landscape and bottles opened at midday, every day, starts feeling normal. Except midday is soon 10 a.m. and sitting in the garden sipping wine in the sun is now drinking from the bottle behind the fridge door at breakfast or hiding empty bottles in the laundry. The desired effect is to feel nothing morning to night.

Another desire emerges. Locked in our house as two clinically vulnerable adults, looking after feral children left to their own devices and surrounded by potential death both inside and outside our four walls, I begin to thaw out from the broken, sexless girl I have become into a horny teenager. Death consumes my every waking thought, and it becomes the blueprint for alchemy. I didn't know Death sitting next to me would fuel so much desire, that to watch the fatalities rise around the world and Greg start to slow down would kill off something of my own self yet birth a new energy. I became a secret sexual being wanting to explore new ideas but with no means to do so. My internal world away from Death became bright and wild, filled with new fantasies.

In my manic desire to redecorate the house, I'm recommended a workman to build a new drive. On a sunny morning, he arrives, and I think Poseidon has just emerged from the ocean. He's tall with long curly hair and most of his skin on show is tattooed and incredibly muscular. He is not someone I would historically have been attracted to, but trapped in the middle of an apocalypse, he is like a Greek god appearing from heaven.

Over the weeks he works at the front of the house, we sporadically chat at a safe distance – about the jobs we've done, about books we like. Poseidon is fascinated by the stoics and dreams of living off grid on a goat farm. I'm not really interested in this; I'm just hyper-fixated on his physicality. He just looks so *healthy*. I sit indoors and watch as he rips out plants with his bare hands and works topless in the heat. I have no idea what to do with myself except flit around the house, talking too fast and two octaves too high, watching the live erotic show outside my window. The hours ricochet back and forth from watching someone vibrate with strength and vitality to watching the person I love grow weaker and wither away in front of my eyes. The difference is abrupt and reminds me of watching Greg as the lead singer of his band; his energy to sing, play guitar and hold court on stage in front of thousands was spellbinding. I could vomit at how painful this memory is now and the desire to turn back time, even for just one minute, to see Greg as a healthy man again, is overwhelming.

Poseidon moves on to another job to fix a neighbour's roof and I can see him from the girls' bedroom. The days are long in lockdown, and while everyone else enjoys the sun in the garden, I climb up to the top bunk and use plastic toy binoculars to watch him work. This obsession is weird because it's not about Poseidon at all; it's about everything he represents and the biological volcano inside me – a deeply ingrained fear of death and ageing, a need to feel young, healthy and vibrant again, set deep within years of fear and suspense. Being around cancer and palliative care has left me jaded, feeling old and unnecessary, other than in my abilities to look after other people. I desperately want someone to look after me in all the ways possible – with their attention, their care, their body, their money. I sometimes fantasise about having a sugar daddy whose aim is purely to delight me, something I would despise in reality, but the need is so strong to just give up and let someone else take over.

I'm so tired of everything – the pandemic, of cancer, of being strong for everyone. I just want to be a teenager again, in my bedroom with my posters and CDs. In lieu of a time machine, I settle for ogling a builder while broken cells quietly take over my husband's organs and my children practise cartwheels in the sun.

Like candyfloss on your tongue

As a teenager, I had a very definite and clear plan for my life, possibly the only time I've experienced such clarity. As a fourteen-year-old, I eagerly showed my textiles teacher the prospectus for the London College of Fashion. 'This is *definitely* where I'm going to study,' I exclaimed, fizzing with the excitement and confidence that lives in those years, on the threshold of choice and freedom.

While my career as a fashion stylist would be ground-breaking, I would also meet The One, a man who would be everything I ever wanted: funny, adoring, clever, and who would love me and all my many faults. You must admire my dedication to the dream, given my only experiences with boys grew more disappointing by the year. No one tells you that crying over posters of Corey Haim and Matt LeBlanc on your bedroom walls will mean you'll eventually alchemise these sugary fantasies into a teenage boy – immature, naïve and no kind of vessel for such bone-china dreams.

Greg kind of fucked up a lot of ideas for me by dying. I don't think he or the universe realised my love trajectory had not included to start dating again in my early forties. While we were in no way the John Hughes movie I had dreamt of as a teenager, Greg and I were something very real and tangible.

Meeting up with other widows is a perk of the new role you've been given, despite never having applied for the role in the first place. Forced into their new life, widows are often candid and explicit, much like the transformation in women when they become new mothers; suddenly, the topics of ripped assholes in birth and cleaning baby shit off the floor of Pizza Hut with your hands are opening gambits. You lose the ability to be embarrassed when you have had your legs held up in stirrups and vagina sewn back together by a team of four nurses, while your mum and partner peer over their shoulders to have a good look.

The cosmic shift of witnessing death gives you a similar amount of fucks left to offer in most situations. You will go into great detail about the projectile vomit and diarrhoea you experienced after the diagnosis news, all happening while you were on the phone to your dad. You will tell people your husband is dead at the checkout in Tesco just to see the look on their faces for your own amusement. You act weird and think even stranger thoughts.

None are weirder than this weird and inexplicable secret – I believed I would find love again very quickly after Greg died. I have no idea why I would think this – there were no reasons that added up to this premonition into the future, but I didn't come to this conclusion on my own. I had an assistant in Greg. We had often joked about my lightning-speed ability to process a situation and move on. When something terrible happened, he knew I would equate it with the end of the world, rant for a while, metabolise the feelings and then act shocked if ever questioned about it again in the future, the event barely memorable anymore.

During my secret consumption of every book ever written by those whose partners had died, my search was very particular – the elusive Happy Ending. I loved the stories where the narrative boiled down to 'things turned to shit, I learnt some life lessons, but now I'm happier than ever in my new life'.

In many ways, meeting someone else would be the worst thing that could happen *after* the worst thing had just happened. Have you *seen* how the world treats women who find love or, even worse, SEX, after their husbands have died? I would be mad to actively choose that situation for myself, but still, in the back of my mind, I begrudgingly accepted I would meet my next love within weeks of Greg dying and would just have to deal with the consequences.

The bizarre nature of this idea only came into full focus in the months following Greg's death. It couldn't be further from how I felt. Just the thought of being in another relationship, either sexual or romantic, made me physically recoil. Even if someone had appeared, they wouldn't have been able to get anywhere near me because of the fizz of invincibility that emanated from my core. Death had caressed and scarred me, my skin pulsing with a scent not of this world. Even wrapped in my dirty bedsheets not changed for weeks, crying in immovable grief, I felt like a high priestess. No human touch would compare to that of heaven.

This armour dissolved from my body over time and what was left was a broken little girl, scared of everything. There was nothing left for anyone else. My children received the remaining scraps of myself. To let anyone step across the threshold of pain would have meant dealing with different angles of grief, ones I had no way of holding when I was already smashing the plates of loss and cutting my feet on the shards.

Also, the confidence earnt from age, experience and the solidity of a long-term relationship dissolved like candyfloss on my tongue. It felt like I'd been cast as Marty McFly in *Back to the Future* – the world was the same yet everything was different. My life seemed as if the past fifteen years had never happened. I had woken up at twenty-six again except now, everyone was married and instead of meeting people organically, you now needed to play small talk ping-pong online with a few dick pics thrown in to meet anyone you might want to kiss. I don't know how to play this game and, really, don't even want to.

I realised I am scared of dating, of the modern dance you need to learn, but even more than that, I am scared to let anyone near me in a significant way. Now I know the heart's true capacity for pain, to love again means to teeter on the edge, knowing how far down the fall could be.

I am afraid of being needed or needing anyone else. No matter how you have constructed your world, I don't know if there is a long-term relationship that won't devour you whole. I wonder if there will ever be enjoyment again in the feeling of being consumed, where merging in love feels sturdier and more robust than standing on your own two feet.

Familiar hands

I am so desperate for familiar hands.

I want touch. I crave the gentle sweep of fingers on my lower back when passing in the kitchen. I want intimacy and the ecstatic peace it creates. I ache for it, but I am afraid to have sex again. I am afraid to have sex again with someone else.

There is so much vulnerability in this space and I am sick of being vulnerable, even with the potential promise of enjoyment on the other side. As has always been the case, there is hesitancy and not knowing what to expect with someone new, as well as the potential for sex to not be very good or for being hurt. I had never thought about risk when I was younger – being pregnant at sixteen showed up that flaw in my thinking – but now, there are so many soft places within myself to jeopardise, the risk feels too high to gamble the weak stability of the nest I have built for my grief to live in, perched up high on a branch to look down at the rest of the world, safe from harm but alone.

I can't tolerate the chance of feeling stupid or incapable with someone else. I'm unsure how much ease I have in my body, last seen by a stranger in its mid-twenties before children, where time and motherly love have moulded its flesh to resemble a clay project my children would bring home from school.

I just want familiar hands.

Mother

The sieve

Why do you need a sieve to give birth?

This isn't a Mad Hatter-style riddle, it's a genuine question while reading the list to pack my hospital bag. The printout from the birthing centre has an extensive selection of all things mother and baby could ever need: six million baby vests, mattress-style sanitary pads, a book (who is reading during or after labour?), a car seat – the list goes on into infinity. At the very end, almost as an afterthought, is the strangest item – a sieve.

'Seriously, why will I need a sieve?' I ask my mum Madge, who is sat with me on my bedroom floor, helping organise and pack my bag, letting me know with every bone in her body how frustrated she is that I've chosen to do this the day before my due date. Despite predicting her annoyance, I've asked for Madge's help because I am as big as a bus and can't move around, but mostly, it's because she is a hyper-organised woman, a trait I didn't inherit. Madge has different packing lists saved on her laptop ready to print out at a moment's notice: one for weekends away, one for UK holidays, one for holidays abroad. They are full A4, multiple-column lists. Even as a teenager in the 1970s, she was known for going out to nightclubs with an atlas in her bag, 'just in case'. My slapdash way of throwing clothes, probably unwashed, in a bag thirty minutes before leaving definitely strains her motherly bond with me. Madge is clueless about the sieve, and if *she* doesn't know, it must be a clerical error. We can't even take a guess. We decide to ditch the kitchen utensils and stick to nappies and muslin cloths.

Much like the sieve, my good intentions for a tranquil

and Zen-style birth go out the window when the real contractions start. The playlist of whale music and seascapes is the first victim when I order Greg to 'turn this shit off and put some dance music on' because I didn't understand how much energy it takes to push a baby out of your body. It's only when I'm in the birthing pool and the reality of the whole situation hits me that I realise in between gasps of nitric oxide what the sieve is for.

'IT'S FOR SHIT,' I shout out loud enough for anyone walking past to hear. 'Madge, it's to scoop my shit out of the water.' The midwife looks at me as if to say, 'Didn't you know?' No, lovely midwife Kate who is rubbing my back, I did not know, and in many ways, I'm pleased I didn't think about my husband having to spoon my faeces out of a bath before I was so far into labour I couldn't give a fuck about anything. Greg could have played bobbing for apples with my shit for all I cared at that point.

Ten years later, I realise that I don't know what happened with regards to this. I phone Madge to remind her of the sieve and ask her what actually happened as we didn't end up taking one. I'm assuming I didn't actually shit myself during labour.

'Oh yeah, you absolutely did,' she recalls, a bit too much delight in her voice. 'The midwife dealt with it all very quickly; it turns out she had her own sieve. Probably because everyone thought exactly the same as us and didn't take their own.'

Hate

I was prepared for The Love. I welcomed the cascade of love-soaked joy that drenched every inch of me when holding my baby. I was prepared for the transformation of self and understood the assignment fully: becoming a mother means to mutate into a totem of love. I was not prepared to discover it also means you become a conduit for hate.

I wasn't ready for how much Greg and I would hate each other. We were inundated with information on pregnancy, giving birth and parenthood, but I saw not one word written or spoken telling new mothers of the extent you will despise your partner after the baby is born, that fact is left to the new mothers to confide in each other over lukewarm coffee and late-night WhatsApp groups. The multimillion-pound industry seems to have omitted that you may seethe with rage when lying next to them at night, with your newborn gurgling in a crib beside your bed. The family you so desperately craved will be all together in one room while you are fantasising about leaving, wondering if they can feel the vibrations of your body shaking with unadulterated hatred through the mattress.

Sometimes, I hate the fact I am my children's safe space. When they hold in all their fear and vulnerabilities during the day, I am the place they return to in order to fall apart. It is a privilege but, sometimes, I want to experience them through the eyes of someone else – the grandparents and teachers who experience the fun and ease of my own children.

Despite having been a young girl myself, I am still shocked at how hate is thrown at me by my own children. I know this mother/daughter dynamic so deeply – there is no one I have needed more or screamed at harder than my own mum. She was the brick wall I have kicked repeatedly in the tough gig that is unconditional love; no matter how hard I have pushed, she has never fallen down. I hate the pain I now understand that I've caused her.

I hate that becoming a mother is the beginning yet is swiftly followed by a million tiny goodbyes, as you discover all the ways you will need to let go.

At least the baby is OK, that's all that matters

A few weeks after Dalí was born, I bundled her up in a hand-knitted cardigan and the enormity of joy as a new mother to sit with women and newborn babies in my pregnancy yoga class and tell our birth stories. The antenatal class had been transformative for so many of us; as pregnant women, we had started out terrified of giving birth and looking to learn a few stretches but left with a newfound confidence in our bodies and their natural ability to grow and birth a human. In my first session, I sat on my mat cradling a tiny bump and stated I wanted all the drugs – I didn't want to feel a thing, very much inspired by the stories my mum had told me of my own birth in a time where epidurals were seen as standard. I had no understanding of the women sat next to me who were considering different types of birth.

Our teacher Aijay was a mystical creature and someone I adored immediately. She was a woman with an otherworldly nature who listened without judgement but slowly unravelled our preconceived ideas on birth. She made us homemade chocolates and massaged our temples with lavender oil while we lay in šavasana. Aijay spoke to us as goddesses who are about to birth a divine love and should be treated as such. It was because of Aijay and her classes that I decided to opt for a water birth involving no drugs except gas and air. Dalí was eventually born a week early with no complications, so I was able to have the water birth I wanted. Despite the intense pain, it was an exceptional experience. I was deliriously happy and couldn't wait to share stories with the group of our joyful, drug-free births.

We sat in a circle on the floor at Aijay's house, drinking

green tea and shoving cake in our mouths, and as we moved around the group of women, it became increasingly obvious not everyone had the birth they wanted or were expecting.

'I had wanted a home birth, but I was near my due date and was told I had to be induced. When I was hooked up to the drip, I immediately went into full labour and the contractions went from nothing to constant with no break between them. I was like that for hours on end, in so much pain, and thought I would die from the craziness of it. I didn't know it would be like that. Sam was born twelve hours later. I feel traumatised by the whole event. I don't know if I want another baby now if I have to go through that but at least the baby was OK and healthy, that's all that matters.'

'I ended up needing an emergency C-section after Harriet got stuck. It all happened so fast. I was scared and didn't really understand what was happening but at least she was OK and healthy, that's all that matters.'

'I begged for an epidural in the end but there weren't enough trained midwives available. By the time someone who could do it was free, it was too late but at least the baby is OK and healthy, that's all that matters.'

I barely spoke through these stories. All I could do was listen to the harrowing moments these women had endured and realise that such scary, painful details were not obscure bad luck – they seemed to be in the majority in the room. In the days after, I thought a lot about my pure good fortune at having the birth I had envisioned and how no birth plan should be declared a choice; it is a hope based on the stars aligning in your labour. As pregnant women, we weren't told the details of the induction drip, of how it would send you into immediate labour, or that an epidural might not be available to you, depending on who is working that shift. I'm struck by how confused these mothers were by what was happening in one of the most intense moments of their lives.

I'm also struck by everyone's final comments – *'But the baby was OK, that's all that matters'* – the satin ribbon to tie up a box seeping with amniotic fluid. Difficult and traumatic births are important to acknowledge without the need for apologetic caveats, all spoken while we leak pints of blood and experience flashbacks. In the ethereal yet brutal transition from pregnant to mother, you lose your ranking of importance in an instant. In the eyes of yourself and society, you move from revered goddess to workhorse. In many ways, this is essential; newborn babies need all eyes and energy directed onto them, but can't there be room for both humans involved in the birth? A mother is also birthed in this moment. A brand-new person in a new role where the initiation is to expend the same energy as running consecutive marathons back-to-back at the same time as a small human exits your body.

As the goddess you were considered only moments earlier, you might assume you would get to rest at this point. Goodness, no. No, this is when the real work starts. It is a stark lesson that women's pain, especially that experienced by a mother, is not only dismissed but considered par for the course. You may be bleeding, exhausted, traumatised and in pain but at least your baby is OK. That's the main thing.

Courage, Dear Heart (for when the baby won't stop crying)

Our first baby came in the most delightful of circumstances, although spurred on by the hand of Death. The quick passing of Greg's grandad – someone who raised him as his own son, always the first to jump from his seat the moment he walked in the room – and my childhood best friend Neil, a brother to me born to a different mother ten houses down the road, changed everything. Greg and I had spent years in a push and pull dance; me feeling the cogs and physical mechanics of a biological clock winding itself into full motion while he felt the pull of all the 'what ifs?' waiting quietly around the corner. What if there was another record deal? What if he wanted to go on tour? The chasm between us fell into deep stereotypical camps: the woman feeling an all-consuming craving for a baby above all else; the man nervous to commit, not understanding these new emotions and dynamics in the relationship.

Two quick deaths in the space of two weeks, of people who were essential scaffolding in our lives, stopped the dance between us mid-song and slapped us around the face. There is nothing like Death close up to force you into the moment and all there is in that space is life – a desperate need to feel alive and consume it like chocolate cake because you can viscerally feel it slipping away. As someone you love dies, Death's scythe also takes a sliver off your shoulder, removing something of yourself, whether that be a feeling of safety in the world, the familiarity of your family dynamic or your naïveté, you now know that loss and grief are tightly intertwined with love.

After being cut by Death as he took away our people,

Greg and I took ourselves away to a hotel that overlooked the sea. We sat drinking tea in silence and, while lying in bed watching *Rocky*, we whispered to each other that we should have a baby. There was nothing left to say but this.

Dalí was quick in all senses of the word: immediate conception, a swift five-hour labour and a child who rapidly took to the world. She brought me along for the ride so, in the first few months of her life, I found motherhood effortless. Yes – effortless. I was tired but in the way you fall into bed after a glorious day at the beach. I experienced all the dreamy, drug-like exhilaration of an overpowering love, a deep understanding of the meaning of life and a calm that I had never previously felt. Greg and I had never been happier or closer, moving seamlessly in a choreographed dance of a young happy family.

I became pregnant with Bay sixteen months after Dalí was born. Yet this magical moment was diluted by a darkness that had prevailed over our home for a year – something was very wrong with Greg. His stomach problems, initially thought of as a childhood milk allergy re-emerging or IBS, were beginning to dominate our lives. He couldn't stray far from home, his life became so small, and he believed that if he could hold himself together in a tight ball at home, nothing could hurt him.

I thought I could carry all of us with my newly found superwoman mother strength, the kind you hear about when children are trapped under cars and their mothers lift the dead weight with their bare hands (has this actually ever happened?). I thought I could hold Greg's pain, look after a baby *and* grow another one while also working full time as a senior lecturer, in charge of a fashion degree course. I absolutely could not.

My pregnancy was similar to living on a rickety fishing boat for nine months. I felt so constantly nauseous that even air passing through my throat made me gag. Every moment I needed to be horizontal, holding my stomach with Zen-like concentration on my breathing, taking in as minimal amount of air through my nose as possible. Next to me was Greg doing the same, but to keep a handle on his digestive system. I barely remember Dalí in this period, an entire chunk of her life deleted to make way for visions of icebergs and still lakes, anything to stop vomiting.

Bay's arrival into the world was even swifter than Dalí's – a sports car birth of 0–60, from drinking lemonade in my kitchen to sitting in a birthing pool with a baby in two hours flat. However hard the previous nine months had been, I loved her on sight. We had been at war together and now the white flags had been flown, my body easing back into itself immediately. Greg was offered a bed next to me during the first night but couldn't bring himself to sleep there with the knot in his stomach grinding his insides. The exhaustion of such a quick birth didn't touch me. I stayed awake all night just looking at Bay, holding her, imprinting myself onto her. This night stands as one of the most magical, transcendent experiences of my life.

And then she started crying.

My parents had told the story on repeat about how I had cried non-stop for three months when I was born. The kind of story told decades later, when the raw edges had faded and was now told as a joke. The tone of the story has always been one of an eye roll, with no real weight given to the experience. I've repeated the story over the years as a weird badge of honour, a way to connect to my mum. Madge is a strong woman. I have rarely ever seen her flustered and she is calm and measured in all the situations she finds herself in. At no point was it inferred that a non-stop crying baby would have fazed her. What I didn't realise was that it would nearly kill me.

Bay never stopped crying. She was perennially unhappy, as if she had been reincarnated from a terrible life, delighted to be freed of the pain of being a human and was now furious to be here again. Her existential pain soon became mine and we fed each other misery.

In the lead-up to the birth of Bay, I became obsessive about a documentary series on SAS training. I watched every episode repeatedly, hoping to soak up some of the superhuman strength these people displayed while trekking through wild terrain in Wales carrying their bodyweight, being kidnapped in jungles in Borneo and evading interrogation. As part of the mental training, they are left alone blindfolded for twenty-four hours with the sound of babies crying piped in through earphones. The chief trainer tells them to forget parachuting behind enemy lines or living off the land for months – *this* is where people crack.

Forget a two-hour labour for a 9lb 2oz baby with no pain relief – which I survived like the SAS. I cracked soon after because the soundtrack of each day was a constant white noise of crying. If she was awake, she was screaming. I sat shell-shocked in front of my GP, gasping for words to describe the endless soundscape I never escaped from.

'It's just what babies do,' my male doctor concluded. I felt like

Mia Farrow in *Rosemary's Baby,* being gaslit by professionals that everything was OK and the issues were in my head. I quickly began to unravel into my own post-natal depressive horror film.

We talk about post-natal depression now, it's not the taboo subject it once was, but it is still often distilled down to fit nicely into the category of 'the baby blues'. The hormone release on Day 3 post-partum gives you a rush of tears, of feeling so overwhelmed and sad by everything you've just experienced, but dissolves after a few days. Post-natal depression is not this. Parenting classes had prepared me for the birth but didn't touch on the aftermath of emotions. I thought after such a delightful time with Dalí, I was bulletproof. Instead, I dissolved.

The word 'depression' gives the impression of being sad and, while there were definite moments of sadness, the most overwhelming emotion was one of total madness, of cascading waves of losing your mind. I would phone Greg – who was painting in his studio at the bottom of the garden – from the living room floor. I couldn't move to get him. He would answer the phone to silence and then a gasp, the sound you might make if you were being murdered. It was at this point the disconnect between us rooted itself in the carpet – my maddening descent clashed with his increasing physical pains, neither of us able to help the other.

In those moments of pure madness, every second felt unbearable. There is nowhere to go to outrun your feelings. When I did try to act like a sane member of society, it would backfire. I decided to take Bay out for a walk in her pushchair one afternoon. In the pouring rain, I left the house with no coat or plastic cover to protect either of us. After ten minutes,

I couldn't cope with the weather, my poor decisions or one more minute of the drill in my head. I stopped to sit in the middle of the pavement and sob, while Bay cried along with me. The senior school had just finished for the day and teenagers had to veer into the busy main road to pass us. I heard some of them whisper to each other, 'Do you think she's having a nervous breakdown?', 'Should we phone the police?' and 'Do you think that's even her baby?'

At other times, people in public would ignore the breakdown happening in front of them. Queuing up in John Lewis to return a jumper, Bay was fractious and screaming. I tried every trick in the non-existent parenting book to help soothe her but her crying intensified. Other shoppers looked on with disdain and withering stares. The queue was so slow, filled with explanations of unwanted Christmas presents. There was a breaking point in my head where everything turned to white noise. I put Bay back into her pushchair, sat on the floor with my head in my hands and cried. No one asked if I was OK or if they could help, they just walked past us without comment to take my position in the queue.

We fill the space in conversation about the needs of new mothers with the safe and easy solution of self-care. 'New mothers need to prioritise self-care by sitting quietly with a hot cup of tea or taking a nice bath' the parenting advice suggests, as if a face mask and a biscuit would quell my main desire, which was to be dead.

I was never suicidal, but I absolutely wished I didn't have to be alive anymore. These are two very different feelings. I didn't want to kill myself even when I lurched around the house desperately looking for a Stanley knife with the thought of cutting myself to help alleviate some of the emotional pain I was in. I just wanted to let the blood and madness out.

I was lucky to bond with Bay immediately and was always able to look after her, but it was this fact that prevented me from accessing the care I needed. When I mentioned post-natal depression to those around me, it was dismissed because the baby was fed and in clean clothes. Her needs were met, and everyone told me what a great job I was doing, except I was dissolving into the ground and no one could see. I considered going to doctor's secretly to beg for drugs to stop the madness, but I thought about explaining this years later to Bay; how would it make her feel that I had needed antidepressants to get up in the morning when she arrived and not her sister?

After five months, her crying stopped as quickly as it had begun, and my madness followed the tears out of the door. I wish I'd had the grace for myself in that period to understand I was very ill and desperately needed help. I wish others had not been scared to hold such big emotions and acknowledge what was happening. I wish we all spoke about the snakelike tendrils of the post-natal experience and how it can break a mother into pieces.

Motherhood in a nutshell

'Dad is best at drawing, painting, singing, writing songs, playing guitar, football and writing poems,' my daughter tells me.

'Yes he is!' I agree. 'What do you think I'm best at?'

Pause

'Driving.'

Pause

'Oh, and writing all the things we have to do in your diary. Although you do lose your diary all the time so I don't think we can put it on the list of things you are good at. So just driving.'

(Insert a witty line about motherhood or a crying emoji face here.)

The road to hell is paved with good intentions

There is often a huge distance between what we think we are representing to our children compared to how they interpret it. We can have the best intentions to protect them but they are often lost in translation.

A large percentage of the decisions I make in my life are seen through the lens of my daughters and how I want them to experience the world. It's important for them to see me actively pursue my interests. I want them to see me working so they can understand what it is to build something for yourself and be financially independent. I also want them to see me prioritise my friends and see how those relationships nourish you. I want to show up in the world as the example I want them to see.

When Greg was ill and in the dire situation of needing to pay privately for treatments not freely available, I consoled myself during the hard work of the fundraising by believing I was being a good role model for the girls. In that period, I worked obsessively, with my main incentive being the Portfolio of Good Intentions I could show them in the future to say 'LOOK! Look how hard I fought for your dad and for us.' There were times I was so busy campaigning for better cancer treatments, organising auctions with celebrities, writing copy – all for my children to be so proud of how I handled this situation in the future – that I often ignored them in the present. I didn't understand that they wouldn't care about any of this. They won't remember the meeting I attended to help decide which clinical trials should be funded by charity funds; all they will remember is the phrase 'hang on, in a minute' as I forever looked down into the screen of a phone.

In many ways, the logistics of motherhood are all about playing the long game. 'You'll understand when you're an adult/parent' was a phrase used by my mum on repeat when I was young. In a cycle as old as the hills, I dismissed it as nonsense from someone who didn't understand me, only to find out that she was entirely correct. I would then end up saying the same line to my own children. But when my mum would say this to me, it was because she didn't think it was a good idea for me to go out in a top that would be generously described as a handkerchief. It is a very different situation for me to say to my kids, 'Don't worry, you'll understand in twenty-five years why I'm so focused on the rest of the world except you in the most traumatic time.' They needed me immediately, when their lives were being ripped apart, but there were times I was too busy trying to raise money by selling Coldplay's gold disc to the highest bidder to see that.

I realised Greg's health was never really in my hands, I could never control the pain I would feel in his death, but the catastrophe of not showing up in the way I needed and ultimately wanted to was absolutely my responsibility. I soon realised my children's needs were exactly the same as mine – for someone to sit down next to them, look them in the eye and just be there.

One-woman band

'Could your husband not come? Is he working?'

The early-morning questions from parents I don't know, sat on miniature plastic chairs either side of me, are not my favourite way to start the day. Shall I just say my husband is dead? Or make a joke about bringing his ashes to sit next to me to watch Bay's school assembly? I start chatting about something else, batting away the explanation of why I'm sat alone in the rows of mums and dads, all waiting to support their children on stage. In fact, there are lots of parents not here; many are working and can never come to any events set in school hours. There are blended families, grandparent carers and foster families all within Bay's one class. I'm not usually aware of my lone status on the school run, but today, here among these teams of two, flying solo feels heavy.

Historically, being a single parent comes heavily laden with negative connotations, especially as a woman. It has been associated with being poor, a scrounger, desperate, alone and a bad mother. We may be more aware of the nuances of this situation now and reject these unhelpful stereotypes, but it was only very recently, in 2005, the official status for those not in relationships and marriages was changed from 'spinster' – a universally disparaging insult – to the more neutral term 'single'.

While I was part of a parenting duo, I assumed the hardest thing about being a solo mother would be making all the decisions alone. How would you make those choices without a second input to help mull them over? As it turns out – easily. When you have made actual life and death decisions, choosing a secondary school or when to discuss sex falls into the same category as what's for dinner. These aren't the things that keep me up at night; I know they will all work themselves out. As a one-woman band, I have slightly different worries to other parents.

First and foremost, there is no safety net left in the infrastructure of our family. I worry about becoming ill myself and – the worst eventuality of all – dying and leaving my children alone. I lie in the dark, calculating a reasonable age for humans to survive with no parents. It's a fruitless task when as a forty-three-year-old with both her parents still alive, my own answer would be 'probably never'. I worry about not having anyone I feel comfortable nominating as a guardian if the worst happens.

These are huge, overwhelming fears that consume my heart in the background but there are more pressing day-to-day concerns. The dynamic of our household altered entirely when we became a unit of three, needing my style of parenting to change with it. As a family of four, I had a definite role within the group; I was the more lenient parent, the one who tried to encourage taking more risks. I was also more often the 'bad cop' as the primary carer. Now there can be no 'good cop/bad cop' parent situation in our house so I need to be constantly mindful to not tip too hard into the disciplinarian and have them hate me while at the same time not being desperate for harmony and letting them get away with murder. There is so little space to be the 'bad cop' when things have been so tricky for most of their lives. I don't want to create a legacy of moaning. It is also hard to care about the small things when you have seen how the world ends because you know it doesn't really matter. As a mother to young children, I had always been a stickler for routine, but as the only adult in the house, bedtimes get later, dinners aren't eaten at the table when laps on the sofa are preferred and things slip because I am so exhausted by being all things to two tiny humans who assume I am infallible.

I also assume there will be times in the future when I will be cast as the devil in our home. I alone will receive the full force of these firecracker girls' spirits when they don't like the parenting decisions I've made. In the child's version of their dead parent, they would *absolutely* let them stay out until midnight whereas the mean, alive one will only allow until 10 p.m. If our future had been different, they would have organically seen when the time arrived for them to have a phone; it's only me who will know they could have added five more years to their wait if their dad was around. Potentially, the dead parent will always be funnier, kinder, more lenient, understanding and generous than the living one in the eyes of bereaved children.

As the remaining parent, I'm aware I'm the main gate-keeper to Greg's legacy for the girls. The empty space in our house that he occupied will be filled with stories, songs, images and memories and, most importantly, what the girls want him to be. Many people become canonised by the living when they die. The dead are raised up to the highest echelons of their best selves to become deity-esque, especially if they die young and even more so in tragic circumstances. It is a societal norm to 'not speak ill of the dead' out of respect and the obvious fact they can't reply or defend themselves.

I worry about the sainthood of Greg through the eyes of our daughters. They would have lived with early-morning grumpiness and arguments, annoying habits and the uncomfortable truth you discover that your parents are just people, trying their best and often getting it wrong. They will never know him as a fallible man who had many faults mixed in with his maddening talents, fast wit and deep love for them. I will need to judge how to delicately sprinkle these stories into their lives to create a richer, fully formed version of their dad, alongside filling our house with the creative legacy Greg left behind. I think a lot about my daughters' future relationships – if they will look in dark corners for father figures, desperate to fill empty holes in their hearts.

Our house has Greg's energetic abstract paintings in most rooms, to represent the very best of his creative talents. So much of his work on display is in lieu of any photographs of him or us as a family; for me, our house would become a minefield, with any glance at Greg's face liable to take me down. At times when our hearts can tolerate it, we will dance to Delays' music, to shake our love and grief out from our limbs. We open the windows of our home as wide as they will stretch, to let Greg's voice out into our neighbourhood, the place he lived his entire life.

We live directly next to an airport, the edge of a liminal space of departure and arrival, yet I am steadily here, sleeping with my head on the runway every night. It isn't an enormous international airport but it's still big enough to have planes take off and land every fifteen minutes and, if you are sat in the garden in the summer, you will need to stop talking mid-sentence because of the engines' roar. Visitors to my house will always comment, 'Don't you mind the planes?' whereas I barely notice their noise anymore. The local paper is full of angry readers' letters about airport expansion plans and fury at more flights being added.

For me, there is no such anger. In fact, I adore living under a flight path and the constant feeling of toing and froing, coming and going. Living on the south coast in a port city, where cruise liners three times the size of *Titanic* line the docks, acclimatises you to a transient state. It is a city of total flux, where it is usual for the night's quiet darkness to be punctuated by the Disney cruise ship horn blowing out the 'When You Wish upon a Star' melody across the water.

Our house sits at the highest point of the city fifty metres above sea level. There is safety in height; to have a bird's-eye view on anything helps to scan for potential danger. Behind our house is a field called Toad's Copse, a protected green space used to encourage wildlife when, in reality, it is the designated emergency landing strip for the airport. I question this every morning when I open my children's curtains and look at the small piece of land: *this* is supposed to hold the violent force of a 747's descent? The homes packed in around its edges would be decimated along with everyone in them. As I walk our dog around the perimeter, it seems crazy to think this gentle field with its ladybirds and wild flowers would stop a 200-ton plane ripping through your living room at 400 miles per hour while you're watching Netflix.

This is how being a solo parent feels. I am not equipped to hold what is expected of me.

They know

'But you're not going to tell the girls, are you?'

The same comment is made by a hundred different well-meaning people. My honesty about our lives puts people on edge when I don't talk in code or translate death and horror with just wincing facial expressions. It's obvious people around me are terrified I will use the truth about Greg's health to destroy my daughters' childhoods.

Every instinct as a parent is to protect. All the maternal fibres laced through your nervous system that grew alongside your first baby will pulsate at the thought of the emotional damage such bad news will have on their tiny selves. As they grow, this dominant feeling doesn't change but, for me, what did change was my understanding of what protection looks like as a mother.

The girls sporadically asked me what was wrong with Daddy, and I told them what we had agreed, using words they would understand – he had a bad belly. They asked if he would get better – I said the doctors were working very hard to help him. This was technically not a lie, but a world of pain was omitted. For tiny children not yet even at school, these answers placated them, and we could all jolly along in a fog of make-believe for a while longer.

However, as children get older, such sleight-of-hand answers tip the balance between who we are now protecting. Using our words to dodge the truth no longer protects them; they start to damage them while beginning to shield us. Children are smart – they understand when what they see in front of them doesn't tally with the flippant nature of the answers they've been given. We use the term 'age appropriate' with no real understanding of what this actually means to children; it can signal much more of what *we* feel we are capable of explaining and tolerating. The problem with hiding important chunks of information from children is *they already know.*

Big family secrets are impossible to hide. Whether it is a terminal diagnosis, a loveless marriage, an alcoholic parent or a mental health issue, the truth will seep into the fabric of the house while the children fall asleep to its whispers. When Dalí was five, she was asked by a girl in her class why her dad was dead. Obviously confused, she asked me why anyone would ask her that when her dad was alive at home. The truth was everyone around us knew Greg was terminally ill, so it was no surprise children had heard their parents talking about it. It felt like an impossible situation when we didn't feel ready to discuss Greg's prognosis with the girls but, at the same time, understanding the importance of such a sledgehammer blow coming from us as opposed to the kids in the playground and any grotesque version of events they had heard fifth-hand.

This is the most important thing about telling children the truth in any situation. The broken whispers and morphing stories mutate into something else in their minds, often more extreme and scarier than the real truth. Children are like scientists; they will pull all their theories, ideas and their own mini-experimentations together to make sense of what's in front of them to create a hypothesis. If they don't receive answers to their questions from parents, they will just look elsewhere, often from the unreliable sources of peers and the internet. To talk openly with children enables a soft space for them to crash-land in. You have control of the narrative; you can answer questions and know any additional information will land gently. It builds trust and gives them a sense of agency in their own lives while feeling safe and secure the adults are handling it.

There is a flip side to this argument though, in the universal idea that children are resilient, often more so than adults. This is so often a lie; one we comfort ourselves with when our children are faced with indescribable pain. What adults see as resilience in children is often the burying of what they cannot understand yet. They don't have the developed cognition to either understand or process such overwhelming moments. Adults relax when they see traumatised children playing, carrying on as normal and label it resilience when the trauma is silently bedding down in their tiny veins, waiting for the time to make itself known.

I would not choose resilience for my children. I would choose a soft life full of delight and ease, not having to break their bones in order to grow back stronger.

Jumpers for goalposts

The arrival of Death's 'save the date' invitation created an immediate and seismic shift in our home. This was most visible in how I chose to parent Dalí and Bay. When I returned from the hospital on the night Greg was diagnosed with cancer, not yet knowing what stage it was at, I let the girls eat Bay's homemade birthday cake on the kitchen floor with their hands alongside the dog, grabbing at the icing with their tiny fists and delighting at what they believed was a fun detour in rules. None of us recognised how this moment shifted my entire role as mother forever.

The self-penned manual of motherhood was set on fire. Those lofty ideals didn't apply anymore. It reminded me of the shifting values from being a pregnant woman and new mother to having a toddler and subsequent children. With Dalí, I would make my own organic vegetable purees then scan ingredients lists of shop-bought products – sugar?! For a baby?! I wasn't yet worn down by having to feed everyone three times a day, before you even include snacks. A day feels like an eternity when you see it through the lens of food. By the time Bay arrived, the first food she tasted was chocolate. I have never liked to offer advice to new mums other than to say, lower your standards and then, once you've done that, lower them again.

Other routines began to slip. Bedtimes became later; we all stopped eating at the table, watching cartoons with plates on our laps instead. We had let Dalí watch the first two *Harry Potter* films when she was five but resisted her protests to see the others, believing they were too dark in tone, but now, how is watching Voldemort on a screen any worse than watching your dad lose his hair, his weight, his life in real time?

When we knew Greg's death was imminent, the girls stayed home from school, floating around with whoever could take care of them at any given moment. There is no good time for your dad to die but Dalí was two weeks into starting a new school. The first day was surrounded by freshly pressed new uniforms and gushing parents. I must have looked like a wide-eyed deer about to have their bones shattered by an oncoming car as I whispered to any authoritative adult I could see that this child, the one who took so much care with her hair this morning and packed her new backpack herself, her dad is dying less than a mile away in a room he used to play with toy cars in. I wanted to scream in the new playground that I didn't understand how this new beginning was happening when so much was ending at the same time.

After Greg died, the girls went back to school four days later and two of those days included a weekend. This fact sits starkly on the page now, something that could be recounted in the future as a strange decision. All I know, maybe bizarrely, is at that time it absolutely felt like the right thing to do.

The three of us spent months scrabbling around in the dirt finding new ways to just survive. Greg's death was at the very end of summer, so the dark nights drew in around us, offering no light to see our way through. There was so much desperation and anger with nowhere for it to go but ricochet off the walls to be absorbed back into us. When the girls struggled, I encouraged them to smash soft toys against walls. Their bedroom became the space where they were allowed to scream swear words as loudly as they wanted, sometimes the only thing able to raise a smile.

It is a mess when a parent and children are all grieving.

In those fiery first days of grief, we took turns in crying on the floor and when it was my turn to not know what to do anymore, Dalí learnt how to use my phone to call my parents to say, 'Mum isn't coping, can you come round?' At other times, all three of us would be sat on the floor howling together in our own personal hole, unable to reach out to each other. There were moments when the slurry of pain cannot help but seep from every pore.

I could see how stressful this was for the girls, their lives already upended by the loss of an anchor. It was frightening for them to see their only parent lose control and detracted from the feeling of safety already in short supply. It is a moment of guilt as a mother, seeing the fear in their child's eyes and sometimes even try to be the adult for a moment, a dynamic that always feels wrong and uncomfortable. Your heart is the bullseye for all their arrows of pain and sadness, shot towards you because you are an unconditional monument of love.

Grief in children feels like a failure. You had one job as a parent and that is to protect them, and you've failed at the first hurdle. I didn't know how to be the lighthouse when the boat was sinking and the headland on fire. I was spread too thin and looking for my own light in the distance to save me from the crashing waves. How are you supposed to save someone when you're drowning yourself? Isn't this how people die in the news? MAN DROWNS IN RIVER TRYING TO SAVE DOG. MOTHER DIES SAVING CHILD SWIMMING IN RESERVOIR.

Adults can process grief with sadness, crying, talking about the missing person, but children don't have the cognitive functions developed to see such a clear path for their raw emotions. Instead, their grief is rage, regression, phobias, meltdowns, separation anxiety and fearing the new. They will find ways to process these feelings at every new age.

This is what happens when we have cold hard proof the world isn't safe. We've seen with our own eyes and felt deeply in our own hearts that bad things happen to good people, those people being us, and life cannot be trusted to play fair – whether that looks like losing someone you can't live without, a bankruptcy, a natural disaster, a messy divorce, an unexpected accident or even how the mundanity of modern life can chip holes into you. It can feel safer to close the blinds, keep your circle small, choose the same meal from the menu and believe you are cursed.

It is exactly this time when we need to take more risks. I often see bubble-wrap behaviour from others around my children as a non-verbal way of saying, 'I'm sorry your dad died!' *Give them the toy* (because their dad died). *Of course you can have the sweets, in fact, take them all* (because your dad died). I don't want the girls to use their dad's death as a crutch or a way to manipulate situations in their favour.

In a world where our children will be broken-hearted and disappointed repeatedly, it is important we still push them out into the rain when we want to wrap them in a blanket. As the last generation who experienced a childhood without mobile phones and the full extent of the internet, we need to help our children live with the same abandon as we love to wax lyrical about; the days playing out with friends, swimming in rivers alone. We got hurt but it was OK because no one gave us the impression it was the end of the world.

In this new messy mother shape I hold, I try to model what truth looks like: making mistakes, forgetting and apologising. I will be the one to encourage reaching for the higher branch or jumping from the larger rock. Sometimes I'm so tired, I will shout because it's easier to blame the children than understand what is really going on inside me. I want to show them love and relationships are complicated and messy, that working at a relationship is no consolation prize to the prince on the horse. I play this long game for my daughters so when they are older and experiencing a world which makes them feel alone or ashamed, they will know they aren't experiencing anything except life.

Bodies

The dress (pink)

We are told Greg is going to die on our daughter Bay's first birthday, an outrageous juxtaposition. At home, there is a table laid for a party, with balloons and a poorly made cake I baked earlier in the day.

'I'm sorry, the cancer has spread to your lungs,' the surgeon tells me, Greg and his dad in the blue-draped cubicle on the busy ward. 'We won't be operating; it will be pointless. There isn't anything we can do for you.'

In that moment, it's my life that flashes before my eyes, not Greg's. A ticker tape of images screams past as old photographs: a baby with jet-black hair in my mum's arms; a shy child; a reckless teenager; a new mother. The innocence and naïveté of these images shatter any idea I have of hope or fairness but now, as a mother myself, on the anniversary of birthing my own child, a maternal instinct is ignited and gives the clear message – if it has to be either of us, it cannot be me who dies. A split-second reconnaissance of our lives all comes down to who could look after the children better. I am the primary carer, I'm still breastfeeding Bay, I can drive/ Greg can't, I have a secure job with a pension. I make the mental judgements as if it's just the two of us in a fatal game of rock, paper, scissors. I am nothing except a mammal, desperate for the survival of her babies.

The comparisons between birth and death become obvious when you are in the presence of both in a short space of time. Birth leaves nothing to hide behind and you quickly realise you are not in control; your body is going to take over. Animal, biological instinct kicks in, imprinted deep within your DNA and your body moves accordingly.

142

You rock, you moan from a place deep within you where ancient ancestors reside; the inner mechanics of your body begin to pull themselves apart, helped by new levels of endorphins and oxytocin.

When I gave birth for the second time, I saw wild imagery. I saw the pink and cream wallpaper of my childhood bedroom printed over everything. Whether my eyes are open or closed, it was there and it lasted for months after the birth. I saw myself walking up the Brecon Beacons holding hands in a row with all of my girlfriends, a line of feminine unity pulling me along. I felt myself hugging my dog, so real that at one point, I screamed, 'MILK!' ('Umm . . . does she want a glass of milk?' the midwife asked. 'No,' said Greg. 'It's just the name of our dog.')

A rhythmic noise that sounded like an animal barking in distress brought me round. I flailed around to see where the noise was coming from, and when I felt the midwife grab my hand, I realised it was coming from me. I was 10 cm dilated and ready and she was coming. I looked at Greg. He looked like a daddy already, so confident. He was slowly nodding, telling me that I'm strong and that I can do this and he's here. I felt the earth move on its axis as Bay was born, the world ripped apart for her to enter. I remember Greg and I looking at each other making tiny gasping noises at the joy of her, an explosive moment of happiness and calm. A year from this moment, I wanted to revel in these memories, at the pure magic of creating a life but, instead, Death has taken a seat at the birthday party table.

In an eerily similar way, Death arrives with nothing to hide behind and you quickly realise you are not in control; your body is going to take over. Animal, biological instinct kicks in, imprinted deep within your DNA, and your body moves accordingly. As Greg is told he is going to die, I saw wild imagery again. A dress. It's bright pink, a jubilant summer fuchsia. A 1950s style with capped sleeves, nipped in waist and full skirt, the Christian Dior New Look. The dress embodies the crisis that facing mortality brings – making everything utterly frivolous and pointless while at the same time, all things that provide joy become the unadulterated meaning of life. Whose dress is this? Not mine. Why is my wardrobe full of black and grey when I could be wearing pink?

I see Bette Midler. Every December, I start each day with her Christmas album. Please live until Christmas. I need to listen to that album one more time because soon, I will never be able to listen to it again. Every year, we have the same argument – I want a real tree because it reminds me of my childhood but Greg is convinced I won't clean up all the shed needles and just throw it out the back door to rot throughout the year. He's so right, that's exactly what I will do, and I so desperately want to have that argument with him again.

The new series of *Twin Peaks* doesn't start until May. It is Greg's absolute favourite, and he has waited twenty-five years to see it and now he won't. How can I get in contact with David Lynch to get a copy?

A rhythmic noise that sounds like an animal barking in distress brings me round. I look around to see what it is and, when I feel the nurse grab my hand, I realise it's coming from me. I'm having a panic attack. I can't breathe and I'm going to be sick. I look at Greg. He looks like a little boy. He is slowly nodding as the surgeon tells him there is nothing more to be done because the cancer is too advanced.

He thanks the surgeon for coming to tell him. He shakes his hand. Greg's politeness in the face of death floors me. WHY ARE YOU FUCKING THANKING HIM? He has told you you're going to die. I fantasise about smashing the surgeon's head into the floor with a hammer. He looks like Voldemort from *Harry Potter*. Has no one else noticed that? A thin, grey face with nothing behind his eyes. The doctors float around the corridors like Dementors delivering death blows.

I can't breathe but all I can think about is the pink dress, where I could buy one and how much I hate the blue of the thin, polyester curtains pulled round the bed. Why is the end of our lives being played out in the middle of a ward? The curtains don't stop the sound of the patient next to us screaming about how he doesn't want a sponge bath and ordering the nurse to get away from his testicles. It's all so outrageous, so bizarre and nightmarish. Greg's dad is sat at the end of the bed in shock and a new weight fills my lungs; Greg's mum isn't here. She is walking back from the café in the last few moments of her life when she won't know her son is going to die. Voldemort is talking about something medical that I'm sure is important but I'm concentrating on ways Greg's mum could delay her arrival into hell. Maybe a trolley could hit her and she breaks her ankle and will need to go to A&E. That could give her a few more hours still in the normal world.

'How long have I got?' Greg asks. He wants to know the number. That number, as innocuous as a card picked from a pack by a magician masquerading as a consultant, but heavily weighted with science and statistics. There is a definitive before and after: that once you are given this weight to hold, you won't be able to put it down; it's yours to carry.

Please don't say a number, Voldemort. I only have so much breath left in me.

'We don't know. How long is a piece of string?' the dark wizard replies flippantly, casually rolling up his shirt sleeves as if he's on holiday. I wish he was dead.

I think about taking the girls camping. This is a ridiculous idea as I hate camping and don't own a tent.

Oh. The girls.

Voldemort and Greg's dad leave the blue box of hell and it's just me and Greg alone. The whole world disappears and all that's left is us, playing out a heaven sequence in a film.

'Life is wild.' The words leave my mouth of their own accord. We talk in clipped sentences in between big breaths as that's all that's available in this new world. There doesn't seem to be much air.

'Don't worry, we'll see each other again when we are space ghosts,' Greg offers up as a condolence. At that moment, this seems a totally reasonable answer and we sink into the bed together in a trance, imagining ourselves zipping around the universe. There was a calm in this space and, dare I say it, even a tranquil happiness. A transcendence of clarity and an immediate understanding of everything – that nothing matters, literally nothing except people you love.

'I won't let the girls grow up afraid.' I think this is a noble, strong thing to say in the moment but later, Greg will tell me how painful this was to hear, that I had already confined him to the past where he wasn't a parent anymore.

We are drifting through time and space, but the absence of Greg's mum starts to pull us down to earth. When she finally arrives and opens the curtains, my body ejects itself from its haze and the sheer horror of where we are comes into focus.

I can never unsee the heaviness of her body as she dropped onto the bed into Greg's arms. I try to unsee it, so I run away out of the ward.

How many people have walked these halls with their mouths wide open and tears streaming down their face? I'm suddenly outside and phoning my family. How do you say these words? In gasps and short words and with a stranger approaching to hand you a tissue because you are standing in a crowd crying and your life is ending.

I sit on the floor with my notebook because something has to come out – either words or vomit:

NUMB.
SCARED.
SICK.
DROWNING.
I can't breathe with fear. I didn't know terror like this existed. Life is wild. We think we know. We don't. Today, from the top floor, I watched cars trying to park. They look like tiny ants crawling around, looking for something. I suddenly see us all like this – wandering around, looking for things. I wonder what I was looking for, before this. I don't know. And what am I looking for now? Hope. And time. And peace and goodwill and energy and grace. Grace to sit in this and not harden or fall apart in a way that I would have done years ago. I can feel the blackest hole nearby.

Let me find the grace and strength and hope from the energy that we know is within all things. It's always there, we just need to see it. OPEN YOUR EYES AND DON'T CLOSE YOUR HEART TO MAGIC.

BEAR WITNESS.
DON'T LOOK AWAY.
EVEN IF IT'S EASIER.
When I go back upstairs, I vomit in the toilets. My body feels the travel sickness from the sharp detour into a new world.

Rites of passage

The patient in the bed behind the curtain is receiving visitors. Greg and I give each other a confused look because what we can hear isn't the forced, overtly happy lilt of any newcomer to an oncology ward. We can hear prayers, three voices intoning in unison, the smell of old habitual perfumes. A reading from *Romans* about co-operation. We sit in silence with mouths open, a mixture of horror and fascination. Is it nuns? A priest? They are here to read the paper-thin old man his last rites.

Simultaneously, the patient's adult daughter is furiously pacing the length of the ward, screaming into her phone, her fast strides and shouting abrasive next to the slow, intentional words of the priest.

'Hallelujah . . .'

'I COULD NOT GIVE ONE FUCK ABOUT WHAT YOUR RECORDS SAY. THE PHONE LINE WAS DISCONNECTED ON THE DATE I'VE TOLD YOU.'

The exclamation doesn't sound as it does in a gospel church, so full of hope and energy. Here, it is flatly expressed as they make a concession to privacy. There are incantations, whispered through a nylon curtain, that land in our ears as though witches are stirring a cauldron and brewing a spell. Perhaps it's a tonic to save the patient, to dissolve the tumour gnawing his bones. Hopefully, God can also save the person sat in the call centre having fire and brimstone hailed at them through the phone.

'The Kingdom of Heaven . . .'

'NO, THAT'S NOT THE CORRECT FINAL AMOUNT. I'M NOT PAYING FOR THREE FUCKING EXTRA MONTHS.'

To those in earshot, desperately clinging onto life, the prayers feel like an imposition. There is no comfort in the endings of final redemptions.

'The fisherman hauled it ashore . . .'

'I DON'T WANT TO HEAR YOUR TERMS AND CONDITIONS.'

Does *anyone* in earshot want to hear such cloistered witchcraft?

'Divine sacrament . . . our servant John in our Lord's Salvation . . .'

'LET ME SPEAK TO YOUR MANAGER.'

John is so polite: 'Thank you ever so much, I appreciate your time.' His daughter finishes her call, bursts into tears and runs out of the room. The nuns and nurses shuffle out together and the ward returns to a pulsating silence. Later, when I mention how quiet it all seems for a Saturday, two separate nurses say, 'We don't mention the Q word here.'

I silently take a photo of Greg and sit on the edge of the bed, not knowing what else to do except document that we are still alive.

Across from us, the man in the bed coughs up blood onto the white sheets. I would also like to speak to the manager.

Holding an atom bomb

My dad found his own father dead, his head in the oven and body splayed out over the kitchen floor. I was fascinated by this story as a tortured teenager. How very Sylvia Plath, I thought. My dad was only two years old when his father Thomas killed himself, so he has no memory of the event, although I have often wondered what bomb-site residue has infused into his subconscious. He had entered the house with his mother and his brother David, six years older than him so, at age eight, would definitely have the scene sketched into his mind forever – except we don't know this because David never spoke of it again. Heavily influenced by my grandma, the event was erased from history, changed into a more acceptable car crash for those who wanted to know what happened to Thomas, including my dad. It was many decades later, after my parents were married in their late twenties, that my mum casually chatted to a family neighbour on the street and the secret suicide was dropped into the conversation like an atom bomb. It was my mum who had to tell my dad there was no car crash in his childhood but many secrets.

Secrets fester like untreated sores and itch under your skin. There is a reason why children who have been told a secret physically blow up like a hot-air balloon – eyes wide, hamster cheeks, up on tiptoes. It is so uncomfortable to keep classified information, the desire to share is enormous, and in children's young, innocent bodies, it becomes unbearable and they want to share the load. Adults are better at holding information but that's not to say there isn't a price to pay, and as a mother myself now holding secrets of my own, I wonder what psychic toll my grandma had to pay for holding such big secrets.

No one blamed my grandma for wanting to keep this information within the four walls of her home. I don't doubt she did this with the best of intentions. There was too much collateral damage; she closed down parts of herself forever to prevent being smashed to pieces and not be able to put herself back together. Her first son David was the result of a fling with an American soldier who Grandma later told everyone had died in the war, a questionable fact now seen through hindsight, perhaps returning to the US to be with his wife. It was 1954 when Thomas killed himself; suicide and mental health were not the buzzwords of today. The societal shame of the time around becoming a single mother encouraged her to put her head down and get on with bringing up two boys on her own.

I think about my grandma often. She died in 2019 at the age of ninety-four. Even though she lived close by, I was never particularly close to her; in fact, I found her way of sugar-coating every situation incredibly difficult, even as a child before I knew anything about her past. Now I look back at her life with such sadness and empathy; she was widowed twice by the age of twenty-nine to then marry the man I knew as my grandad, who was mean and controlling. I want to wrap that young woman up and protect her from the cruelty of the universe; she endured so much and kept a large part of it secret. Our situations were different but the act of keeping secrets and its wear and tear on our psyches over time is something we have in common.

For me, the mental juggling of remembering who knew what about Greg's illness and prognosis and deciding who had the capacity to deal with what on any given day was exhausting. I needed to create differing versions of the same thing, like making the same dinner but serving the adults, cutting up the meat for the kids and pureeing the whole thing together for the baby. To hold all the information meant to be split in half, often having wildly different conversations in the same house but in different rooms. I could be making a cup of coffee and discussing how probate works then deliver the drink to those who are discussing when we should sell our house and where we would move to. I played along, planning an imaginary house move in an imaginary future because even though I couldn't know what carefully constructed version of reality others had created for themselves, I knew enough to know it was not mine to break. Everyone had tentatively built their own personal shelter from this storm; rudimental nests made of feathers and tissue paper, which the weight of reality would crush immediately. By a process of elimination as the holder of facts and secrets, I couldn't build myself any shelter because I had to be on constant watch and needed a clear view of oncoming threats.

How important is the truth compared to the importance of not knowing? Greg had told me the story of a school assembly where a teacher had begun by saying, 'So we all know Santa isn't real and is just our parents . . .' as other children nodded along while Greg sat stunned in silence, his childhood dreams shattered. I was always furious when he spoke of this event. 'Who the FUCK was that teacher to take that away? He had no idea what that idea meant to any of those kids.'

The truth is often simple yet incomprehensible. I regularly saw messages to Greg on social media or in cards with the same words sent with good intentions but which left me wondering if I was gaslighting myself: 'You can beat this', as if biology is merely a battle of wills and a decision you can make.

As the years rumbled on and Greg became frailer, I remember sitting with Dr Baggins in his office and asking him how Greg could possibly not know he was going to die.

'He will,' he said, with a soft, knowing smile, as if he'd had this conversation many times before. 'His body will tell him.'

I can see why you would want the most violent truth to be kept a secret from you. I can see why people live in the past; there are no surprises there, you already know all the ways you'll be crushed. I can see why my grandma wanted to keep certain times of her life locked up. There are now thoughts, memories, places inside I have decided to never visit again for fear of what lives there now. There are rooms in my heart I have padlocked shut. They feel like haunted rooms. I will walk the long way home to not have to pass by them.

Just get on with it

I learnt very quickly as a woman that you are not allowed to become sick, especially in the roles of mother and carer. In the early post-partum days, there was a bleak night where I lay on the bathroom floor, delirious with dehydration from vomiting and diarrhoea. In the dark, Greg brought me the baby to breastfeed as I was the only one who could nourish her. I puked in the toilet while twisting my body around so the baby's head wouldn't be covered in sick as she drank every nutrient from me. When she was finished, she was taken back to bed and I was left alone to shiver on the floor.

You are also not allowed to be sick as a pregnant woman. We may acknowledge that morning sickness exists but refuse to allow women to actually *be* sick. Working through pregnancy illness is a special kind of torture, forged in the hell of the patriarchy. Growing a human, needing to throw your guts up and fall asleep through exhaustion while working full time is a fresh kind of purgatory. In my job as a fashion lecturer, I sat in tutorials with students who earnestly showed me their work while I vomited my breakfast up into my mouth, silently swallowing it down because I didn't want anyone to know I was pregnant yet or question my ability to do the job.

After my pregnancy was announced, I sat in work meetings with other senior academics as silent tears flowed under the unbearable pressure to hold down my job when I hadn't held down a meal for weeks. I felt like a small child at the table, wanting the adults to take away all my responsibilities and let me go to sleep. Unlike when a child cries in desperation, no one knows how to deal with an ill woman who is saying

155

no, that she can't carry on being stoic and needs to lie down before she passes out. I had to leave the room, throw up in the toilets, fix my makeup and come back to the meeting to let the group know how I was going to shoehorn eight weeks' worth of work into two and make up for the time I'd had off. *Please stop crying, little girl, you're a woman now, soon to be mother with a child.*

* * *

I loved being ill as a child. To have a day off school with a duvet on the sofa, daytime talk shows on TV, on-and-off snoozing and food brought to you was my idea of heaven. This was only for light illnesses; anything above a fluctuating fever or headache was no fun but this weird revelry in sickness and recuperation played out over many years, although I fell in love with being ill much earlier.

I developed chronic asthma as a three-year-old, a wheezing kid whose airways would become agitated and close most days. Its inflammatory nature started so early in me, I don't remember a time where I wasn't reliant on inhalers and steroids to be able to breathe. I also don't remember the few occasions where I nearly died because of it. Madge tells the stories of driving through red lights, her normal calm demeanour screaming at drivers to move on her way to A&E because I had turned blue and stopped breathing. She would throw her keys at nurses to move the car she had left abandoned in the spot saved for ambulances while she carried me inside for emergency shots of steroids and nebuliser masks. I don't remember being in intensive care with pneumonia. I don't remember having no good veins left for IV drips because my body was so small and overused by needles.

I can only remember comforting snapshots of the few years I lived in hospital; the mothering nurses who let me join them on their rounds as I pulled my drip on wheels behind me like a sad dog. Every day began in the same way: you were given a menu for the day to choose your three meals from, each served in bed with a huge bowl of ice cream as dessert. The rattling sound of the tea trolley which meant hot drinks for my mum and biscuits for me. The playroom filled with toys, books and brightly painted walls featuring Bugs Bunny and Minnie Mouse. A doctor dressing as Santa, giving gifts to the kids who had to be in hospital over Christmas. Everyone I came into contact with, whether in or outside the hospital and the brief moments I was at school, treated me as if I was made from the finest glass that would shatter; that I was a precious cargo in transit to protect and look after at all costs. Illness in a child might feel similar to being a child star; people treat you differently, with an aura of reverence, and you can get away with more than your normal peers. This cocooning and deferential treatment led me to become addicted to being ill.

As any good addict will attest, manipulation is a key ingredient. As a child, I had little to do all day lying in a hospital bed except watch people: how people reacted to me coughing; how other parents would jump from their seats if their child raised their hand to their chest. There was an easy flow to my days in hospital that I enjoyed and became used to, so much that when I became stable and could be discharged to go home, I would feel sad and scared. The hospital was my safe place where nothing was asked of me and I could do no wrong. At school, I was bright but began to feel different to the other kids. I learnt that I could avoid everything if I was ill, and I taught myself how to do this. My asthma symptoms would confuse doctors when they would suddenly worsen as I was leaving the hospital so I would need to be seen for observations. My desire to stay would be so intense, I faked an asthma attack in the car park of the hospital so I could be readmitted into the safety of the ward, with my books, my colouring pencils and my team of people to look after me. If I couldn't fake asthma, I would hold thermometers up to lightbulbs to show I really did have the fever I complained of the moment I looked at my school uniform.

My addiction to being ill was facilitated by one of the greatest gifts my parents gave me – they never, ever showed me they were afraid. Their calm demeanour while watching their tiny daughter stop breathing undoubtedly saved my life on many occasions. They knew the rules of the illness – panic and fear will close the airways tighter and quicker so fought every parental instinct to make sure I never saw how terrified they were. Mixed with the security of nurses, I learnt that illness was nothing to fear, that everything would always be OK, no matter how drastic.

As I grew up, my addiction to being the sick kid diminished; it became harder to catch up on school work and I wanted to be with my friends to build a normal life. However, the behaviour I learnt as a child is hardwired and fused into my personality with a soldering iron. Even now, as a middle-aged woman, I revert back to a small child when I'm ill; my body language becomes that of a kid auditioning for a character in *Oliver Twist* – a crumpled disposition, small high-pitched voice, a pained look.

As an adult, no one has time for this kind of behaviour, and rightly so, because it is pathetic and annoying. Greg hated it and was often angry with me for morphing into a toddler in front of his eyes. Madge, once my guardian angel as a sick child, will now tell me in a stern tone to 'speak normally' when I'm moaning about any aches and pains. It is a delightful mixture of deep-seated trauma at a young age, a developing brain's way of learning how to cope and stone-cold victimhood. I didn't really know anyone else with a chronic, serious illness until Greg became sick.

Despite my role as professional patient as a child, I've shocked myself by being a good nurse as an adult. There is nothing more galvanising than a child vomiting in the night; I've relished walking to the shed at the bottom of the garden in nothing but underwear at 3 a.m. to hunt down a fan for a child with a high fever. It feels like the ultimate moment of mothering, exactly what the alchemy of birth was supposed to do – transform you into someone who will tie their hair back despite it being covered in sick and make some toast.

The doubting sickness

Greg's death certificate states he died of metastatic bowel cancer but the finishing blow was cancer in his liver. Years before this, I secretly asked people, as it's never discussed – how do you actually *die* of cancer? What happens to the tumours that can sit happily in major organs for years, sometimes totally undetected, to suddenly plummeting down the slippery slope to the end? There are many reasons – different people, different diseases – but often, it comes down to your liver. If your cancer has spread to arguably your body's most important organ after your brain and heart, it begins to shut down and poisons you, turning you delirious and yellow with jaundice.

People develop diseases for a variety of reasons: genetics and family history; lifestyle; environment; sometimes just bad luck with no rhyme or reason. With a diagnosis, we often immediately reach for a reason, we want to know *why*. Why us, why our husband, why our child, but also why *not* us? We want someone or something to blame.

After genetic testing, we knew Greg had none of the genomes that indicate he had a hereditary cancer, so we were left with the unanswered question of why he developed it at such a young age. He immediately asked the consultants if years of lying in bed using his laptop on his chest would have drawn the cancer up to his lungs, as if Wi-Fi connections could lasso cancerous particles from his lower body and drag them through his lymphatic system to set up camp. Was it his limited diet of white bread, processed ham and crisps on the rider list backstage of every venue in every city while spending years on tour? We were told we would never know a definitive answer; it could be many factors all mixed into one revolting, catastrophic soup.

There is one ingredient that I believe played an enormous role in his death that is missing from the list of contributing factors. One that is overlooked in its ability to stealthily destroy you from the inside out: OCD.

Obsessive Compulsive Disorder is a well-known disorder. We may have even referred to ourselves as suffering from it if we like to have our tins all facing forwards in the kitchen cupboards or make sure there are no dishes left in the sink before bed. We may even know about the darker side of OCD, about those who have cracked hands because they need to wash them 200 times a day or who never leave the house because of their resolute belief they have left their hair straighteners on, and their house will burn down.

It's ironic the public persona of OCD is so clinical and minimalist, based on pristine visuals of cleanliness when its reality could be represented by pulsating, knowing worms underneath your skin, dissolving your brain matter with battery acid until the neurons between rationale, logic and comprehension break down and you don't believe your own eyes or mind anymore. It's important to say I do not know what this feels like personally; I have never experienced OCD and don't want to commandeer a disorder with authority, but I've had front-row seats to watch in horror how the worms wriggled under the skin of Greg, metastasising like cancer before the real deal arrived and ate his sanity like slugs in spring gnawing at fresh green leaves.

Greg developed OCD decades before we met; in his early childhood, he would clear his bedroom floor at bedtime, sleeping with every cuddly toy, Lego brick and *Star Wars* figure because he believed they would be lonely on the floor. In the late 1970s, no one talked of mental health issues or disorders; such traits were seen as funny idiosyncrasies. By the time we met, Greg was twenty-nine and the worms had set up camp permanently. At night, he would come to bed much later than me and, as months passed, I grew confused about why he was downstairs for up to three hours every night on his own. Greg finally told me of the rituals he had to complete every night before bed; he needed to unplug every socket – linked to a memory of his grandad doing the same, telling Greg it was necessary in case the house was struck by lightning. He would tap every plug switch thirty times and say the number out loud, needing to start again if he mispronounced the word, something that happened often in the post-midnight ceremony. He would tap every hob ring thirty times to make sure it was turned off. Every locked window and door handle would need to be pulled, almost wrenched from its hinges to prove again and again they wouldn't magically open in the night and let in a host of monsters. At its peak, the OCD convinced Greg to leave the house in the dark hours of early morning to repeat the dance of his childhood but, in this adult version, he would be in his underwear picking up litter in the street because he thought it might be lonely.

In the nineteenth century, OCD used to be referred to as 'the doubting sickness' because of its insidious nature, working its way through your synapses and gnawing on your ability to judge or trust what is in front of your eyes. For Greg, his mind was so often in freefall, distrusting the simplest of things. He could close and lock a door himself multiple times, even with me as a witness, and believe it was still unlocked.

We hear our work colleagues, our neighbours, our friends

declare they are 'a bit OCD' because they like their bins to line up outside. These traits are almost seen as a medal – who *doesn't* want to be seen as clean and tidy? The desire to have things 'just so' might be seen as slightly anally retentive but, in recent years, we have bowed at the altar of Marie Kondo, of a minimalist lifestyle where we declutter and organise our lives and spaces. This is often advertised as a method to gain mental clarity, as we all know 'a tidy house means a tidy mind'. We try to gain control of an overstimulated, chaotic society by making sure we have clear worktops and that our spices are well organised.

It is the lesser-known strand of OCD that broke Greg in half. In his adult life, he was plagued by intrusive thoughts that tortured him in all aspects of his life. To an OCD muggle, the term 'intrusive thoughts' might mean thinking you've fucked up your driving test as you pull away from the curb, or wondering if your partner is having an affair because they came home an hour late. You might think it's a constant negative voice in your head, shouting abuse at yourself for not feeding your children enough vegetables this week or not being able to fit into the jeans you bought last year. These thoughts, while often unhelpful and based on very little, are normal and part of living in a society hell-bent on us feeling less than. However, the intrusive thoughts of OCD are a different breed.

When you cannot believe your eyes and doubt everything you think or do, a dark intrusive thought will immediately become amplified and be fed from the dark roots the OCD has grown. There are common areas the roots will twist around and pull into focus – those that are the most abhorrent, resulting in people believing they are paedophiles, murderers or rapists. They believe they are HIV positive and have AIDS despite negative tests. OCD gives the sufferer the impression it is keeping them safe in a world that's out of control; it offers a bargaining chip to dream of security and control, the irony being the payoff keeps you small and frightened. In Greg's case, the lifelong disorder took more than his sanity and freedom. I believe it to be a contribution to his eventual death.

Greg had symptoms of cancer for three years before he was diagnosed at thirty-six. To have stomach pains periodically didn't seem like an issue, especially with someone who had lived his whole life with a dairy intolerance. He was diagnosed with IBS by the GP, which was later confirmed by a gastrologist, and Greg was advised to eliminate inflammatory foods. As the months rolled by, Greg began to feel a more continual sense of illness which OCD spun into full-blown health anxiety, terrified these pains meant something more sinister. He believed he was HIV positive. This was despite blood tests showing no traces, my own negative AIDS tests, the wrong symptoms and no history of drug use, unprotected sex or blood transfusions. To witness this felt like pure madness, a sign Greg was so lost in a fog trying to rip him from reality, he couldn't find his way back. I tried to straddle the tightrope of calming his nerves while surreptitiously pushing him to beg for a scan for the real problem hidden deep underneath the madness. I had been Googling his symptoms for months, trying to ignore those syncing with bowel cancer because, ultimately, I wasn't looking for the real cause – I just wanted to find something like Crohn's disease or a perforated bowel, to prove OCD to be an insidious liar.

It was during this time I had an epiphany on the bathroom

floor. I was twenty-four hours into a sickness bug, my cheek resting on the toilet seat, vomit dripping from my lips and my stomach muscles tender from hours of retching. In one bleak moment of the night – while everyone else slept and I emptied the contents of my stomach until nothing was left but the very obvious truth – from nowhere, the thought came:

Greg has bowel cancer and he's going to die.

I had spent years steering Greg away from all the catastrophic outcomes the OCD directed him towards. I tried to be the perennial voice of logic, explaining the wiring set up to believe the worst. There were years of whispering, shouting, crying, 'EVERYTHING IS OK' because I thought the doubting sickness was our worst enemy, not knowing that one more deadly and sinister was growing inside Greg's body.

The bees

Greg always bought me jewellery for special occasions. He loved to pick pieces out himself and always did well in his choices but, as he became more ill, he asked if we might choose something together for my birthday. In the past, I had always gravitated towards vintage styles or super modern one-offs, pieces I knew no one else would have, but something drew me to a delicate rose-gold bee pendant necklace by a well-known designer.

I've never loved bees; they have always been too similar to their evil cousins wasps for me, but the recent narratives around them have given me pause for thought. We now know how important these insects are to the human race. If bees become extinct, we have around four years left to live because of their critical role in food supply and keeping famines at bay. They have no idea how essential they are. They have no clue how their tiny bee lives, unconsciously buzzing around pollenating and propping up an entire eco system, mean that we can go on wandering around department stores looking at jewellery.

For me, the bee became a sign of hope – they act as a symbol of everything we don't know about how life works and how we need to be OK with the huge unknowns. I wonder how bees would cope with the grand realisation of their power and responsibility. Badly, I imagine, just as humans cannot handle any real explanation of why we are here spinning around on this planet and how our actions have a wider impact on everything around us. We just have to place our trust in the unknown and hope for the best, that the universe is working perfectly, even if it very often doesn't feel like it.

Hope is a balance as delicate as the wings of a bee and isn't

167

as simple as being the beacon of light it's portrayed as – it will ask a lot of you in return. In the context of illness, to not allow death or other unfavourable outcomes into the realms of possibility means to become blindsided. You can become caught in the harsh machinery of constantly fighting, battling and other verbs we love to use for those whose biology has turned against them in an internal war that was never a fair fight to start with. You will need to stand on the highest ledge to hope for a miracle, meaning the fall is much greater. To live within the rigid nature of these cogs of pure hope can rob you of something beautiful.

Hope requires us to be comfortable with disappointment and reconcile what you have already imagined. It will teach you how to dredge the river of optimism inside you to learn how to cope with impossible news and complex situations. The expectation of good things happening has entitlement attached to it, but if we don't hope and believe in *something*, we may as well kill the bees off now. Optimism without attachment feels lighter but when the Hard Stuff arrives at your door, you will crave a stronger anchor and might need to put your trust in the fuzzy logic of the universe.

I find hope so complicated. For me, there needs to be tangible action attached to hope, as it can sometimes be a passive emotion and become what we *want* for ourselves rather than what we are *doing* for ourselves. Semantics seem to matter a lot here. To have 'faith' means believing in something bigger than you, to willingly hand over an outcome – not something I'm a fan of. I don't like hope's relationship with its less steady friends, 'chance' and 'luck'. I also struggle with the word 'belief', the issue being the need to tie your flag to it and be all in whereas an idea tends to be more transient and flexible. Like writing in sand, you can let the sea wash it away if you want to and not end up bereft when it disappears.

So, what is hope to me now, when the next chapter of my life has already been written in indelible ink? I hope for some agency, to move gently, to find grace to sit with what is.

Ultimately, there is so little control in life. I can hope myself and my loved ones are spared as much pain and suffering, but this feels like betting on a racehorse – there are too many variables I don't even know about, let alone have any influence on.

I hope I can stay soft in this space, to not become brittle in an attempt to stay strong against the winds of change. It is so easy to feel alone here, as if you are the first person on earth to feel how you do.

I hope to feel ease again, like a bee buzzing around the flowers in July.

Death

'Alexa, play the death rattle'

I magine a new colour. Close your eyes right now and try. Focus on a brand-new colour you've never seen before; nothing that is slightly blueish, not a green-yellow or a wild aurora borealis. Sit with your eyes closed and imagine it.

You can't. It's impossible. Your eyes have experienced all your retinas will allow.

Watching someone you love die feels like a similar impossibility. When tragedy happens to someone else, we say, 'I can't imagine' because no, of course we can't. You can try but the concept is so abstract, so unimaginable to fully conjure in your mind's eye, even if we have experienced something similar.

I imagined Greg dying when he was first diagnosed five years ago and every day since. I wrote his eulogy in my head during the car journey home from the hospital when we were told he would die. Every morning when I woke up in those initial months, a silent voice would scream, 'I'M GOING TO HAVE TO WATCH HIM DIE' on repeat in my head. It was The Thing I was most terrified of, a torturous nightmare guaranteed to happen – *when* not *if*.

I continuously tried to conjure Greg's last hours: what I would say to him, what he would say to me, his last breath. My most frequent scene imagined us lying in a hospice bed together, holding hands, all his close family circling around by dim light as if in an oil painting.

We go to great lengths to explain what birth looks and feels like. Women are told contractions feel like bad period pains (if period pains felt like ripping your insides out with a scythe), the 'ring of fire' will sting as the baby's head crowns, the hands of a surgeon delivering a baby through caesarean will feel like you are a human washing machine. And yet, still, we can't imagine what this is *really* like until we have either experienced or witnessed it ourselves. Imagine if we didn't talk about waters breaking in labour or if delivering the placenta was a secret. Imagine how terrifying and traumatic it would be to experience and witness. It would be an ungodly horror show of blood and surprise but, quite rightly, we have framed it as necessary as billions of us give birth or will witness it. We need to know what is going to happen to us.

Before I gave birth to Dalí, I woke up in the night lying on soaking wet sheets. 'It's happening!' I whispered to Greg in the dark. I wasn't stressed by this; after all, I'd paid hundreds of pounds to attend NCT classes to prepare me for my waters breaking because This Is What Happens In Labour. I felt comfortable having an internal examination at the birthing centre, confident my baby was on her way.

'No, sorry, you're not in labour, that wasn't your waters that have broken, it's your back waters,' said the midwife, her hand so high inside my vagina, it felt like she was tickling my tonsils.

'What the fuck are back waters?' I shouted between contractions, struggling to understand how this baby was not about to arrive. Lying on a table with my knees up by my ears was not the time to discover brand-new information on the mechanics of birth. I had invested in all the books and apps that supposedly tell you everything – the main topic covered was the size of your baby week by week by comparing the foetus to an increasing size of fruit. Also provided were photos of different types of nappies, demonstrated with smeared pesto, Marmite and chicken soup in them. None had bothered to mention the seemingly vital information of what back waters were. I was sent home with the advice to put labour out of my head as it could be days yet. This threw me entirely and I had to mentally work hard to get back to a confident place to give birth, which eventually turned out to be the next day, my 'real' waters breaking at the exact moment Dalí arrived.

I needed someone to tell me what back waters were, just as I needed someone to tell me what death would look like because here I am now, as underprepared as I was as a heavily pregnant woman, scared to give birth for the first time. I am about to watch Greg die and I'm not ready in the slightest, even though I've imagined it all in great detail but, as it turns out, in no detail at all.

This is where we are at with death and dying. We go out of our way to avoid thinking about what death looks like, despite it not only being guaranteed to happen to us but if we are lucky enough to love and to live a long life, we will watch it happen on multiple occasions. We assume the portrayal of dying in TV and films will be all the education we need. Much like the TV version of birth, we need some better teachers.

The end arrives like love – like a dream and then we fall fast. Greg stopping his treatment months before did not let the abstract concept of death truly materialise. I knew he would die but maybe, somewhere in my subconscious, I didn't. On paper, I understood everything, but how do you fully imagine something so foreign, so unspeakably strange, that someone will just *stop existing*? I had originally thought he would die months after he was diagnosed, when his bones jutted out from his back, his frame as frail as tissue paper. To think he would survive five years at that point was utter madness. And yet, he is still here half a decade later – reading the news, making cups of tea. The momentum of life can lead you to think that maybe this could go on and on forever, like a chronic illness instead of a terminal diagnosis.

The beginning of the end starts on a summer evening no different from any other. On that day, I'm so overwhelmed by everything I need to do – how to help Greg, who has seemed more tired recently, how to entertain the girls as it's the start of the summer holidays, how to protect them from the steep view over the edge of the cliff we are all about to fall off together. The first step towards the edge is remarkably symmetrical to the evening five years ago that began Greg's walk towards a diagnosis – with sickness in a plastic bowl from pain, by the dim light from a bedside lamp. The difference now is that I am not phoning for an ambulance in panic, I'm phoning the hospice in resignation. Hospice is a Big Deal. It is many things, but to someone with a life-limiting illness, it is mostly seen as The End.

I had secretly visited the hospice in the months leading to this moment. It had morphed into a brooding slaughterhouse in my head and I wanted to see what it was really like on my own terms. I had never been to a hospice before and I walked in as if in a trance, as nurses led me around like you would a small child meeting a big dog for the first time, explaining there was nothing to be afraid of. I am desperately afraid though. I'm afraid of the clinical plastic seats, the insipid peach-coloured walls, the sandwiches made with cheap white bread, the flowers everywhere and the deafening quiet. What are you supposed to do with all this silence? Despite this, I feel more prepared now I have the co-ordinates to hell.

On the phone to the hospice, they tell me there are no beds

available. We sit up all night in the revolting reality. The next morning, with Greg finally exhausted and asleep, I drive the girls into town to throw money at cheap plastic toys to keep everyone buoyant and distracted, all while on speakerphone to the palliative nurses, trying to convince them Greg is unwell enough to be admitted, talking in a bizarre code the girls won't understand. Standing in Claire's Accessories, jostling with excitable kids and harassed parents, I try to whisper down the phone with urgency that I think my husband might be dying and could they phone me back when some of these other sick people die so that he can have a bed, please?

We are in the changing rooms of H&M when the call comes in – someone has died. Brilliant! Greg has a bed! Someone has died and I'm happy about it. All the big life events seem to be on a conveyer belt; just as when you leave a registry office or a crematorium, the next set of families are lined up behind you, waiting their turn to celebrate or commiserate in a whiplash-quick turnaround.

Later that day, after dropping the girls at their grandparents, Greg and I drive to the hospice. You would never have detected the fear beneath our skin, our conversation jubilant, a well-crafted defence mechanism against the pain of the steps towards new unknown events. Greg's bright room faces the gardens with huge open French windows leading out to a courtyard, almost quaint with its rustic table and chairs. The doors are kept wide open to provide much-needed air as all the oxygen has been drained from the room, inhaled by us talking faster and in high-pitched voices to give the mood of bright confidence. I have imagined this room in my mind's eye for years, but now we are here, I can't quite believe it's real and I don't know how we got here. Everyone is so kind and it's unbearable because this much kindness means you're screwed. Being offered an alcoholic drink from the trolley on its rounds at 1 p.m. means you're in big fucking trouble.

We have told ourselves and everyone around us this is a quick stop to get on top of pain, but I know it's not. This is The End, but I must keep pretending that it's not because to say it out loud feels impossible. I know Greg needs to keep up the pretence and there are so many other people to protect from this revolting truth. I am exhausted by the weight of this game we've played for years but I want to carry this false hope on my shoulders a bit further.

Greg finally sleeps with the help of morphine, and I leave his room to sit alone. The hospice feels like Venice – an unreal film set, floating in its own orbit, where you can sometimes feel the ground move beneath your feet. Where I'm sat in reception, there is a large TV on the wall, which I discover is always on, blasting daytime mindlessness into an empty space. Weirdly, there is also a fully equipped kitchen here with more drinks to choose from than a café. I suppose there is logic here – hot drinks are the backbone in any crisis to the English; we can prop up any disaster by popping the kettle on. There is often a group huddled around the communal biscuit tin, gushing over the wonderful choice of donated spoils – anything to focus on other than Death leaching out of the pastel walls. There is a kids' area with plastic toys and books littered in a corner of the lounge. People have donated books to the 'library' and an absurd number of them are by Jeremy Clarkson.

The nurses realise I haven't eaten for two days and bring me a sandwich without asking, a display of kindness that almost breaks me. I eat it listening to *Homes Under the*

Hammer and the conversations of a family on a neighbouring sofa talking about the death rattle and what it might sound like. They finally Google it and play the sound through the phone's speaker. At a different time, I may have vomited up my sandwich in horror, but I was one step ahead, researching the same question days before and asking Alexa to play it loudly in my kitchen when I was alone. We all need a map when trekking through this new territory.

The next day, the slow drip of truth turns into an unstoppable flood when I am told to sit down on a plastic seat in a corridor. A consultant with a kind face sits opposite, looking straight into my eyes while nurses sit either side of me, holding my hands. Much like a shot of whisky in a plastic tumbler in the afternoon here, hand holding is no sign of good news.

'I'm so sorry, Greg has a few weeks to live.' The consultant is straight to the point, and I laugh. In this moment, I can see a new colour. It is one I will never be able to describe or mix with paints.

This moment reminds me of the midwife, kneeling down to look me straight in the eyes to confirm she can feel the baby's head and I am about to give birth. The time is now. The time I had secretly talked about for so long, had planned for but also had looked away from. There is the deepest sadness in this, a resignation to nature but also, a strange relief that the monster had now finally been unveiled. This feels like steadier ground than when you don't know when the enemy will attack. The suspense of waiting for the end is over. I can let my guard down because it's here. Now, I can break.

The boxing match

I am watching a film.

I am walking down a corridor with walls covered in large stickers of flowers. I'm not sure I can feel the ground beneath my feet. Am I floating?

He is going to die soon. He will die here, between the sunflowers.

In these few steps, I imagine a soft falling into each other, in tears and in love. I imagine poetic truths or even a profound silence where no words are needed. There is nothing but this moment with each other, floating in time and space.

I slowly open the door to the beginning of the end and make eye contact, knowing we both know.

(*Inhale . . .*)

I did not imagine an argument, the very worst I have ever had. I did not imagine questioning if anything at all was real or true because I had lost sight of reality.

I did not envision the alchemy of both our emotions would become too poisonous to hold or that Death could take so much from the living. His toxic concoction of desperation, urgency, anger and disbelief created rage and vitriol in us.

Drunk on Death, we scream at each other. Has this soft room ever seen anger before?

This fury isn't just directed at each other, it is at the universe because this is about the girls. They are the raw nerve, the sharp intake of breath. We want to smash the universe to pieces *because* of the girls, *for* the girls because they are young, so very young. Greg will die and there is nothing to stop this baring down on their soft skin.

I did not imagine being dragged backwards from the

bright room on the floor by nurses, screaming and crying, back out into the tunnel of sunflowers to lie on the lap of a nurse who strokes my head while I howl like an animal in pain. The peach walls close in.

What if he dies now like this, with us in separate rooms being soothed by nurses, as if we are boxers in opposite corners of a ring? All is lost. Death has won. It has broken the bones of us; the delicate ribbons of love we have woven have been ripped apart to wind round our bloody hands to fight each other as opponents. We are too far apart to come back together. We don't have time.

We are brought back into the same room by the nurses, as if they were teachers mediating a fight between children. When we speak again, it is in quiet, hushed tones with tentative hugs. I don't know how to reach him; everything is just too big and heavy. He's already gone, not physically yet but his presence has flown elsewhere. Everything I want to say hangs heavy in the air and I sit with my mouth hanging open and hope the words will fall out onto the floor.

I want to say how much I love him, how I cannot stand the thought of what is about to happen.

Selfishly, I want him to soothe me too, to tell me everything will be OK, even though he is the one who is about to die.

(*Exhale . . .*)

A ghost in the throat

The girls and I come to visit Greg. In the foyer, we are met by a very old woman in bed, having her last rites read to her by a priest soundtracked by *This Morning* blaring on the TV. She could very possibly be dead already, considering her skeletal body and open-mouthed translucent pallor.

'What are they doing, Mum?' Dalí asks curiously.

'Saying some lovely words to make her feel better,' I weakly offer.

I have no idea what is being said. We pass through this Catholic vignette to get to the squash and biscuits. I might treat myself to a warm glass of white wine from the 24-hour trolley as it's 10 a.m. and I've already witnessed the first trauma of the day.

The bubble

I didn't realise how much energy it takes to die.

Greg doesn't want to talk. He is in front of me, still flesh and blood surrounding the cancer slowly shutting down his organs, but he is alive and yet, I can't find him.

I want so desperately to know what Greg thinks about everything. I want to know if he believes in heaven, if he's scared, if he thinks he will see his grandad after he dies, who does he forgive, what were the best times of his life, what did he realise were the most important lessons. I push him to talk but he can't engage, in a way that is so reminiscent of our late-night conversations in bed. It is the same back and forth where I am too much, trying to orchestrate big conversations that Greg doesn't want. I want to drink the last drops of life from him but they aren't mine to have; I realise the dying need all of their dwindling energy to actually *die*. Like an animal who will retreat under a dark bush to fade away, humans go in on themselves too. In antenatal classes, you're taught that the most desired place to give birth is in a small, dark room without lots of people watching you. I would have wanted to kill anyone who tried to have a full-blown conversation with me when I was in labour. I suppose this makes sense; in our intimate, vulnerable moments, we mostly want quiet without lots of eyes and distractions. We are often drawn to sex with one person in a shaded bedroom. Public bathrooms are for one occupant. We are led to believe that death is the stage for huge euphonies, to make and receive huge statements of love, apologies or wisdom. It is only now, standing in front of death, that I see it's not any of this; it is a place for stillness. Greg has retreated into a bubble to process how all he has known and loved is about to disappear – that he is going somewhere else alone.

I understand this, I do, but I also want to scream. I have never felt more alone than now. It felt like claws ripping at my chest and I can hear a voice shouting NOW! NOW! NOW! This is about to end, there is no way to stop it and you can never have him back. I am desperate for Greg to share and describe his mental landscape so I can visualise where he is, but I only ever catch a glimpse reflected in his eyes.

The bubble is violently popped by the tasks of the dying. I am asked to sign a Do Not Resuscitate form. The nurses explain in detail the grotesque physical realities of trying to bring someone back to life when their body wants to die. Everything is life and death, life and death, switching between the two and straddling the fine line between them. I sign it with a scrawled signature written on the floor, the ink made to dance by tears. It feels like signing a death warrant and I have become the person with the axe.

The sharpest knife

Humans adapt so quickly. Greg feels like he lives at the hospice now, despite his stay being less than a fortnight. The girls barely ask about him in their childlike ease of the summer holidays, except to hint at their understanding of the severity by asking, 'Will Dad be home for Christmas?', which is over four months away. There are times when Greg feels well enough to leave the hospice to sleep in his own bed for the afternoon. The journey back to our house, on the familiar roads of our neighbourhood and songs playing through the tinny speakers of our phones could lead you to believe you are driving home from the supermarket or from seeing friends. It's during one of these sleepy visits that we have to do the very worst task we ever had to do as parents – to tell our children Greg is going to die soon.

The girls knew their dad had an illness called cancer, that it meant he needed a lot of rest and couldn't play all the games he wanted to with them. We told them the doctors were always trying to make Dad feel better but the full stop on the horizon was never discussed. I can see Greg could not bear to speak that vile truth out loud because then it became a real and solid entity, the knife you already know will rip through the fabric of their childhoods. The alchemy of becoming a parent means you will prioritise them over yourself and Greg so desperately wanted to protect them over everything.

As the long days slowly rumbled on and Greg's health was so obviously deteriorating, it was harder and stranger to *not* tell them what was happening. He had always been in control of what we told the girls but, as we edged closer to the edge of the cliff, I felt a distinct tipping point. The scales began to move when I realised it was me alone who would need to parent them for the rest of my life. I needed them to trust me and know they could always rely on me for the truth. To lie when it was so obvious felt like Greg and I were performing in a play, with the girls sitting in the audience looking confused.

In retrospect, I can see now this situation was never about truth or secrets; it was the most treacherous, disgusting task for a person to be asked to do. It signified the absolute end of everything, not only Greg's life and of any scraps of hope he had left, but the end of our children's innocence. To witness your words land with such brutal destruction goes against every parental instinct. Instead of their shield, we became the scythe to cut through the delicate naïveté of their childhood.

Greg sits the girls down in front of him while I silently watch on, floating like an angel witnessing the Rapture. I hear the words. Time stops. In real time, I see their eyes slowly dim and change as they take in the news. Immediately, I want to take it all back and pretend none of this is real. I am wretched, my eyes dry from not blinking, being held open too wide. There are no words for this kind of horror.

The girls' reactions are very different: one sobs on her dad's lap and the other runs to the kitchen to fetch glasses of water and snacks for us all, picking out special bowls she knows we like and making jokes to stop us crying. This thoughtfulness and the inability for her tiny brain to be able to fully comprehend what is being said is the sharpest knife. She is just so small and wonderful; I want to set fire to the world for putting her in the situation where she sees her family are falling apart and she attempts to fix it in the only way her five-year-old self knows how – with crisps and silliness.

The maddening

No one tells you about morphine. We are comforted by the phrase 'they are being kept comfortable' and hope there is a cocktail of drugs ready to obliterate the pain and awareness of our own demise. In films, it looks like drifting into a gentle snooze, with slower speech and a weak smile. All pain disappears and you slip gently into the abyss. In reality, a concoction of pain relief is a hard mathematical equation to understand and produces very different effects.

To watch the pain in someone you love as they slowly die is a very particular seat in hell. My view was to encourage all drugs available, but I didn't know that to feel nothing through palliative drugs is to be in a coma and have no communication; ultimately, you give up your goodbyes for peace. In trying to find the middle ground, we found a terrifying place we didn't know existed – an opiate madness.

In this space, we go round and round, one minute talking of potential treatments and chasing up results, all of which are pointless. The next, Greg will ask me to fulfil impossible dying wishes, so bizarre and inappropriate in their nature. I wonder if Greg actually understands what is happening; he tells me he's not afraid to die but then talks of where we could go at Christmas. I don't know if it's denial, the drugs or if maybe this is just what death looks like – a confusing tussle to not let go of the life you so desperately don't want to lose.

With increased doses of morphine flowing around his bloodstream, Greg's demeanour changes overnight. He seems as though he has developed late-stage dementia in a heartbeat – he broke glasses and absentmindedly walked across them, wandering the corridors of the hospice at night; he talks of seeing things, has conversations with people who aren't there and cannot remember those who are. I am sat down in a quiet room with a consultant and a box of tissues to be told that this might just be it, that cancer raging through a body can upset its chemistry and affect the brain like dementia would. There is an outside chance it could be an adverse reaction to morphine, so the drugs are changed. Like a biblical miracle, our Greg comes back to us as quickly as he had left, although as a more terrified version by the maddening hallucinations he has witnessed.

I don't remember the specific conversation, but as Greg was so agitated at the hospice after this episode, we all decide that he is going to come home to die. Secretly, I'm horrified at this thought. I am scared Greg will ask to die in our house, in our bed. Ultimately, I will do whatever he wants, but I quietly know this will mean never sleeping in my bedroom or possibly not ever setting foot in our home again. Death will be in every corner of our small house, giving the girls front-row seats to witness their dad's demise. I don't know how but it's decided Greg will return to his parents' house to die, back to his childhood bedroom. I am torn between relief and putrid guilt; as his wife, I should be the person to care for him, but the reality stares us all in the face. All of our roles have changed. They aren't vocalised but silently understood by everyone: my focus will be on the girls; the focus of Greg's immediate family will be on him and Greg needs only to focus on dying. Living three minutes away from each other makes this arrangement work seamlessly, and we set about the task of helping Greg die in the best way possible. It feels as though we were leaning over the edge of the world.

A liminal space

It's not lost on me that we are in this liminal space during my favourite month of September. Working in academia for so many years has shaped the rhythm of the months, September representing a new year to me much more so than January. You can feel autumn's slow approach, in the air's slight chill early in the morning and in the subtle differences of how sunlight hits the pavement. Your body acts like a body of water under the moon, sensing the shifts in current as the seasons rotate.

I am a huge fan of change. I am a Pisces, born under a star constellation which harnesses alterations, signified by the two fish connected yet pulling in different directions. Like them, I can be transmutable at a moment's notice and live for the novelty of change, although what is on the horizon is of tectonic proportions. But for today, there are only slow movements – the colour of the leaves in my garden warming to orange, my girls growing, Greg's health declining further, my heart adding extra beats.

I don't want this season to change. I want another chance to cradle my children as babies, to sit with the sun on my face, to pull Greg back from the abyss. The seasons move on and have never been ours to stop. I tell myself to be here with eyes wide open. This time will never come again. Swim, little Pisces, and if you can't swim, float. Dead fish may float but I'm not dead yet.

Greg is back in his childhood bedroom, this space that the girls had claimed as their own. A weird dichotomy of his childhood mixed with theirs, making the entire situation even more bizarre and unsettling. The juxtaposition of it all – where he grew up and slept as a child, the posters, his mum and dad gently caring for him as they did when he was a baby all makes me feel like I will combust. Is it possible to implode with poignancy and just the entire madness of everything? There is an intangible pain in me that isn't physical, somewhere deep inside. It feels like my subconscious is being ripped apart and there is a distant scream echoing from a place I never knew existed.

I need to keep moving the goalposts of what OK means. One day, we will exchange only a few words between hours of sleep and the next; Greg is sat downstairs and wide awake, eating biscuits and full of opinions on the documentary he's watching about the history of hanging in Britain. Some days, he will seem pregnant in his cravings for tastes: Farley's rusks, blue Slush Puppies, ice cream Coke floats. All tastes that remind him of his childhood and holidays with his families. Other days, he wants only a drop of water squeezed into his mouth with a sponge.

Again, I envisage a constant vigil, easier to create now that we are all more relaxed in a familiar space, but Greg still doesn't want anyone to sit with him. Everyone outside the inner sanctum assumes I will be by his bedside day and night when, in fact, the children and I visit Greg for no more than ten minutes a day before it becomes too physically exhausting for him to engage with noise or emotions. Instead, I'm spending my time at the zoo, at the supermarket, at the park, at soft play on playdates because life and the summer holidays carry on regardless of Death. I will be pushing Bay on a swing or reaching for a packet of pasta on a top shelf at Sainsbury's and think, Greg is dying and I'm not there, and I will want to puke my guts out and run to him.

Greg's insistence to be in almost total solitude includes everyone, something no one was prepared for. As hard as this is for all of us, he craves control and agency where he has had none for so long, so there is nothing to do but agree. It is the last gift we can give him. Sitting around restlessly gives me the space to think about this exchange and its impact. I would do anything for Greg, and he has asked me to do this one last act for him – to leave him alone. Of course, I will honour his wishes but there is a payoff. I know what the psychic damage of this will do to me. I will leave him alone and it will destroy me.

Everyone understands that Greg sets the pace here, but when I do get my chance with him, I dance around like a court jester, asking if he wants music playing, something to watch, something delicious to eat, a scented candle to enjoy but he wants nothing except solitude and silence. This shouldn't surprise me; Greg's general introverted default in life was to be on his own with his own thoughts. I am projecting onto him the circumstances I would want in my own death, an exact reflection of all the ways I am comfortable living – lots of noise and constantly surrounded by people. I grew up with every member of my family listening to their own music in different rooms, with TVs on in empty rooms creating a sonic soundscape. To this day, I need to have music playing all day and spoken word as I sleep to be able to relax. The silence in this liminal space is so enormous, too enormous to sit with, so I fill it by telling inappropriate jokes, making endless cups of coffee that jangle my nerves further until I burst into tears before starting the dance again.

I have never witnessed a truer love and strength than what I see in Greg's parents and Aaron. To gladly accept the inhumane task of caring for your dying son and brother is a weight too heavy to carry but I witness them do just this every day. I see how the ravines of pain rip deeper into their skin as they navigate the new tasks arriving hour by hour. I see how graciously they receive new medical staff who arrive on rotation, warmly greeting them like old friends. It is a humbling experience to watch.

I spend a lot of time in our family house alone. I am homesick while sat in my own bedroom. I am nostalgic for a time that isn't gone but yet isn't here. The word nostalgia comes from the Greek 'homecoming' and 'pain'. This liminal space spans time and emotions, giving the impression that I'm floating above all the chapters of my life where these different versions of myself still exist.

These weeks blur into a hurricane of hysterical children who can't understand what is happening, quizzing nurses on doorsteps for timelines, hunting down fentanyl around the city at night and talking about chapels of rest. At the same time, it can involve taking the kids swimming, eating pizza with friends and analysing an episode of *RuPaul's Drag Race* by voice note. This anticipatory grief feels like a pendulum, swinging into a sticky abyss before ricocheting back into the mundane and usual. I don't believe the heart could withstand living in the dark permanently. The normal moments allow the space to take a breath and move back from the cliff edge, to look away from the tsunami wave that is now so close I can feel the droplets of water in the air.

All I can think is I want him back. I want to reach into the void Greg is in and thrash out some cosmic bargaining for one more conversation about ghost hunting, one more coffee in a bookshop, one more night of ease, sleeping next to each other. It is inconceivable that I will never have these everyday moments again. In my bedroom, a place I barely recognise anymore, I am yearning for a moment where I don't feel like I'm playing a lead role in a horror film.

The tipping point

The doctors had estimated Greg wouldn't live long but we are now over a month into end-of-life care. It would be a gross understatement to say this is a cruel torture of the highest degree. The sadness and fear of the suspense often spills over and my body cannot contain everything I feel. There is a day when Madge comes over to help me clean my bedroom and just being in the space leaves me catatonic on the floor. No words, just convulsions and screaming. She drags me up into my bed with her, pulling the covers over both our heads and holds me like a baby, pushing our hearts together so I can feel hers to slow mine down. This is a technique I have used with my own children since they were babies to regulate their emotions when they can't manage it themselves. I cry at the ache of wanting to be a child again, to have my mum look after me forever.

This place is madness. In one moment, I am picking up others crying on the floor and giving pep talks worthy of *Dead Poets Society*, the next, smashing a fan against a wall because the sound of its blades whirring becomes the most unbearable noise on earth. I am picking out the clothes for Greg to be dressed in when he is taken to the funeral directors without tears but losing my mind when putting children to bed and running outside barefoot to scream into the night, much to the confusion of my neighbours. I am sitting on the front doorstep in the sun, eating lasagne with my hands as my children beg me to take them swimming. En route to the pool, I am having an explosive argument through my car window with anti-vax protesters lining the streets. There is no time or space to process anything. I'm blowing up like Violet Beauregarde while trying to fit through the eye of a needle.

The slow drip, drip, drip of this time begins to feel holy. The air is heavy with reverence, holding a vigil that's not even bedside. It is a dreamlike world that feels so alien despite the surroundings being those of my own life. Sometimes, I feel like I will wake up as a sixteen-year-old and go downstairs to tell my mum over breakfast about the weird dream I had about my life as a grown-up.

* * *

I wake up in my own bed to the sound of wolves howling. Maybe not wolves but the sound of animals crying somewhere outside. There's no sign of any nocturnal beasts as I look through the window, only the full moon. I gave birth under two full moons, its power seeming to pull my babies from me. It can move oceans so it seems reasonable it can keep me awake for hours, feeling at sea on my own ocean. I feel like I'm floating high up with the moon, suspended in space and looking down on what's happening, my phone beeping constantly with messages from down on earth. *Houston, we have a problem.* I still dream about ex-boyfriends every night, anxious that I'm back with them and desperate to find a way out.

Greg comes to stay at our home for a night, just the two of us like it was at the beginning of our relationship. I want it to be a lovely special time but the weight of knowing this will be his last time here makes me bloated with anticipation. We sit in bed, drinking tea, dunking biscuits, listening to political podcasts and, for a moment, I'm back on earth. It is beautiful but absolutely brutal. Every moment is a slow deep bruise.

Greg returns to his parents and normal life goes on. The school year commences and new uniforms hang up in wardrobes next to our old lives, hanging on by a thread. The normality of everyday life is a balm for my heart. I drink in making breakfast, the school run, the idle gossip with other parents before visiting Greg, as if this routine is normal.

But here is the weirdest thing – I have never felt more alive than now. Alive in the sense of the most heightened awareness where no sense is dulled. Everything is now and now is everything. My eyes are wide open, as if they are being pinned back by the universe, who is shouting 'LOOK!' To be this close to Death makes all living things throb and pulse. You begin to see all the molecules vibrating, holding everything we believe is real together. The seams of reality are fraying but there is a streamlining of consciousness and focus; everything is so clear, and nothing exists other than what is in front of you. It reminds me of being newly in love. An exquisite pain, unlike any other. Death becomes an unlearning, an exercise in relinquishing control – of expectations, of my own wants and needs, of my person and the family I had. But if I must let go of so much, what can I hold onto? I'm just here, wide-eyed and waiting.

The pink karaoke machine

The scene unravelling looks nothing like the world told me it would be.

There is no Big Talk or Big Epiphany or Big Heart-to-Heart.

Greg's childhood bedroom feels claustrophobic and tight, clawing at the back of my throat every time I quietly enter the room. Weeks of the same view, the same diffused glow through the drawn curtains, ticking down the hours of the same day in slow motion. Despite the cloudlike nest created of multiple mattresses, duvets and blankets, Greg is the Princess and the Pea, every fibre acting as a sword into his exposed spine. He wants to move beds, the only option being his parents' room. There is a moment of sharp reality; if this happens, this is where he will die. A child dying where his mother and father sleep. Burn the bed, burn the room down to the ground immediately with the revolting pathos of this image.

We had sung out 'In sickness and in health, till death do us part' and here we are only three years later, living the vows that no bride seriously entertains on her wedding day. As Greg's wife, I am powered by love to move his limbs gently out from the covers to rest his feet to the floor. The marathon task of only a few inches takes everything and we need to sit on the edge of the bed to catch our breath. We hadn't been next to each other since I asked a nurse to take a picture of us together at the hospice; sat on the bed with weak smiles looking like crumpled old teddies, knowing this would be the last photograph of us together, a bookend of images. It had only been a month ago, but I have lived and died many times over since then, so to be sat, legs touching, felt novel and reminded me of the intense fascination I had with the nearness of Greg's legs and hands as we sat next to each other in the cinema on our first date.

On the floor directly in front of us is our daughters' karaoke machine. Its plastic pink glare is blinding in the darkness of the moment, a light shining on the enormity of what we are about to lose: the hope and joy a young family represents; the years Greg will miss with his children. Their childhood feels frozen in time, their spark and irreverent joy encapsulated fully in one pink object. Its playfulness is taunting as we stare in silence at the symbol of our biggest loves; we may have been severed into strangers from each other over time, but we still share the most sacred and important commonality – we love the same two people the most.

For the first time in weeks, Greg reaches through the sticky moment for my hand, his fingers shaking.

'Our girls,' he whispers as he squeezes my hand with the recognition of everything that has joined us together. The slow knife which had pierced my flesh repeatedly for the past five years lurches forwards to finally slice my heart open with ferocious abandon.

There is bile in my throat as the wall between us for so many years, built up of confusion, sadness, frustration and resentment, breaks into pieces and we are here, alone together at last. Greg lets me hold him as we shake in Siamese sobs, a specific type of cry reserved for parents watching an oncoming truck about to hit their children with no way of stopping it. It is the purest of pains, almost transcendental in feeling, elevated to a holy place of agony. A cascade of pure devastation, two tributaries of grief joining together to flow over the love for our children. In this black space,

I'm surprised to find a lick of ecstasy; I craved this moment for so long, to share the grief of our doomed future with the person I lay the first bricks with instead of devouring the fruits of sadness in our own separate rooms.

We shuffle together to Greg's final resting place, and he lets me lie next to him. The slow, staggered walk from his childhood bed to his parents', a literal time machine taking him further back in time towards where he was created, a realisation that makes me recoil in horror while also deeply understanding the circle of life. He will die in the warm nest of his parents. I cling to his broken frame as I realise I have found him again, just for a split second. In the mirrored wardrobe doors, I watch us as if floating above, looking on as a bystander marvelling at the extent of human fragility. The past fifteen years scroll past like a birthday compilation and ends with us here, a crumpled mess of flesh, bones and morphine, wrapped together with deep love and sorrow.

'I need to sleep,' Greg whispers, his eyes already closed. I gently unwrap myself and make my way out, slowly closing the door to the now ill-fated room and the path back to us.

An unoriginal hot take on Death

The universality of death is a comfort, a clear fate we can all agree on. But each death being different, or rather each progression towards death being unique, keeps us under the illusion of dying being a bespoke kind of misfortune. Yet, the ultimate outcome is so commonplace, it could be seen as mundane. The finality of all our days amounting to the same thing: the unalterable 'plainness' of our no longer existing.

It's in this unifying fact that I find comfort. I liken it to the comfort of a storm when everyone needs to take shelter, driven inside to form a new community of observers with an elevated sense of care for each other.

I also take refuge in the unity of suffering: this is so selfish, that I might feel better about my own suffering and mortality as long as others are enduring it too. How scared do you have to be to entertain this? There is no schadenfreude here, no gloating – these 'others' include my most loved, whom I would spare the slightest pain if I could. So, I find solace in, what, disaster? No, the point is surely that something so natural as illness cannot be a true disaster. I'm reminded of 9/11, being glued to the news with the entirety of the world next to me; to look away would have meant I would need to process the enormity of it alone.

Pain and suffering enhance the idea of death as The End but doesn't allow it to be considered in isolation, merely as contrast. What is death without the idea of pain accompanying it? An absence, just stillness? Neither so terrifying on paper, like the dreamy abyss on the edge of consciousness before anaesthetic. Death being reached through suffering is where the real fear lies. After all, we can only imagine non-existence.

I doubt an original thought on death is possible but that in itself is a relief. It's boringly normal, the most average topic but, to the individual, it is an exceptional moment of their lives to be revered and cower from at the same time. We are desperate for our lives to also be exceptional and hold meaning so our deaths take on the mantle of ultimate individual tragedy.

We are taught we have control of our lives and believe the laid-out plans for a certain trajectory will blossom into fruition; the map and compass direct us to the qualifications, the vows, the big decisions, but like the devastating realisation as a child that your parents are just humans, not the infallible beings you believed them to be, there is the heavy understanding we are only a part creator, an apprentice merely whispering suggestions into the wind, hoping we might be listened to.

Making memories and other nonsense

In a therapy session, I was asked to sit with my eyes closed and gently let the very best moments of my life rise to the top of my consciousness. It was made clear I shouldn't try to force or choose what was expected; it should come from a very authentic place within. I sat quietly and let those moments reveal themselves to me.

I'm walking out of the main entrance at senior school. I'm on my own, classes are still in full swing, but I'm Head Girl so I've managed to worm my way out of maths to walk the corridors as if on important business. It's summer and, as I walk outside, I smile to myself as the sun hits my bare arms and legs. It's lunchtime soon, so I can eat with my friends and gossip about the day so far.

It's early morning in the summer holidays. I am around seven years old. The sun is bright in a way it seemed to be only in childhood, the quality of the light becoming different when you're an adult. My main objective is to be out in the street as early as possible. All the kids spend every day playing football, hide and seek, riding bikes. Today, I am the first one out and I walk down to the corner to wait for the rest of my friends to eat their cereal and appear for a full day of playing. I sit on the ground and the concrete is already hot under my legs.

Greg and I are in my car driving to the New Forest. The windows are open, we are listening to Hulk Hogan's wrestling theme tune and we are laughing so hard, we are crying.

I met Death on a clifftop

The writer Anne Lamott suggests grace is a mixture of exhaustion and running out of good ideas. She also says, in any situation it bats last. Here we are at the very end, and I can feel notions of grace creeping up on me like a spring breeze. Grace feels like letting go again and again, especially of the expectations I've realised I have so many of. I've held on for so long, tried to move mountains with my bare hands, but now there is a desperate relief in letting go. Grace is the light touch; to let the butterfly in the summer rest on your fingertip without trying to catch it. Anyone who has ever tried will know butterflies are made of dust and dissolve when touched. Better to let them fly away and watch their magic from afar, knowing it was never yours to own. In this room, I let go of Greg.

There is a shimmering veil at the end of the earth, a translucent border between this world and the next, as delicate as dew-covered spider webs found in the sun on a September morning. We are in the crossover section of the Venn diagram, where our world and the next mix like oil and water. The frailties of the human body become laughable in this space; our indestructible energy held in such a delicate vehicle feels like faulty design. We only get to experience a first kiss, the full moon, road rage, the joy of stroking a dog because the mechanics of our body keep working. When that begins to falter, all things disappear, and the veil starts to twinkle in the low sun. This is all there ever was; everything else was just a distraction.

In this room, I'm watching the last moments of my own life. My body won't physically die alongside Greg but a distinct part of me will. Versions of ourselves die all the time, but slowly and without detection. Or maybe they don't die, they are just absorbed. Maybe every age of me is kept inside like a Russian doll, waiting to be drawn on when needed. Right now, I feel young and old at once, so naïve to life but gaining wisdom at the rate of knots. I will need the sixteen-year-old version of myself when I need wonder, lightness and silliness in the future to combat the hardening crone I can feel myself becoming.

I'm witnessing myself dissolving in fast forward, as if I can see the atoms that make up my body begin to vibrate, my own life force shimmering against Greg's fading energy. It is a physical feeling; part of me is ripping off my flesh and the thin-skinned version is birthed. Perhaps that part of me will walk through the veil with Greg and what's left will walk back down from the cliff edge to begin again and start a new life.

The disintegration of the human body is a confusing event to witness. Ultimately, we are just weird bags of bones and goo, injected with magic to animate us like a meat puppet. When we die, this magic moves elsewhere, and our vehicles become useless. It becomes laughable to think of how much time, effort, money and brain power we spend on decorating them. You begin to understand euthanasia and the desire to help end suffering, as you would put a dying animal out of their misery for far less. It can feel cruel to know that there is no other ending available except death, so close you can taste it, but watch on as the body and spirit wrestle to free themselves of each other.

Greg has now let us sit with him, not enough of this world to argue. He lets me give him a foot rub, the only physical contact he can handle, and I remind him how we used to do this every night when we were obsessed with watching quaint English mysteries on TV. He smiled, something I hadn't seen for weeks, and whispered in a barely audible voice, 'Such lovely times.' All the moments he has spoken of over the last few months of his life have been tiny, quiet snapshots – watching *Jonathan Creek* in the winter under a blanket, walking through our neighbourhood at night in the snow, band rehearsals in his parents' garage and playing football in the field behind his house. Such small, seemingly insignificant moments offered up as if they were jewels.

This moment, rubbing the feet of my dying husband, talking about the plot points of the *Jonathan Creek* Christmas special is one of the most beautiful moments in my life. I didn't imagine I could experience any new emotions, but this is a heady cocktail of wonder, love, simplicity, heartbreaking sadness and a crash course in what really matters in life.

Foot rubs become the way for us to connect. Sometimes Bay helps me, taking great care to be gentle and wet a cloth to bathe Greg's feet and ankles. Even though she is only five, I can see how important this is to her, to have a role here. I know how she feels. Just to witness what is happening feels so helpless, so to actively help soothe the transition feels like love in its purest form. Dalí, ever the representation of sunshine, will fill the room with excitable chat from her day, making Greg smile and, suddenly, there is summer in the room mixed with deepest winter.

I secretly record the girls' last moments with Greg. Their tiny voices match Greg's new softer sound. The juxtaposition of their youth and vitality next to his dwindling life force is a masterclass in humility. I can see fear begin to creep into their eyes now, wary of how their dad is physically changing.

They tell him about school, about a funny video they watched on YouTube as the bright September light moves shadows across the walls.

When they leave the room, I ask Greg if he's seen his grandad yet. He had always said he believed he would see his beloved Grandad Tony when he was about to die, not thinking it would be this soon. He gently shakes his head. Greg hasn't blinked in hours, and I can see his forgotten contact lens fused onto his retinas. He turns to me suddenly and whispers the last words I will ever hear him say.

'Have I changed yet?'

I think he's asking if he's still human or has he changed into whatever comes next.

We are told by the nurses Greg, has hours. It feels like waiting for a gun to go off to begin a race, the anticipation so bitter and metallic, it tastes like coins in my mouth. I leave my parents' house to drive towards the biggest moment of my life, my dad following me in his car in case I drive into a wall. When we arrive, he gives me a silent hug before leaving, as if I'm about to go to war. I take a picture of the early evening sun, the last blue and pink sky that Greg will be alive under.

I move around erratically, setting up the house as if for a party; there's dim lights to put on, people to phone to come round, snacks to put out. My nervous energy is through the roof and as people begin to gather, I laugh more than I have done in years. I have tears running down my cheeks as we tell funny family stories to break the tension.

We have an unspoken two-in, two-out policy with Greg while everyone else sits under blankets and drinks tea downstairs. My overriding feeling during my turns is fear. I watch his breath while I hold mine, so terrified that it might be his last. Why did I light these candles? His parents' room now feels like a mausoleum. I can physically feel an energy swirling around the room. Soon it is the early hours of the morning and people are beginning to bed down for sleep wherever they can find a soft space. Everyone comes to say goodnight and I realise that my designated place to rest is next to Greg, that I'm on the whole night watch. I am terrified. I don't want to be alone with him when he dies. I don't want to be the person to tell his parents their son is dead.

I lie in bed next to Greg, whose consciousness has already flown away. The candles flicker; there is silence in the rest of the house. Framed pictures sit either side of the bed: of the girls and our niece; of Greg and Aaron with their grandad. These photographs stare back at me, an animation of our lives. I can't even close my eyes, let alone sleep, my body rigid in fight-or-flight response. I fill six hours with watching the shadows of candles dance on the walls and trying to remember to breathe.

In the end, there is nothing left but breath. It all comes down to heart, blood, lungs, air, breath and then nothing. I can feel Greg isn't really here anymore. His organs have all stopped working except his heart and his lungs. Slow, deep mechanical breathing, as if he is a wind-up toy waiting to run out of battery. My own lungs feel broken and are heavy with a familiar asthmatic wheeze, an indication I am stressed beyond capacity. I keep breathing through the fear, just like I did as a child in the back of my mum's car, speeding towards the hospital.

I want to tell you a million tiny things. Of why I love you, of why I have always wanted to be where you are. Every grain of sand running through the hourglass left of your life has a story of us encapsulated in it. I hope you are breathing them in, seeing them play out in the moments before you die. I hope you can smell the grass from the field you played in when you were a boy. I hope you can hear the sounds of family parties ringing in your ears. I hope you can feel the adrenaline of singing on a stage and hearing a crowd sing back to you the lyrics you wrote in your bedroom when you were sad and didn't know what to do with yourself. I hope you feel loved and that although I can't go where you are going, my love is going with you.

At 6 a.m., I feel a shift in the atmosphere; I know it is my time to say a final goodbye and leave. It is a deep knowing, that it was not me meant to be there when Greg takes his final breath, that my place is now with the girls. I get up from the last bed we will ever share, pull back the curtains to the midnight-blue morning and open the window, placing the photographs of Dalí and Bay either side. I lean over Greg and whisper, 'Go be in the universe with the stars. I'll see you later, my boy', and drive home to be with my babies when they wake up.

What does eternity look like?

The night has felt like an eternity but, somehow, it is still pitch-black outside, and I need all the car windows open in order to breathe. I drive on autopilot with my mouth gaping like an apple-stuffed pig waiting to be roasted, as wide as it can possibly stretch because I am desperate for oxygen. I am driving but also flying, or maybe floating. The familiar streets are still shrouded in shadow and disappear from view altogether. All I can see is eternity.

'You can't possibly see eternity,' Greg had said to me years ago in a discussion about time and space. 'The very fact that you think you can imagine it means you absolutely can't. It is the impossible. You are only imagining what you have already seen and what you know, like imagining a new colour. You can't see what you can't see or know what you don't know. I bet you are just imagining space, black, emptiness, aren't you? Like the beginning credits of *Star Wars*?'

'Yeah, but so what?' I replied indignantly. 'That's what everyone thinks eternity looks like, so how can the whole human race be wrong?'

I think Greg was right. If I was to draw eternity from my view at the edge of the world, it wouldn't be dense black marks scrawled on paper. It is light and wispy, almost translucent – no, not like heaven. If it were paint colours, it might be called 'lavender haze' and 'oatmeal dream'. Eternity is a loud silence that suspends your heart in treacle. The connections holding atoms together, the edges of all things fall away while, at the same time, every version of myself, every person I have ever been fuses into one being. Everything is in hyper-focus. I understand everything. Is this what enlightenment feels like? Is this the place Greg and I tried to reach when we would sit in the dark of our bedroom every morning, practising the *oms* and the *ahs* of the universe in our phase of meditating every day? I understand it all: Greg is here and there, where he always was and where we are all going. There is nothing to fear.

And then the searing pain at the sight of my parents' house.

PTSD o'clock

I'm sure it won't come as a huge shock to hear that waiting for a phone call to let you know your husband has died is weird. As in, fucking weird, the weirdest, most surreal moment. It's especially weird when you so desperately want it to happen, to pop the black balloon that's over your head to end your time in Death's waiting room.

Greg is still alive. I had fallen into bed as if in my own coma.

'There cannot be anything worse than this,' I had later whispered to my sister-in-law Michelle as I sat in her kitchen the next day, drinking coffee as if it were water. I'm a furtive fox on alert; twitching eyes looking at the girls through the window jumping on the trampoline with their cousin, all of them knowing Greg is on the edge of death and yet still able to play and laugh. Eyes back down to my phone, twisting hands in my lap again and again.

I am here and he is there. Everyone understands that my place now is with the girls; they need me with them but, at the same time, it's not a choice I've made. I cannot be there to watch him die. I imagined this moment for so many years, played it out as if it were a film scene – where I would sit (at the top of the bed, with Greg leaning on me as I held his hand), his mum, dad and brother sat at the end with hands on his legs. It would be transcendent, otherworldly and, as Greg took his final breath, we would feel his spirit ascend, maybe even see a mist rise from his body and know that he was finally at rest. We would be sad but moved in a spiritual way that would change us forever into better people.

When it came to the end, I couldn't go through with it.

I couldn't because I didn't know the dying don't always look like themselves and just drift off into a heavenly slumber. No one tells you what death smells like – of medicinal biscuits, a clawing sweet stench that catches at the back of your throat.

Maybe it has nothing to do with this. Maybe I am not brave enough and have left the job to others to be there who might not feel brave enough themselves.

My phone rings. It's Aaron. There is silence because there's nothing to say. He's gone.

I run upstairs, the sudden burst of adrenaline telling me to run, run anywhere, towards this or away from it, it doesn't matter, just run. I click my fingers. Click, click, click as I listen to the words describing the scene. Greg took one final breath as he listened to fail videos on YouTube while Aaron and his cousin Jason laughed about stupid stories from their childhoods. It is not what I imagined but it is perfect. A modern deathbed, one that would rival religious tableaus in paintings.

I'm still clicking my fingers. Adrenaline, keep breathing. Sit down, don't hyperventilate. The fabric of the chair I'm sitting on is frayed and faded. He's dead. Click, click. What does he look like now? People say the dead look like porcelain, their skin rewinding time as the muscles underneath relax in a way they have never been able to. Will he look young again? He's dead. Dead, dead, dead. No, he's 'gone'. That's what I tell everyone as I sit on the faded chair and call my family. He's gone. Gone where though? I'm glad no one asks me this question.

I have to tell the girls their dad is gone/dead/gone/dead/ which one? We sit on the floor in a circle, on a Persian rug surrounded by their cousin's plastic horse toys, and I say the words out loud. Somehow, it feels less harrowing than telling them Greg would die soon because then, they had no idea what was coming, the news acted as a freight train hitting their tiny frames without warning. Now they are braced, knowing the words would come, waiting for the impact but, at five and seven, not really knowing what they mean. Do they know what to be dead means? Do *I* really know what it means?

Someone starts humming the *Indiana Jones* theme tune and the focus turns to how do these children know it? We are laughing at the break in tension, at the absurdity of an eighties film score bursting into the set of the Worst Moment of Your Life. There are tears, there are jokes, there is pretending to ride horses and it is madness, perfectly fitting the insanity of the moment.

A big realisation looms into view, one that makes itself known like thunderclouds shading the sun enough for people to look up and wonder where the light went. I must see Greg dead. I desperately wish this wasn't what needs to happen, but I know I have to see him. I have to know this is real.

I drive along the roads I drive every day – on the school run, to the shop to buy oat milk – to see Greg's dead body. I think about how I've forgotten to buy oat milk and I can't possibly drink coffee with cow's milk. This suddenly seems the most pressing matter.

I'm too scared to walk upstairs on my own so ask Aaron to come with me. I hold his hand like he is my parent. The stairs are lined with black and white framed photographs of the band: Greg at Rockfield Studios playing his guitar with headphones on; the four band members under a full moon. It feels as though we are walking backwards through time and space with a visual representation of Greg at all ages, young and healthy.

Greg is the other side of the door. I try to summon the energy of all the people who have walked into a room to witness the death of the person they love. Billions of heartbreaks have gone before mine, but it is as novel as a snowflake.

A gong rings in my head as we walk in the room. I have never felt anything as still and silent as this place. It feels like a transient space, existing in time only for this moment then it will disappear forever.

The nurses have dressed Greg in the clothes I had chosen and covered him from the waist down with a burgundy blanket – a blanket that will unknowingly be repurposed as a sun shield the following summer by Greg's mum, and Aaron and I will look at each other and know that inanimate objects can break your heart.

The stillness of death is extreme. Last night's oppressive feeling of heaviness and fear has been replaced with a feeling of PTSD being formed inside you in real time. The image of Greg's dead body on the bed, his face and absolute emptiness packaged up and swallowed again and again with every blink, travelling to a place in my subconscious, each image compounding on top of each other, burning into my psyche, lying silently to grow and waiting to be born into full-blown trauma.

Aaron and I laugh at something. We say lots of inappropriate things, things we know Greg would have found hilarious. Saying the most ridiculous statements feels like the only thing to do in this absurd place. There is nothing else to say except crude jokes when you are looking at the dead body of your husband, hand in hand with his brother who sat with him as he died.

It is done.

The truth is a delicate thing

I found my great-grandmother dead in her bed when I was a small child.

I remember walking slowly up the stairs of my grand-parents' house, the same house my mum had grown up in and shared with all three generations of her family. The décor of the house hadn't changed from my mum's childhood: swirling patterned nylon carpets, brass ornaments on the wall above the electric fire – the only source of heat in the house. I can remember every detail of their home so clearly as I spent so much time there. It was the perfect house for children to explore; my brother and I loved it there because our grandparents let us do anything we wanted. Grandpa Noel let me rummage through cupboards, emptying the contents and playing with his war medals and Nanny Louvain spent hours with us making inedible pastry that would be put straight in the bin and playing hunt the thimble, when the tiny piece of metal would be in our pockets.

The details of their house are so emblazoned in my mind that I can perfectly picture the cup of tea I carefully carried up the stairs to my great-grandmother's room. I can hear my mum and nan chatting in the tiny kitchen downstairs, Nanny Louvain's Welsh lilt obvious compared to my mum's Hampshire twang. I can smell the tobacco coming from my Grandpa Noel's pipe in the living room, his spot to watch snooker on a black and white TV.

I gently knock on her bedroom door and twist the large wooden knob, careful to not spill any hot tea over the tray. The room is bright through yellowing net curtains and softens the enormity of the solid, dark wooden bed in the middle of the room. My great-grandmother is lying under the multiple nylon sheets and heated blankets, eyes closed and mouth slightly open, head tilted to the side. She looks so peaceful that I feel like walking back out; I was old enough to know adults don't particularly love children waking them up. I set the tray and hot tea on the bedside table and gently touch her powdery hand to wake her. It is icy cold and hard, like a wax candle. This is confusing as my nan's main role in life has always been to keep everyone at a sweltering temperature, especially in bed. Nanny Louvain didn't know about cotton; she believed in the insulating properties of nylon and any other man-made, itchy fabric. When my brother and I would sleep over, I would peel back the thick sheets of my mum's teenage bed to reveal a rubber hot water bottle and an electric blanket on full to warm the bed for my arrival, no matter the season or temperature.

My great-grandmother's hand was icy – something wasn't right, I knew that even as a child. I remember knowing that she was dead and that I would have to walk back down the stairs to tell everyone. My memories of this moment end there; they were probably too torturous for my young brain to contend with. To tell your family you have just found a dead body upstairs as a kid scores high on the trauma meter; thankfully, our brains have a magnificent way of protecting themselves from the deep-seated traumas we experience, choosing to blot them out from our conscious memories. I've spent my life believing the moments after finding a dead body are kept in the dark recess of my subconscious for a reason.

Except they aren't there because I didn't find my grand-mother dead at all.

One day, Madge and I are chatting about her long since dead parents and their house when I throw into the conversation how strange it was that I had found my great-grandmother dead. Madge looks at me as if I have shapeshifted into another person.

'Sorry . . . what?' she asks, confused. Madge is known for her terrible memory, both long and short term, so this isn't a shock, but I'm fairly surprised she doesn't remember her own daughter finding her dead gran, as it feels like it would be quite a significant moment. Maybe her brain has processed the event in the same way as mine – by deleting it, never to be considered again.

I relay the details of that day earnestly, as if I'm talking to a small child. I take her back to the moment of walking up the stairs with a cup of tea on a tray and finding her dead body in the bed.

'Stace, she died in 1982,' Madge clarifies. 'You were two years old. You were a toddler who had only recently learnt to walk. You weren't carrying hot drinks up any stairs or anywhere else. We weren't even *there*. We got a phone call in the morning to say she had died in the night.' My great-grandmother had died of old age in her sleep at the ripe age of ninety-two. She had been bedbound for a while but there was nothing wrong with her, surprisingly as she insisted on smoking legions of untipped Woodbines right up until her death. She had been found in bed by Nanny Louvain in the morning.

Madge may as well have told me I was adopted for how shocking this information was, that the memory I had concreted in my head wasn't true. The scene is full of colour, texture, scent, emotion, totally fully formed and real. I didn't understand how I could have believed this or where I had got these images from in the first place. I had told so many people over the years this story and, in doing so, changing history through the eyes of others.

In writing this story, I phone Madge to ask some questions about what *did* happen on that day and to check the spelling of names. Nanny Louvain had been named after a Belgian city her Uncle Gomer had fought in during the First World War and her mum had loved the name. Ignoring the fact that the name was chosen of a place I imagine he would like to have forgotten about forever, I found that the city is in fact spelt Leuven.

'Who knows?' Madge resolved when I asked her about the different spelling. 'They didn't have Google then. They couldn't look it up so probably guessed.'

How many of our stories and beliefs about ourselves, our families and our lives are based on stories that have been twisted and mutated through time? The 'truth' becomes fuzzier with time for a multitude of reasons. All memories of our past are seen through the lenses of the general passing of time, decreasing cognitive function, conscious and unconscious personal agendas, loyalty, alcohol/drugs and the general passing down of stories over the years and generations, each telling moving slightly further away from the original.

In the post-truth world we live in at the beginning of the twenty-first century, we are now wary of how we can define the term, especially relating to the relaying of information through news outlets and governments. It feels like it shouldn't be hard; the definition of the word truth is 'that which is true or in accordance with fact or reality'. Surely, a fact is a fact is a fact? We all live in the same reality after all.

It feels extremely urgent and almost sacrosanct to make sure the truth is told about those who have died. It will make no difference to my dead great-grandmother that I've told friends over the years I was the one who found her body but, for Nanny Louvain, the person who *did* discover her mum's body and experience the trauma and reverence of that moment, it snatches away her experience and agency over a pivotal moment in her life. I didn't purposefully invent a far-fetched story to impress my friends or want to be the main character of the event; I imagine it may have been a mixture of a child's undeveloped brain overhearing stories about the event, possibly mixed with images from dreams, which produced a Frankenstein version of events.

In a conversation with a friend about politics after Greg died, they recalled conversations with him on the topic and stated with authority Greg held polar opposite views to what I believed he had. In that moment, this felt outrageous; Greg's thoughts on politics were solid in liberalism and he was well known for engaging in online arguments about the topics of the day. At first, I laughed at the absurdity of the idea, but when it was insisted that this was THE TRUTH, that my version of Greg was wrong, I felt angry and defensive. My first instinct was to act as a barrister would – collecting evidence from the years of Greg's social media accounts with proof of the contrary. I could almost feel Greg in the room with us, horrified that he could possibly be attached to views he found abhorrent.

Our friend believed his truth about Greg's views as vehemently as I did. Why did this matter so much to either of us? In many instances, it doesn't matter; I recently heard someone say Greg's favourite colour was blue when I knew it to be orange. I didn't correct them because . . . *it really doesn't matter.* Maybe he had told them different to me. I have different favourite colours on different days. Perhaps the concept of truth begins to matter when the slight trajectory moves away from the essence of the person, the incomparable nature that made them who they were but, even then, who is to judge what that even was?

Some changes to the truth may be purposeful, made with good intentions to soften the blow and dilute the real event. A revised story may offer comfort and solace for someone who is broken, and when there is nothing else you can do to take away someone's pain, it might be delivered as a gift.

Depending on who is doing the telling, we may be the hero or the villain in the same story. Others have memories of us that may be truer than our own. Truth is often the first victim of self-preservation; we have all kinds of needs to finesse the truth of ourselves to make it more palatable – to help us cope with guilt, shame, embarrassment, moments we would rather forget. Our memories are filtered through the lenses of our childhoods, politics and beliefs. Tiny denials are added over time to keep us blameless. If you could quantify the value of memories – the fidelity to the moment and the details – someone's memory of us would be as valuable as our memories of ourselves. They have witnessed us and hold a specific version, all accounts singular and rarely overlapping with another, never to be repeated.

In writing about someone who has died, I am acutely aware of the control I have over their narrative. After all, a person's legacy is always a mixture of what they left in the world and the stories chosen by others to tell about them. *My* truth is not everyone else's and even my own version of events is marred by time, memory and trauma. Our stories will only ever be from our current viewpoint but they morph over the years, a time capsule fed and metabolised by changing perspectives. The more life happens, the more nuanced and fuzzy the past begins to look.

Dove rivalry

It's harder than you would imagine asking a terminally ill person what they think the best Beatles song is or their favourite tune from the nineties. It's impossible to let the questions trip lightly from your tongue as if you are only asking if they would like a cup of tea.

'Is this a panic interrogation?' Greg would ask when I posed any such questions and I'd have to overact my nonchalance, making it even more obvious I was inquiring for his funeral.

Greg and I had roundabout ways of talking about death over the years, with dark humour often leading the way. During this time, we seemed to live at the hospital and would spend whole days there, waiting around on plastic chairs and discussing the strange choice of using prints of *Titanic* to decorate the walls in an oncology ward. In similar bad planning, the walk to the hospital took us through a large ominous graveyard. Walking from one side to the other was a twenty-minute jaunt through history; the headstones in the darkest corners were covered in moss and illegible writing worn away by weather and time, and, most disturbing – the children's graves were surrounded by concrete teddies holding balloons and fairy lights everywhere, perhaps so the kids wouldn't get scared at night.

We had seen all seasons through different years here, admiring the cherry blossom pink in the spring, and had been terrified in the dark winter months at 5 p.m. when you couldn't see your hand in front of your face, waiting to see ghosts appear from behind the headstones. We would bring Dalí's wind-up torch to guide the way, a plastic yellow duck with a light in its beak to keep the ghouls away.

There is nothing easy about walking through rows of graves when you are giving Death a piggyback and he's screaming 'YOU AND EVERYONE YOU LOVE ARE GOING TO DIE' in your ear. To counteract these voices, Greg and I would concoct ridiculous fantasy funerals. This was a silly game to make us laugh in a tense situation but also a way to tiptoe into the conversation. My future funeral would include black-plumed stallions carrying my body in a glass casket, where I would be in full view wearing a white Victorian gown and holding roses to my chest. Everyone would be asked to wear all black. No exceptions, none of the modern 'wearing colour to celebrate her life' nonsense – this is a funeral, it's time for absolute MOURNING. In the candlelit church, eunuchs would be hidden in the rafters to sing a melancholic serenade, as if their voices were coming from the heavens. There would be no happy, jaunty playlist, only emotional heavyweights like 'Memories' by Elaine Paige or 'The First Time Ever I saw Your Face' by Roberta Flack. I might also insist the Death March is played as the congregation leaves and my casket will be opened for each person to kiss my cold, dead cheek as they pass. Everyone will leave a broken shadow of their former selves.

Greg opted for his dead body to be put in a cannon and shot at a wall in public, his innards covering passers-by. We wondered if that could even be physically possible if you're dead – doesn't your body go into rigor mortis? We filled an entire walk through the graveyard discussing if his body would explode into slushy pieces or shards of glass.

These stories were needed for what often felt like entering the gates of hell. The graveyard itself was a beautiful oasis of calm, so lush and green while the ominous brutalism of the concrete hospital loomed over the trees. We once saw a man sat on the hood of his car there, drinking beer at 10 a.m. and blaring Tina Turner's 'Simply the Best' at a volume that felt disrespectful to the dead.

'Sorry, I'm having a bad day,' he sobbed as we walked past and gave a polite smile.

I had driven past the funeral directors a million times. I quietly always knew they would be my choice when the time came. A traditional, independent family-owned business somehow felt more palatable. I couldn't bear the thought of a corporate chain taking charge; it would feel like a march towards a battery hen slaughterhouse.

Throughout the years of Greg's illness, I would make a point of averting my eyes as I drove past, trying not to think of myself standing on the forecourt, finally needing to go in. Greg wasn't privy to any of these feelings, even when sat in the passenger seat next to me. It never sparked any kind of recognition or initiated any deep and meaningful conversation about his death or what he wanted for his eventual funeral. It was as if he didn't notice at all though it loomed large for me and increasingly occupied space in my brain as time went on. I wondered what he was thinking, never wanting to ask as we watched the hearses sat outside waiting for the final journey to begin.

I was still shocked when I finally needed to speak to the funeral director. When someone dies, their body needs to be taken *somewhere*. If that sounds vague and illusive, that's because it is. Just like when you arrive home with a newborn baby, put them down in their car seat, so tiny and unthinkable, and quietly say, 'What happens now?', you hope a *real* adult will take over. Unfortunately, when it's either your baby crying or your husband who is dead, the real adult is now you.

I had the job of organising Greg's body being removed from his parents' house. I had seen silver private ambulances driving around for years, knowing exactly what was in the back of them, always driven by men in black suit and tie as if on their way to a formal dinner. Dead bodies casually in the same lane as parents and kids on the school run. Once you notice them, you can never unsee them.

The funeral director answered the phone and I immediately burst out laughing at the absurdity of it all; I had no idea what to ask. I went straight to court jester mode because grief is weird.

'Hello. HELLO!!! (*Too loud, too jovial.*) How are you? (*Laughing hysterically.*) Umm, so . . . my husband has just died and I suppose he can't stay here, can he? (*Stop making jokes.*) So what happens now? (*More laughing, they must think I'm drunk.*) I've never had to do this before so I'm a novice. By the way, I hope you don't think I'm a psychopath, this just all feels so strange and for some reason hilarious.' (*Only psychopaths would say this.*)

I'm hoping they must have heard this insanity before. Those answering the phone must have heard wailing, screaming, laughing, urgency, lack of emotion. We've now gone from calling Greg by his name to 'the patient' to 'the deceased' in less than a few hours and I want to correct them as he's neither of these – he's Greg or Dad or G – but I can't because I'm laughing too much, a nervous reaction because this is all impossible. The men in black arrive in their blacked-out death carriage and we shut all the doors and curtains because none of us can stand to see Greg's body leave the house. Even though I know he is dead, to watch may have resulted in rugby-tackling them to take him back. I haven't really thought that through because what on earth would I do with a dead body?

Walking into a funeral director is a bizarre experience because it's set up like your grandparents' lounge. Perhaps the interior decorators thought the business of death becomes a softer blow with chintz and a delicate teacup. Much like medical settings, they love a peach-fuelled colour pallet but, unlike the hospice, it finds a way to calm me. Michelle is my partner here and we are giddy going in, half in shock protecting us from the enormity of it all, half in hysterical laughter to act like a shield. I'm trying to ignore the fact Greg's body is in a freezer somewhere in this building. I wonder if he's cold.

Planning a funeral is very similar to organising a wedding – you need a ceremony, a venue, guests, a speech, but here I am as the lone bride with a groom who will arrive at the altar in a box. We meet the funeral version of a wedding planner – David is in his twenties, so unnervingly professional and respectful that I want to tickle him just to make him smile. The death buffet starts with choosing a coffin. I'm finding it quite difficult to say out loud. Just the word itself feels claustrophobic.

Is Greg going to be able to breathe properly in a coffin? Can they drill holes in the side so he can get some more air? I suppose it doesn't matter if he's about to be burnt inside? Urgh, but won't that hurt?

Thankfully, there is a catalogue to just point at. The coffins all have names sounding like grand English country estates. I joke that Greg would have hated to spend money on something that is immediately destroyed, and David directs us to the eco-friendly cardboard coffins. They look like large Amazon boxes.

I wonder if the congregation would laugh if we drew the Prime logo on the side as a dedication to the never-ending stream of books Greg used to order? Maybe this is too much of an insider joke? Why do I just want to make this entire event funny?

'What if it rains?' I ask. 'Won't the cardboard just dissolve?' All I can think of is the scene from *Jackass* where they pretend a dead body falls out of a coffin onto the road while they film the reactions of passers-by.

'No, this is special reinforced cardboard that can carry up to twenty-eight stone,' David reassures us. I try to picture what carrying a coffin this size would look like and decide cancer coffins must be easier to carry after all the weight their occupants lose at the end of their life.

We decide on the cheapest coffin made of fake wood that looks identical to those costing thousands made from imported oak and have gilt-gold handles. I can understand how some people would feel the quality of the coffin needs to be in direct correlation with how much they loved the dead person. Capitalism and consumerism exist even in death.

The details of the funeral are lost on me during the conversation. As David talks, I'm distracted by a photo frame next to the tissues on the table beside us. An illustrated bird is being thrown up into a blue sky with the words 'DOVE RELEASE – STEVE MALONY' and a mobile number. It feels unusual to frame an advert for deathly circus acts. David tells us about the showmanship of dove release and the workings of a world I didn't know existed.

There are strict rules within this sphere – the doves can't

be released in a certain postcode as, instead of circling the congregation, they will just exit the basket to fly straight home, much to the chagrin of those who have paid hundreds for the poignant moment of reflection. There is a fierce turf war; those in the dove-release world know not to cross county lines and onto another dove's patch. David has worked with Steve Malony for years and trusts his avian abilities but tells us of some local rivalry on the scene – another dove breeder who has upped the ante. The new guy in town has grown the sides of his hair, bleaching and gelling it up into doves' wings. I wouldn't know who to choose but I would definitely like to see them in a dove-off. Greg would have too, so it's annoying that this is actually his funeral.

What are Steve Malony's doves called? Do the doves behave differently at a funeral compared to a wedding? Has David seen them shit on the heads of the bereaved?

I have so many personal questions for David. His youthful professionalism fascinates me and makes me want to get him drunk and crack open all his secrets. I want to know that he is a real person, that who pumped Greg's veins full of formaldehyde is not an automaton. He has been in an intimate moment with Greg's body, so I feel I need to know him more intimately.

David tells me he was intrigued by death as a young teenager and worked in a funeral home at age fourteen. His girlfriend is also a funeral director; they met at embalming school, where their first conversation was over a dead body. He is one of the top embalmers in the country, winning a gold award at the funeral version of the Oscars and has embalmed every member of his own family who's died. Michelle and I listen to a detailed and rich history of funeral directors, happy to be distracted. My favourite story is about how they don't wear top hats and canes anymore because they become cumbersome in having to dash forward when someone inevitably faints.

For as much as I have turned David into a character to play a starring role in the sitcom of my mind, it is he who offers a tower of strength on the morning of Greg's funeral. When the hearse arrives outside the house and we are all in various states of falling apart, it is this young man who takes soft control. He kneels on the concrete in his morning suit to talk gently to Dalí, he makes small talk and jokes with my dad, he offers me a look of deep knowing and understanding. He guides us like sheep towards our cars and towards Greg's final destination.

We didn't hire the doves. There seemed no point if Greg wasn't there to laugh with us.

God wears a Hawaiian shirt

Greg barely spoke towards the end but, when he did, he asked to see someone 'churchy'. He was not religious, and neither am I. This wasn't what I was expecting. Where do you quickly find a priest to pop round?

The nurses who were caring for Greg at his parents' house told us the hospice had their own resident chaplain. I felt a mixture of rising anger and nervousness. These were Greg's wishes but how dare God turn up right at the very end for any kind of claim on his life. I was already scared of the otherworldly nature of Death; I was now terrified of religion entering the ring as well. I was tired of everything being so enormous.

Ted the chaplain arrived with a quiet reverence that sat in a stark contrast to his lurid floral shirt. My heart sank. *Oh God (fuck, I can't say that around him, can I?). He's a 'cool vicar'. He's been sent out into the community to show the Church isn't a stuffy institution stuck in the past.*

I didn't want to hear how Jesus would spread the Good Word through TikTok if he was around today. I wouldn't be fooled by bright colours; if there was any kind of God, I didn't want his Club Tropicana messenger in Ted. Everything about my surly teen body language screamed 'IMPRESS ME'.

And he did impress me, in a way I wasn't expecting. In the first five minutes of talking, Ted swore, mentioned his divorce and laughed at Greg's dad's inappropriate jokes, all while exuding an aura of much-needed calm and ease. He smiled so easily, and I was compelled to rest my head on his shoulder. As I quietly led Ted upstairs to meet Greg, I whispered, 'I expected more dog collars and beads, maybe less tropical flowers', unable to keep my disdain for his calling under cover.

Ted laughed under his breath. 'Yeah, the full black cassock tends to scare the shit out of people.' As we get to the door, I whipped round and hissed, 'NO JESUS SHIT.'

Greg slowly opened his eyes as we tiptoed into the room. No words were said; he just reached out for Ted as I had seen both my children reach out to me when they were babies, arms out in surrender, in need of comfort. Ted moved forward to take Greg's hands and the two strangers smiled at each other, speaking a silent language I couldn't understand. The language of the living sounds of Saturday afternoon shopping centre, the unspoken language of the dying translates as a flower's petals opening in the sun. I had believed there were no new colours to see but this was something I'd never experienced before – holiness. The shedding of all human attributes built over time, with only the simplicity of our essence left.

It was claustrophobic in that small room because in it was me, Greg, a priest in a Hawaiian shirt, God and Death. It was only by being in the presence of all of them that I could see the obvious – God and Death were the same person. Well, not a person. They weren't in Gandalf and Grim Reaper costumes, facing each other and waiting for the bell to ring for the boxing match to begin. I felt like the bees; simultaneously stood in front of the beginning and the end with no understanding what my place is in its enormity. This intimate moment was not meant for me, so I quietly removed myself from the biblical scene and returned to the land of the living, where my children were dancing to 'Gangnam Style' downstairs.

It's a unanimous decision that Ted is to be the celebrant at Greg's funeral. He is a perfect pick and mix of reverence and irreverence. I'm so pleased to be enamoured with someone who can do this job because it had been worrying me. It's not an exaggeration to say I despise funeral celebrants. The older you get, the more funerals you attend, the more I grind my teeth at their faux relationship with the dead. I want to scream when they giggle to themselves at Uncle John's penchant for a tipple and give a knowing look to the coffin. Of course, I am the one totally in the wrong here and an idiot for having these feelings, but this is the possessive hierarchy of grief.

On the night before Greg's funeral, I receive a text message from Ted.

'May creation hold you this night to her bosom, as you hear her words, "Do not fear, do not be afraid, for I am with you sharing in the yoke of despair and all that you are, my child, I am fucking well pleased." You as you. You've got this.'

I wonder if his priest pals would think he'd go to hell for blasphemous use of a prayer.

I arrive at Greg's funeral and might as well be dead myself for how present I am walking up to the crematorium. The silent scream I had heard ringing in my ears when watching Greg die has returned and I stand behind the hearse with my mouth gaping as if it's coming from my own throat. Ted appears in front of me, dressed in full-length cloaks of the clergy and his hands clasped in front of him, as only men of God seem to do.

He leans forward to whisper in my ear. Please give me a balm, Ted. *Please say something to explain how I'm here, how my husband is dead in a coffin in front of me. Please ask God what I'm supposed to do now.*

Ted whispers, 'Fuckety fuck, this is shit, isn't it?'

I have never heard more calming words in my life.

I barely listen to Ted's words during the service. These words aren't for me anyway, they are for the other people here, all of them box-fresh to Greg's death whereas those in the front row are weary from its constant company. There is one part of the sermon I want to hear though.

Ted talks of what a legacy of love really looks like. How the different hues are so expansive, we cannot use the restrictions of organised religion to understand them. He remembers that in his meeting Greg, there was so much warmth and humour, and even in such a desperate moment, there was still permission to laugh. With that statement, Ted whips off his white collar and cassock like Bucks Fizz at Eurovision to reveal a Delays T-shirt underneath. I have never heard whoops at a funeral before.

The dress (black)

It seems unlikely that waking up on the day of your husband's funeral would feel like Christmas morning but there are few other times where an entire house will not have been able to sleep, only to have what rest they have managed to be cut brutally short by eyelids pinging open, as if mechanical and without blinking.

Staring blankly into the lavender walls of my childhood bedroom, I realised this configuration of people had last slept under this roof for my wedding three years earlier. My brother has been ousted from his own childhood room by my daughters, relegated to sleep on the sofa with feet hanging over the edge. I'm the only one with a bed to themselves, a silent gesture of kindness.

There is a frenetic energy about the morning that almost borders on the twisted excitement of watching a disaster unfold on the news. You know it's horrific but did you see the second tower collapse? Everyone has a new outfit they secretly plan to throw away or send back the following week when the fabric becomes too tainted with Death to wear again. I had spent the weeks between Greg's death and funeral obsessing over what I would wear to an event that felt weirdly more important than our wedding day; it was a moment to make a statement on my enforced captivity in a role I never wanted – the widow. Dripping with centuries of tragic stories and desperate imagery, the term is defined by tropes of either the bitter spinster, the emotional wreck or the femme fatale out to steal everyone's husband. None of these comparisons appeal, but as someone who spent her teenage years obsessed with gothic culture, cocooned in her bedroom reading vampire fiction with curtains drawn, I could see the allure of creating an elaborate visual spectacle to represent such bleak existential pain.

I created a Pinterest mood board – Pinterest! How postmodern! – for the look I wanted and titled it 'Italian Mafia Widow'. Everything needed to be as big and dramatic as I felt. Everything had to be black – from the delicate lace gloves, to the synched-to-within-an-inch-of-my-life dress, to my veiled fascinator. I wanted to be Morticia Addams and Lily Munster. Parcels arrive and black lace is everywhere, all over Bay's LOL Dolls bedcover, the juxtaposition making me dizzy.

'Do you think I should buy a black lace parasol?' I ask Madge as I showcase another dress for her and the girls, this one with black rose-petal bodice and skirt with a train. I'm fully aware I'm deep in the sweet spot after death, where no one will challenge me on anything for fear of a breakdown.

'Maybe not,' she replies, trying to be tactful while looking the dress up and down. 'I'm also wondering if a dress with a train is too much?'

'Why?' I cut back defiantly. This is the provocation of grief, calling upon the spirit of my younger self who wore what I wanted to school and would argue with teachers who challenged me. If I'm going to have to be a widow at forty-one, I may as well be a fabulous one, to take the title and run with it.

When the final dress is chosen, I stand in front of the mirror to look at myself, in the same spot I had stood to look at myself in my wedding dress. I could hear Greg's voice in my head: 'Here she is . . . making sure everything is at a dramatic fever pitch.' He gave me the first smile of the day.

I had let the girls choose whatever they wanted to wear. Dalí had gravitated to a very cool outfit of biker boots and a plaid dress while Bay has chosen a Halloween costume, a huge ball of black netting.

We left my parents' house to congregate at Greg's family home. While everyone busied themselves with nothing indoors, I stood outside the house with Aaron, the road eerily empty as all cars had been cleared as a mark of respect. We stood watching and waiting in silence and fight mode. I needed to see it coming, to see the hearse carrying Greg's body so it couldn't sneak up on us. The first sign of black polished chrome hits like an animal with its prey, slowly creeping along with the suspense of a tiger that might pounce to rip your throat out. The cluster of sunflowers obliterates the shiny wood and brass until it's in view and I wonder what Greg looks like inside.

Does the embalming mean his flesh won't rot? Have his nails and hair grown like in horror films when you see corpses? I'm pretty sure he's dead and I'm sure he must be in there because why would the funeral directors want to keep him? Maybe for experiments? I had sent clothes for him to wear today and now, with everyone dressed up as if going to a wedding in hell, the blue and white striped T-shirt and jeans now seems a bit informal and inappropriate. Do people buy suits for their dead to wear in their coffin, just so they are smart? Did I send trainers? Why does he need shoes at all? I think I would feel claustrophobic with shoes on in a coffin. This hill is very steep, maybe Greg's parents should move before they get too old, how would they manage a car up here? Greg used to run up this hill to train for football. Walking up in summer midday sun was enough for me. I wonder who dressed him?

NOW IS NOT THE TIME FOR FLOWERS

I say *him* as if *he* is there. He's not. We are all here in this human dance of endings, with our new shoes and brushed hair while he is flying.

242

The Boy (eulogy)

I wrote Greg's eulogy in my head on the drive home from the hospital the day we were told his illness would end his life, five years before he died. The final edit was a very close match to the words that fell into place as I opened my eyes extra wide to not crash. I want to be regal. Everything became crystal clear – I know the words for the closing scene of our life because I've been in every scene. All things distil down into images, metaphors, words that need to just be put in the right order.

* * *

I held my breath the first time I heard The Boy's voice. 'Can you hear the knocking in your soul?' he asked. An angelic cry held a spotlight on me in a crowded room.

The first time I am alone with The Boy, he tells me secrets. He wears a T-shirt with a lobster on it. He orders tea. He does the best impressions I've ever seen and can talk in any accent under the sun. He is easily the funniest, sharpest person I've ever met but this is held undercover, his knowledge and outrageous talent standing taller than giants next to all his other traits.

To be around The Boy is to be in the presence of another world. I'm not sure he's from here. An ethereal being, his aura radiates creativity, and something flows through him that I have never seen in another person.

At the same time, The Boy is deeply human. His politics are coloured by his care of others, a champion of fairness and equality. His deepest loves are his family, the urban myths of St Denys and 1970s Christmas tinsel. He was born nostalgic and carried this on until his final days, with his last drink being a soda float, like he drank at The Savoy on the Isle of Wight on his childhood holidays.

He owns an unshakable knowledge that he will achieve everything he wants to, that the story of his life how he envisions it will tumble out of his head and onto the canvas with ease. There is no plan B. Yet The Boy is humble beyond reproach. His nature is quiet and gentle like leaves in autumn.

The Boy's attention on me feels like sunshine in June. His belief in me is unwavering. I love who I am in his reflection. He calls me magnetic, oceanic, and in him I feel all these things. He helps me stand up when I want to sit down. He asks me what I'm reading, what I'm scared of, what my favourite colour is. He makes me feel so safe in our world of private jokes, magical thinking and stupid names for our dog. We drive around together laughing. We sit and talk about ghost hunting for hours and there is magic all around.

The Boy once wrote that the last night on earth is for living but he was only partly right. He showed us that the time for living is now, that we only have this moment and there is no time like now to wear the silver boots like Marc Bolan.

The Boy has so many achievements to be proud of but his biggest by far are not hung on a wall in a gallery or played through a speaker, they are sat right here. Dalí and Bay – you are Dad's most glorious creations.

I am so thankful to have been in the orbit of such a wonderful person, who filled my world with such wonder and magic. For The Boy is himself pure magic and always will be.

Grief

Lies I have told myself about grief

On the morning after Greg's funeral, I woke up and thought, This is going to be the worst day of my life. This is what I had been told by others – that straight after the funeral, the initial grief is still visceral and sharp but is also accompanied by an untethered void that comes from now not having anything to do or plan. Your aimless life spreads out in front of you as a dry wasteland. I lay on the camp bed in the girls' bedroom at my parents' house and stared at the boxes of their toys and clothes.

This is it, I thought. This is as bad as it's going to get. And it *was* bad. In fact, it was awful, but I thought this was day one and all subsequent days would get incrementally better, as if grief is a sickness bug to flush through your system.

It was absolutely not the worst day by any stretch. The worst day doesn't have people making you hot drinks on repeat or allow you to stay in bed with no questions. It doesn't include your phone vibrating non-stop with well wishes and heart-warming stories of the day before. I desperately wanted to believe this was how it worked, that the infamous five stages of grief were neatly packaged days to get through as if you were crossing off a calendar for a holiday. I didn't want to believe in grief's ability to hit like a wave, giving such little reprieve to catch your breath before your eyes and lungs are filled with water again. I wanted to believe the hardest times were behind me. I had no interest in learning how to be resilient. I had the most desperate urge to be a child again or, at the very least, be treated like a child – picked up and carried to bed, left warm and snug with the sound of the 'real' adults floating in from another room, knowing it is safe to rest.

I wanted to be bulletproof and never let myself be hurt like this again. I wanted to fast-track everything as if grief was a transaction – if I can do all the therapy, give all the TED Talks, write all the words, I could outrun all the real pain. Self-deception matters least when you're in fear of annihilation – no jury would convict you for cherishing comfort and needing a raft to cling on to.

The pink drawer handles

Death and grief are not Siamese twins bound inseparably together; they are two very separate experiences. I knew I was grieving Greg long before he died when I found myself lying flat out on the floor in John Lewis, crying over kitchen drawer handles. In an attempt to fix everything – which I had reluctantly realised didn't include curing cancer or saving Greg's life – I had decided to decorate our entire house. If I couldn't alter the multiple tumours in his lungs, I could at least give us luscious soft furnishings and mood lighting. I believed it was because I wanted things to be nice in our home when, in fact, I just didn't want Greg to die or to watch the inevitable move towards us like an approaching war.

I threw myself into colours and textures; a focus on paint charts and fabrics became a powerful distraction and I became obsessive over how transformative this needed to be. I wanted to start from scratch and erase every indication of who we were 'before' because it was too painful to live in, like a film set of your own past life. I wanted every colour changed, everything new, nothing that had been marked by the dark stain of illness; a futile act as it was very much ingrained in us.

The kitchen was the first to go as it was literally falling apart. One day, the awkward swing of a kitchen cupboard door had sent me over the edge so I cancelled all my plans and instead visited immaculate showrooms that transported me into an aspirational life, where I could leisurely cook for my family in a space I would never keep as clean. No one would be sick, I would be happy, life would be easy – all this would be possible with new cupboards.

The illusion was dramatically burst by choosing the colours for the kitchen. My heart wanted black units with dusky pink walls, but I was painfully aware of a growing inconvenient truth: I would not want to live in my house after Greg died. I realised I couldn't paint my personality over the walls and choose a kitchen that would make selling the house harder when, in reality, I wouldn't be able to live there much longer.

Grief is often slow, starting as a groundswell but begins to rear up like a Hokusai wave to pick up pace at inopportune moments, such as looking for kitchen cupboard handles on a Tuesday afternoon. I had decided against the black cupboards, opting for a more neutral and, most importantly, sellable cashmere colour. In lieu of what I actually wanted, I obsessed over incredible drawer handles I'd seen made of rose quartz and old gold. They were so over-the-top and expensive, so impractical for a kitchen, but would be my nod towards my original design and I would get to take them with me to a new future house.

I found them in John Lewis's furnishing department and began counting out the thirty needed when I suddenly felt I was going to throw up and needed to sit on the floor. Just looking at the beautiful jewels made me panic and opened up everything that I'd kept inside, all my tears and limbs splayed out on the floor. The ridiculous turmoil over pink drawer handles boiled down to this: I couldn't bring myself to share so much of my identity at home when I was decorating death row. It felt like anything of myself I put into the house – my creativity, my love of design, my money – would be taken with Greg when he died, and I didn't know how much of myself I would have left.

This is how anticipatory grief can sneak in through the backdoor of your mind. You might be able to chat over coffee with a friend about your husband dying in a very matter-of-fact way but then, when out looking for a new sofa, you have to almost climb into a wardrobe to hide your tears because everyone else there is a young couple who will get years instead of months to sit on their purchase. You doubt they are taking measurements thinking about where it could move to if they need to fit a hospital bed in their living room. They wouldn't be wondering where the nurses will sit and if pink velvet is a good fabric choice when you don't know if Death stains.

I didn't expect grief to feel so much like physical illness. We believe grief in all its guises is essentially sadness, but its tentacles unfurl into deeper aspects of our lives. It feels like sadness, heart attacks, morning sickness and influenza. It feels like being drunk and hungover together mixed up in a toxic cocktail. Humans have spent their whole existence trying to capture the complicated facets of abstract emotions like love and grief, amorphous clouds of feelings holding so much more than one eternity. Try to describe a colour and it will pale in comparison to its appearance in nature, in a painting or a flicker in the eyes of the person you love most.

I could see the pain of grief as a black hole in the distance – an endless drop into darkness and the unknown. I couldn't bear to sneak a look; it felt so vast that, if I did, I would have slipped and fallen in like Alice. Perhaps Wonderland was a representation of grief, where nothing makes sense in an upside-down world and you can't get home – except Alice did get home, everything was exactly as it was before, and no time had passed. I often wondered if that could happen to us;

I could wake up as if from a daydream, at the moment when Greg first told me about the pain in his abdomen. We could have chosen a different action, a different conversation and, maybe, there would be a different outcome.

The waves of that distant tsunami were growing higher on the skyline as Greg's pain and discomfort increased over time. All I could do was stand on the shoreline and watch them roll in. Those who were watching the waves felt the air catch in their throat while those facing away, not seeing or acknowledging the impending doom, would carry on as if nothing was happening. But like any storm on the horizon, where the air feels oppressive and claustrophobic, you can sense the change in atmosphere. Sometimes I doubt whether the best way to face what's coming is to imagine it again and again. It's hard to know if this fear is our own or a patchwork monster of what we have been shown. Perhaps we need to dwell on our worst-case scenario to pre-empt an unseen attack in the night.

Anticipatory grief becomes a painful stringing out of time, a hand in your chest slowly reaching around the sinews of your heart and pulling it through your ribcage. You watch your loved one make a cup of tea and try to take in every detail to burn it into your memory, hoping it's deep enough to be recalled when they aren't here.

The emotional destruction of our family was a slow torture, a communal death of a billion cuts. I was the matriarch, the one to comfort and care for everyone but my go-to reaction while waiting for Death to materialise was abandon. I let the girls start primary school with their hair dyed bright fuchsia pink, almost willing someone to challenge me so I could explain that it doesn't matter, that literally none of what we consume ourselves with matters. My nails were bitten and bloody, my stomach felt forever empty despite filling it with sugar and salt on a constant rotation, and my mind needed the buzz and obliteration of alcohol.

I felt Greg was already like a ghost floating through the house, lost in his own thoughts, battling silent demons he wouldn't share. I was the perennial cheerleader, dancing on demand and keeping energy up for the crowd despite crying behind the bleachers. They all looked to me how passengers on a plane look to the flight attendant when the oxygen masks fall down. I had to calmly ask what they wanted to drink because falling out of the sky might be a bit bumpy. This *danse macabre* ricocheted between a denial based on the abstract concept of death and hysteria. I wondered how I would get out of bed with this knowledge but still I did, every day. To other people, this was viewed as insurmountable strength when, instead, it was born out of a cocktail of numbness and responsibility. I was told all the time how strong I was, how emotionally literate I was, how good I was at processing things but that left no space for just being sad. Sadness, the very deep and alone kind, is the hardest emotion to witness and fights to get a seat at the table. Being strong publicly became like inspiration porn to others who benefited from seeing me not just cope but thrive.

Our minds, bodies, hearts and organs aren't separate entities. Their connection with each other lets us know that we are human, we are alive and that we are loved. Sat in my new kitchen with plain black drawer handles, I didn't realise love can also feel like excruciating yet exquisite pain.

Now can you please draw God for me?

No one really knows how to deal with bad news. Sympathetic faces offer 'I can't imagine what you're feeling' as they struggle to visualise a reality different to theirs, a way to acknowledge you without the risk of imagining their own life smashed on the floor, to peer into a ravine that produces immediate vertigo. People don't want to know how others really feel. It's too much, the pain and fear of what could potentially happen to any of us.

I don't think their statement is a request for a description, just a way to quickly move on to less disruptive topics. I don't attempt to articulate anything; hopefully my silence implies a load-bearing corner of my brain has collapsed. It feels pointless to put words or give voice to an emotion so abstract, like being asked to draw God.

This is something I was asked to do in an art class at school. As an eleven-year-old with no interest in any religion, I lazily drew a multi-coloured haze while my classmates around me huddled over their detailed Gandalf/Dumbledore portraits, making sure the beards they all sketched were long and white.

'This isn't what God looks like,' my teacher said to me as she wandered through the tables. 'I don't think you're even trying.' My abstract mess was seen as a defiant stance, instead of an interpretation of having no idea. I felt alone in not knowing when everyone else seemed so sure of themselves.

Ask me now to draw grief and I would recreate a similar image.

Ask me what grief feels like and I will tell you it is a precious bruising to the heart, but I can barely move with my chest so tender. A pain like this undermines and colours everything about the world, and it cannot be compartmentalised. As a result, the world becomes more glorious, imbuing it all with such delicate poignancy. This isn't a fast pain but rather slow and methodical, precise and measured, which ratchets at an inclined pace.

Grief feels like being drenched in love, arms to catch me everywhere. I feel held yet amorphous and undone, everything I'd so desperately held together now loosened. I'm not alone, just an element in the world. All the hurdles are rushing towards me with no time to leap so I smash through one by one like a competitive kid on sports day. I'm a bullet in a gun chamber, nestled into the electric potential of death.

The pain of grief is so deep, it becomes almost an exquisite agony. Philosophers believe the limitations of the human brain couldn't cope with a meaning of life, but this must be the nearest thing to it. You can see everything with X-ray vision, noticing every atom shaking. It takes us away from the trappings of our modern lives that keep our attention focused elsewhere on mundane matters we obsess over. In the expansive space of grief, there is nothing but love.

Love at the edge of death feels like fear, sadness, regret, joy and anger all mixed together to drink down. It tastes like nothing you've ever tried before; even if you've previously been here, you receive a new bespoke cocktail each time.

Like love, grief is a word that needs description rather than definition because both are so expansive, so fluid and abstract, it becomes inadequate to summarise them. Within such huge energies lies a spectrum of their capabilities; grief can level you to a shadow and yet enhance your experience of life, just as love can create joy, fulfilment and safety and yet utterly destroy you.

It is love that will lacerate us and leave us with the wound of grief to tend to.

My own tsunami

Sitting in front of Greg's hospital bed as he slept, I breathed a sigh of relief.

At least this is it. This is the very worst thing that will ever happen to me. This is the pinnacle of pain. Nothing will get close to this again. I have reached my quota for bad things.

There was a weird comfort in this thought; I would have to watch Greg die but as the killer had removed his mask, there would be no surprises.

The universe must have heard my thoughts and placed a newspaper on the table I sat at in the hospital café the next morning. In among the stories of the day was a photograph of a couple in hospital beds side by side, pushed together so they could hold hands through the cannulas and tubes. COUPLE BOTH DIAGNOSED WITH TERMINAL CANCER IN THE SAME WEEK shouted the headline. They had four children under the age of ten.

There are no rules anymore. The concept of fairness is a myth. Is everything just pure luck?

In the space of two years, one of my mum's closest friends lost her husband very quickly to cancer, her son to a brain aneurysm and her daughter to kidney failure. Her entire family dead in a heartbeat.

Grief is no tsunami, it is tidal. The powerful tectonic shifts of a tsunami will hopefully be a once-in-a-generation event. We are going to have to ride the power of the moon back and forth and encounter pain on repeat, especially if we love and want to live an expansive life. The moon never made this pact secret; twice a day, she plays her hand, so formulaic and like clockwork. The tide will pull away from the shore to offer the land to walk on in the sun, to lie on the golden sand and bask in the warmth and ease. As time passes and the sun and moon move the shadows like puppets, the tide draws close again at such a slow incremental speed, you will need to squint to see the direction of the waves. It will be when your attention has been drawn back to your sandcastles that you notice the water is nearing the edge of your blanket. This is the exhale of water, a cyclic breath and the heartbreaking rhythm of loss we must live with.

The Shit Olympics

Honorary mention

I was eighteen when my grandpa Noel died. He was very much a man of his time – a quiet figure who refused to discuss his time fighting in Africa during the war yet exuded an ease with life rarely seen in most people. Noel and Nanny Louvain were exceptionally content with an uncomplicated life, potentially influenced by both growing up in the small coal-mining village of Aberfan in Wales, despite the coal spoils disaster in 1966 killing some of Noel's family. They were delighted with their daily routine walking to the pub hand in hand for a pint and a trip to the bookies to bet a few pounds on horses, Noel looking at form, Louvain creating categories like 'has a colour in its name' to choose. My grandpa died eight years after Louvain. We had wondered how he would cope without her, but he did. He created his own new practical routines and simple pleasures, teaching himself to cook and making sure he moved his body every day. He was always so lovely, but I didn't feel very close to him, the mixture of emotional and expressive young girl and stoic old man never quite gelling.

At Noel's funeral, I wandered around the real adults and smiled politely at strangers from Wales who wanted to tell me how they remembered me as a baby, how they couldn't believe how old I was now. The more people I spoke to, the more I hated everyone there. I decided to lay down on a sofa in the hotel the wake was held in, covering myself in other people's coats while strangers ate sandwiches around me. I pretended to sleep so I didn't have to talk to anyone. Under the coats, I silently raged at the strangers talking about a member of my family.

Bronze medal

When I was nine, my best friend who lived opposite me died of leukaemia. I didn't understand what cancer was; all I knew was Kelly had to stay indoors in the summer while all the kids in the road had water fights. All her platinum blonde hair fell out, and on the days she did go to school, Kelly wore a baseball cap that stated: 'bald is beautiful'. When we did play together, we loved to collect Garbage Pail Kids stickers, which were the envy of all the other kids. We each had an impressive amount but realised if we pooled our efforts and co-owned them, we would have the best collection in the whole school. We took turns to look after them; every other day, the big box would swap houses across the street. We spent hours talking about which ones were left to collect and which ones we could swap.

After spending so much time in hospital as a kid too, I wasn't worried about Kelly's constant disappearances until, one day, she disappeared forever and died. During her illness, I don't remember anyone ever telling me she was going to die; either they were hopeful she could recover or the parents of all the children decided not to tell us. When my mum sat me down to explain Kelly was dead, I was confused. How could she be dead but, more importantly in the mind of a child, what does this mean for our joint card collection?

This question silently burned in my brain as her funeral was organised and it was decided by all of our parents that no children would attend. I watched through the net curtains of my parents' bedroom as a hearse pulled up to the house with Kelly's small coffin in the back. It was fascinating; was she *actually* inside? I imagined her pushing the lid up, waving to us through the windows. I watched the adult neighbours file out of their houses and into cars to follow the death procession, wondering if they knew Kelly's favourite ice cream flavour because I did, yet somehow, I'm not allowed to join in. When the funeral party returned, I resumed my place hidden at the window and watched as Kelly's sister had to be carried by their dad out of the car and into the house, too broken to walk.

The next day, I brought up the issue of the cards to my mum. A tricky proposition – even though I didn't want to lose our collection, I knew how inappropriate it would be to ask Kelly's family for them. I had to let them go and cross my fingers I would see them again.

Silver medal

A week before Christmas, I received an early evening phone call from a number I didn't recognise. 'Hi, it's Chris Gooding,' said the unfamiliar voice of someone I went to school with many years ago. At thirty-two, I was still naïve to the nature of out-of-the-blue phone calls and what they inevitably mean.

'I have some bad news.'

A pause.

'Neil's dead,' said Chris tentatively, already knowing this was sledgehammer news.

Neil was my oldest friend. We were born a month apart, grew up on the same street where our families still lived, went to all the same schools and stayed very close as adults. Neil was my blueprint of platonic friendships; he was my evidence of how important it is for girls to have boys as friends. We always rowed like siblings; as kids we would physically scrap with each other but, as we became teenagers, he took on a big brother role. I would phone Neil at 2 a.m. when I'd had too much to drink and needed a lift home. He would diligently arrive with Kenny G blaring to try to embarrass me outside the indie clubs.

'But I spoke to him a few days ago,' I said. There was no way Neil could be dead. We had just messaged each other; he had been writing his wedding invitations while watching *The Muppet Christmas Carol*. He was thirty-two and wasn't ill. While I didn't believe it, I sobbed on my bedroom floor, thinking the world had gone mad. I had a desperate need to be back in my childhood home, back where we had grown up together. I drove in a daze past Neil's house and fell through the front door in front of my parents, feeling like a child again.

As the news of Neil's death spread and gushing tributes appeared on Facebook, there was one strong emotion I felt over all others – rage. The outpouring of grief from people we had been to school with, those who barely knew Neil then, let alone now, made me furious. I felt possessive of him and hated everyone who said they had any kind of attachment with him. I had a clear idea of whose words were appropriate and, in private messages with Beth and Anna, I acted as judge and jury for those whose tributes rang hollow. 'BUT THEY DIDN'T EVEN KNOW HIM AT SCHOOL! AND THAT WAS SIXTEEN YEARS AGO!' Grief tourism is big business and pulls a crowd.

Walking towards the church for Neil's funeral with my parents either side of me, I stumbled around as though I was drunk through crying so hard, my dad needing to steady me. I could see Neil's parents and siblings stood outside, greeting

264

everyone and shaking hands. Their smiles were gentle and solemn. I realised I couldn't arrive as a carnival of chaos, wailing and hyperventilating while they held themselves with such grace in the face of their pain. The only place to hide was the bushes surrounding the church. I threw myself in between the branches to hide, my dad having to pull me out when I'd calmed down. Eventually, I took a seat on the back row and silently shook with non-stop sobs throughout the entire service. The only time I stopped was when 'Return of the Mack' by Mark Morrison was played as we slowly trawled out of the service, offering a moment to laugh and remember how ridiculous Neil's taste in music was.

At the wake, a memory book was passed around. I held it and stared at the blank page, willing the words to come that could fully express the nature of our relationship. I needed my words to be incredible and poignant, for any future readers to think, Wow, they were so close. I wrote about the day when Neil got the first pairs of Nike Air Jordans ever released from America. It was a Saturday morning in the late eighties and he immediately came to my house to gloat. 'These new trainers can make me jump just like Michael Jordan,' Neil boasted as he took a run up into the road to jump over our front garden wall. On the way over, one trainer flipped off his foot when it made contact with the bricks and he fell face first onto the concrete. I laughed uncontrollably while Neil picked himself up off the ground, grabbing the lost shoe and ran home crying. It was the first and last time I ever saw him cry.

To me, this story encapsulated everything I needed it to: the dynamic of siblings that grew between us over the years; the delight in each other's fails; the jokes at each other's expense while, underneath, our loyalty and love for each other was as strong as the wall that took Michael Jordan down. To anyone else, it would read like a silly kid's story. I had the visceral need to prove how much he meant to me that others could see but, ultimately, after thirty-two years of being next to each other in life, there was nothing that described us better.

I thought about what Neil would have written in my book of condolences had our roles been reversed. He would have revelled at the time he told the boy who fancied me that, in the evening, I would sometimes stand on my bathroom window ledge naked with the light on. For weeks, James Forrester would ride round to my road on his BMX with his shirt unbuttoned to the waist to show off his dad's borrowed gold medallion for extra panache. Instead of flaunting any nubile body, I was usually sat outside with all the kids from the street, kicking a football around and eating crisps. Neil would be a wheezing mess collapsed on the very wall he tripped over, laughing at his best plan yet to embarrass me in front of as many people as possible, like any older brother.

Gold medal

Greg and I sat in silence in the hospice room. The French windows were opened as wide as their hinges would allow, letting in an August breeze while also offering an escape route to the suffocating truth in the room – that he was going to die very soon and there was no way to ignore it anymore. The centrepiece of the bright room was a vase of huge sunflowers, acting like the real sun for us to orbit around. They were a gift from an acquaintance fifty times removed who heard Greg was in the hospice. They had arrived as if they would be welcomed in and offered a front-row seat. Instead, they received confused looks and an invitation to leave by nurses with no review to write for the Grief Tourism Board. We kept the flowers though.

The flower heads made a mockery of death in their explosive scream of joy and delight in the bleak atmosphere. I silently thanked a god I didn't believe in that Greg was going to die in the summer. The thought of being here, doing *this* during the desolate grey of a quintessential English February filled me with horror. Although it didn't seem to matter, as apparently Death wears yellow, not black. Everything in the room was sunflowers and daffodils: the paint on the walls, the sunlight landing on the table full of uneaten food, the jaundiced colour of Greg's skin and discoloured whites of his eyes.

Time moved like honey as I rummaged through my head to find something to say. Something poignant felt too heavy, a nail in the actual coffin to cement my acceptance of our fate. All I could think of were all the inappropriate jokes I could make: 'At least you won't have to clear up your Dad's shit when he's old and infirm!'

I didn't need to fill the void with any stupid commentary because Greg whispered something very clearly while staring straight ahead at the sunflowers. Four names, as clearly as if in the witness box being asked to identify the defendant.

'What about them?' I tentatively asked. I hoped this was another hallucination. Please don't say you want to see them or ask me to contact them. They had never visited Greg or made any real contact during the five years of his illness, despite living nearby and spending every childhood holiday and weekend together. Greg had brushed this off with anger, but I had seen something rise within him during quieter moments – the young boy who was so sad and hurt those he had loved couldn't be there for him when he needed them the most. I'd read about this at the end of life – grudges are buried, forgiveness is offered willingly, all past misdemeanours seen through the lens of grace and understanding.

Greg turned to look me squarely in the eye. 'I don't want them at my funeral. Make sure they are nowhere near it.'

This was the first time in the five years of having a terminal illness he had ever admitted he was going to die.

I nodded solemnly. 'They will have to walk over my dead body first,' I confirmed.

I danced down the aisle to Prince because I didn't know what else to do. It felt impossible to walk so slowly in a solemn bow, so I just danced. 'Raspberry Beret' had been Delays' walk-on song when playing live and, after hundreds of gigs on the sidelines, my muscle memory flushed me with anticipation. I remember Madge telling me she had walked down the aisle of her wedding laughing and swinging her bouquet as if it was a bat because she was just so happy and excited. When we were much younger, I had said to Greg if we ever got married, I would like to dance down the aisle to Deee-Lite's 'Groove Is in the Heart', anticipating the same rush as my mum. I never did get to dance at my own wedding.

I danced now because I didn't know what else to do walking behind my husband's coffin, holding the hands of our small children. I thought of all those who couldn't make it and were watching the live stream at home – how confusing it must have been to see the coffin's soft arrival from the bottom of the screen followed by a go-go dancer draped in black lace, swaying like a gothic Victorian ghost.

I was very aware I could do whatever I wanted; literally nothing was off limits because I was The Widow. While my grief or connection to Greg was no bigger or stronger than that of our children, his parents or his brother, it is me who receives a new title, a new outfit, the best seat in the house. I realised today will be the only time this label will be revered; in all the days after, the term 'widow' will be met with pity.

Sitting in the front row at a funeral is a Big Deal; it holds enormous weight. When organising the day, we had no idea of how many people would come but, estimating a lot, we asked the funeral directors if we could reserve the first three rows for closest friends and family. We all scrawled out who would be in our own Fantasy Football team of mourners, only to compare them and realise there was little crossover. It all became irrelevant when our wedding-style seating plan was dismissed by the crematorium, stating they had never been asked to do such a thing and reassured us there is a strict etiquette that people understand at funerals.

Thank fuck I had chosen to give the first eulogy because I couldn't physically house any more adrenaline. I could see my hands shaking as I held the order of service between black lace fingertips, looking between the photo of Greg's handsome and healthy face staring back at me and his coffin covered in sunflowers. In the photograph, Greg had straightened blond highlights – a stark difference to the dark-brown locks cut from his head by palliative nurses for us to keep in tiny taffeta bags, tied with yellow ribbon. The bright sparkling eyes that danced when talking about books and politics looked back at me. They were nothing like those who had last looked at me, the sallow yellow globes fused with dried-out contact lenses because they had stopped blinking. I tried to bore this healthy version of Greg into my brain to override the image of his dead face. I would have used my fingers to pull my eyelids back to drink in his face but my widow's fancy dress costume of enormous sunglasses indoors and lace gloves made it impossible.

As I tell my children so often, fear can also feel like excitement. I had butterflies to be able to stand in front of our family and friends with Greg next to me, to publicly declare how I loved him in a way I never got to at our wedding. My vows were handwritten, my last love letter.

I stood to say my final words and anchored myself to the altar, taking a second to peruse the congregation of familiar faces for encouragement. I could see none of my best friends' faces. Infact, none of my friends were in the packed crematorium. Instead, I saw rows of people I didn't recognise. I saw old fans of Greg's band. Sat in the second row, I saw two of the people who Greg asked not to be there. This wasn't so much of a surprise – it had eventually been agreed by everyone, including Greg, that telling them not to come would be one too many problems to deal with, but the audacity of choosing second-row seats felt outrageous.

Everything was too quick to process this or to even care in the moment but, as I gave my entire heart into the microphone, the dizzy adrenaline was replaced with white fury. I spoke my last words to Greg imagining a ghostly version of him, swimming around our heads, furiously screaming at me, 'You promised me you wouldn't let them come.' I read the eulogy while planning the enormous argument I was going to have outside because I had nothing left to lose except the guilt and sadness of letting Greg down. The rest of the service was a blur of heartache and beauty.

Suddenly, it was time for the corpse bride and groom to kiss. I was escorted up to the coffin, with unknown hands on my waist and arms as if waiting for me to collapse. I didn't want to faint or break down. I wanted to climb on top of the coffin and wrap the sunflower stems around my legs. I wanted everyone there to disappear so I could talk to Greg one last time, as if we were reading in bed or leaning against the kitchen counter. I could feel the hundreds of eyes on my back, the hands being squeezed of loved ones, silently comforting each other that it's not them stood up there, as I had done at funerals in the past.

I pressed the wood of the coffin to my lips and squeezed my eyes tightly in an attempt to dilute the intensity of the moment. I bowed my head to the holiness of death, to admit a final defeat and humbly accept the fragility of life.

I love you so fucking much.

There is no hierarchy of grief and yet, there absolutely is. It is subtly ingrained in us; sometimes understood and sometimes wilfully ignored. People so often caveat any problem they tell me about with, 'Oh, but it's nothing compared to what you've gone through', as if I have won the grand prize of the Worst Hand Dealt on Earth. I don't like that narrative; partly because it feels very different to everyone else but mostly, I just don't agree with the sentiment. I can't deny that your spouse dying is exceptionally terrible and affects every single element of your life, but as I listen to others tell their own stories that I haven't lived – of infertility, child loss, coercive relationships, estrangement, racism, domestic abuse, bankruptcy – I find myself with the same phrase I hate on the tip of my tongue: 'I just can't imagine'.

There are no medals at the Shit Olympics and, even if there were, with all the deep pain and senseless tragedy in the world, my own experiences wouldn't get a place on the podium or even be on the sidelines clapping the gold, silver and bronze medallists. I wouldn't make the team or even get through to the try-outs. My place in the hierarchy would be sat at home, watching on TV with tea and biscuits.

How do you marry a ghost?

You can heavily rely on the appearance of certain things when someone dies – flowers, homemade lasagnes on your doorstep and psychics.

A few months after Greg died, a friend I hadn't seen for twenty years messaged me out of the blue to say she had bought me a session with Simon, a local spiritual healer. I knew what this meant – a psychic who would try to connect me to Greg. I had been to see psychics when I was much younger, almost as a teenage girl rite of passage. When you have seen a few, you become familiar with the patois and realise there are lots of the same stock phrases thrown around at people who are often in the depths of grief and desperate to believe there is a chance to talk to their dead loved ones. I understand why those left behind would seek out and believe these people; the comfort gained from their words supposedly from the afterlife can't be understated but those wanting to hear them are vulnerable and often willing to part with money to have that chance.

Greg and I had been obsessed with those who claimed to be clairvoyant and the analysis of how cold reading works. We spent hundreds of hours watching programmes and reading about popular psychics who had been debunked. I may not have believed that Simon was going to be able to talk to Greg, himself the ultimate sceptic, but decided to go along out of curiosity.

Simon lived in a row of semi-detached nondescript houses. When he opened the front door, he was wearing a crisp white T-shirt and jeans, very 1980s 'Born in the USA' Bruce Springsteen and, most shockingly, looked a lot like Greg's dad. He was jovial and chipper, not 'spiritual' or wearing the robes or long beads I'd imagined. As he led me up the stairs, I caught a glimpse into other rooms in the house: a small dark toilet; a kitchen upstairs where a bedroom would be, with piles of mismatched and stained mugs similar to the shelves of a charity shop. Simon explained his work room in the house was just a space he rented but had been allowed to decorate to his own taste. His area was painted a pastel lilac and filled with framed images of Jesus and the Buddha. Huge crystals sat on the floor, and behind where Simon sat cross-legged on an old sofa was a cork board with dozens of photographs of babies pinned to it.

'I chose this colour on purpose, to calm people,' Simon reassured me as I perched on the edge of a tatty armchair. Nothing about the room was calm. Simon couldn't make eye contact with me at all; in fact, his eyes darted around wildly. When he talked, he clicked his fingers, tapped his legs and waved his hands in the air. There was an alarm clock on the table next to him but facing me, as if this was a timed therapy session. Simon explained the format of the session – his spirit guide Liam would move through the afterlife to beckon forward anyone who wanted to speak to me, while Simon would act as an interpreter.

'I feel like you've been feeling low recently, you've had some hardship.' His first line from the afterlife was textbook. I immediately regretted coming. The classic cold reading continued with tried-and-tested phrases.

'You're a sensitive soul, you put on a brave face but, underneath, you're very fragile,' Simon continued. 'You're a very private person, you don't like people to know your business.' This was promising as he obviously hadn't Googled my name and discovered my writing career had been based on telling everyone everything. My willingness to have a more open mind was abruptly closed when Simon continued with a list of direct questions.

'Does the name Christopher mean anything to you?'

'No.'

'Crystal?'

'No.'

'Terrence?'

'No.'

'Jeremy?'

'No.'

'Michael?'

'Umm . . . yes.'

Simon's eyes widen. 'Who is he?' he asked. (*Um, shouldn't you tell me this, Simon?*)

'He's my father-in-law,' I replied, feeling like I had already given too much away in only a few minutes.

His wild eyes widen even further. 'Someone here wants to talk to him.' (*Um, what about me, Simon?*)

'Who is it that wants to talk to Michael?' Simon asked outright. I thought he was asking Liam in another realm but realised he was speaking to me. If talking Simon and Liam's language of the afterlife, the actual answer could be one of many people in Mike's life who have died but the most obvious was Greg.

I gave him the golden ticket.

'His son.'

The cogs whirring in Simon's brain were audible, trying to work out what this meant.

'So . . . it's your husband's brother then?' he guessed.

'No.' The questioning felt like a ghost edition of *Guess Who*. The cogs had stopped.

'So, who is it then?' Simon asked, him and Liam both giving up. I couldn't answer with anything other than the truth at that point.

'It's my husband.' A flashing lightbulb should have appeared above Simon's head in this moment.

'AH, NOW IT ALL MAKES SENSE!' he shouted. (*Does it, Simon? Now I've told you who the dead person is and that my card is Greg, the man with the brown hair, beanie hat, blue eyes and striped T-shirt?*) We left *Guess Who* to move on to spiritual *Twenty Questions*.

'Is there a birthday in April?'

'No.'

'Is someone an Aries?'

'No.'

'There's a birthday in October?'

'No.'

'Is there a birthday in either August, September or October?'

'No.'

'Is there an anniversary in one of these months?'

Greg died in September but that was only four months earlier so there hadn't been an anniversary yet.

'Someone died in one of those months,' I offered up.

Simon finally just asked outright, 'What month was it?'

'September.'

'Is it recent or a while ago?'

'Fairly recently.'

As Simon had struck gold with Greg, we moved on to how he died, which felt quite unnecessary as information I was very confident about and offered freely on a death certificate.

In the videos Greg and I had watched about cold reading, it was explained how this question is a home run as most people die in the same handful of ways.

'He's telling me something about the lower half of the body . . . prostate? It's his testicles? Testicular cancer?!' I caught Simon glance down at my hand to see if there was a wedding ring and the cogs started working out how old I am, how old Greg would have been. Testicular cancer is often a young man's disease so it was a good punt.

Simon gave up. 'What did he die of?'

When I said bowel cancer, he's alive again, jumping up to distract from losing that hand of 'Guess How the Dead Person Died'. 'AH, THAT MAKES SENSE, THAT MAKES SENSE NOW.' (*Does it, Simon, does it?*)

'Did you ever talk about children?'

I absolutely would not give him this.

'Yes,' I confirmed. This wasn't a lie, it was technically true, we *did* talk about having children. I just missed out the few steps afterwards of having them.

'Was there a discussion about sperm?'

'No.'

'Did you talk about keeping sperm for you to use in the future?'

'No.' This was going nowhere fast, so Simon moved on.

'He was in a lot of pain, wasn't he?'

'Yes.' (*He died of cancer, Simon, of course he was.*)

'Liam is showing me morphine, did he have morphine?'

'Yes.' (*Alongside everyone else in end-of-life care, Simon.*)

'He's telling me he looks fine now. He's got all his hair back and he's saying, "Didn't I look bad at the end?"'

This comment got under my skin. There is so much trauma

deep within me from witnessing Greg's physical demise – how cancer and chemo but ultimately death gnawed at his body and made him look like a macabre waxwork of himself. Greg as a healthy man was a beautiful vision; he had always looked young for his age and the thought of his vibrant, not-ill, not-dead self made me choke up. Simon's next vision brought me round quickly, though.

'He's speaking about the film *Ghost*, with Patrick Swayze always hanging around Demi Moore. He said he's like that with you. He mentions the word "ditto". Have you seen the film?'

In the few months since he died, I had never wanted Greg to not be dead more than this moment. I wanted him there next to me so we could have laughed together at such an outrageous and cheesy line, obviously said to many others who had sat in the same chair. I suppose Simon used it to comfort people, to offer a popular reference that would resonate with the bereaved. That he would reference a rom-com was hilarious; he didn't realise Greg's taste was obscure to say the least, his favourite being a nine-hour silent film about the slow, meditative daily lives of monks where literally nothing happens. I thought the film was torture, Greg thought it was a masterpiece.

'Any reference to the number eight? Or eight, nine or ten? On a door? Or any combination of those numbers – eighty-nine, ninety-eight, nine hundred and ten, nine hundred and one?'

'No.'

'Have you got a pet?'

'Yes.'

'Is it a cat or dog?'

'Dog.'

'The dog senses him.' This was stated as fact.

'Um . . . OK.'

'Have you got a new car?'

'No.'

'Are you getting one?'

'No.'

'Has anyone you know got a new car?'

'No.'

'He's mentioning a Mazda.'

'I don't know anyone with a Mazda.'

'What about a Citroën?'

'No.'

A swift detour. 'Are you training for something?' Simon asks.

'No.'

'He's telling me whatever it is that you start, you just have to go for it. He's showing me a bell, he's ringing that bell and shouting, "You ring that bell, girl."'

I wondered if people change entirely when they died as this was not language or imagery Greg would ever have used.

'You're not well emotionally, are you?'

I lost the will to answer because it's such a stupid question.

'He's saying that he doesn't want to see you sad, that he wants to see you happy. It makes him sad when you're sad.'

Brilliant, I'm shamed from the afterlife. There's no break in conversation, straight into the next unexpected question.

'What's your connection to the Canary Islands?'

'None.'

'Greece?'

'None.'

'Italy?'

'I worked in Venice for a while.'

'AH, THERE IS THE EVIDENCE!' (*Of what, Simon?*) Any-thing I agreed with, Simon jumped up, shouting, 'SEE! THERE'S THE EVIDENCE!' as if we were part of a science project or a lawsuit.

'Do you have a connection with London?'

'Yes, I used to live there.'

'AH, he's telling me about the connection with London. HE KNOWS!' (*Of course he knew I had lived in London, Simon.*)

'Do you have any connection to the Celts?'

'No.'

'He's telling me about railways, do you have any connections to railways?'

'No.'

'Do you live near a railway?'

'No.'

'Do you know a pub called The Railway?'

'Yes.'

'Do you know anyone who works there?'

'Yes.'

'Did he know them?'

'Yes.'

'THAT'S IT!' Simon exclaimed, without telling me what *it* is and moves on quickly.

'I'm seeing a house. Or a flat. Have you moved house recently?'

'No.'

'Are you thinking of moving house?'

'Not at the moment.'

'Have you ever lived in a flat?'

'Yes.' (*Is the next question 'HAVE YOU EVER EATEN FOOD?'?*)

We then entered my favourite set of questions from the session.

'Do you have any connections with a department store?'

'No.'

'What about Jasper Conran?'

'No.'

'Upholstery?'

'No.'

'Have you bought any designer clothes recently?'

'No.'

'Has anyone you know bought any designer clothes before?'

'Yes.'

This sparked an interest. 'Who?' Simon asked. Many, many people, including myself, but I said the first person who sprang to mind.

'Greg's brother.'

'SEE! He wants his brother to know he's with him.'

Simon was sweating and became quite manic. 'He's doing well, it's his first time communicating with the living.' Greg would have been happy to know he would become such an effective ghost.

'He was very into walnuts, wasn't he?' I had never seen Greg eat a walnut in the fifteen years we were together except the Walnut Whips his mum sometimes bought him for Christmas. This was a stretch.

'Were you married?'

'Yes.'

Simon looked down at my left hand again. 'But where's your ring?' he asked. He didn't need to know that other than on my wedding day, I had never worn my ring. That I couldn't bear the feeling of being the doomed bride. That it felt so claustrophobic and I couldn't breathe with it on.

I lie.

'I don't have one.' I thought I saw a hint of pity in Simon's eyes.

'Well, he's down on one knee right in front of you, he's kissing your ring finger and asking you to marry him.'

Simon must have thought this was a huge romantic gesture but the idea of a marriage proposal from beyond the grave felt more of a bizarre horror film. (*How do you marry a ghost, Simon? Will I need to inform teachers at parents' evening to address both me and my dead husband who is hovering above the pencil pots?*) Greg's initial late-night proposal had been lacklustre; his second – dead, speaking through a charlatan in a room full of baby portraits – wasn't much better.

The thought of Greg shuffling around in the afterlife next to self-acclaimed psychics to pass on obscure messages offers me no comfort whatsoever. Ultimately, I have no fixed idea on what happens after we die. I'm very happy to assume we will find out when we get there. I don't need or want Greg's ghost to be keeping me company or waiting around corners to drop white feathers at my feet. I absorbed him while he was here just by living life next to him; by chatting in the kitchen, driving to do the food shopping and playing with our children. I take this ecstatic loss with me because it all exists in the same space. It is the seesaw equivalent of falling in love; they are equally weighted. He is woven into my life forever – I don't need to see a robin to remind me. In fact, the thought of Greg being reincarnated as a robin is terrifying. What a total comedown after being a human. My bubble of reverie was abruptly burst by another question from beyond the grave.

'Does someone you know have a sweet tooth?' Simon asks.

Identity

What's in a name?

One of my favourite places to visit as a child was a gift shop, the type at zoos and theme parks that sold giant pencils and glitter rubbers that erased nothing. My most beloved items were the keyrings with names emblazoned in holographic text – it was the 1980s, and, back then, you could still find ones with STACEY. (In choosing the names for our girls, I voiced my very real concern to Greg that by picking Dalí and Bay, they would never be able to find a personalised keyring or mug with their names on and what psychological damage that might have.)

In every gift shop of my childhood, on the keyrings for STACEY would always be the clarification 'short for Anastasia' and the meaning – 'of the resurrection' or 'she who will rise again'. I loved this. It made me sound like a mystical wizard who slayed dragons or an elusive Russian princess. I tried to make my parents refer to me as Anastasia, even asking my mum to shoehorn the nine letters onto my sixteenth birthday cake. It never caught on, at least not until I switched the keyrings for a legal document and changed my name by deed poll when I was twenty-two. In the flat I shared at the time with my boyfriend and best friend, I wore a paper crown and signed the documents in bed, legally changing my name from Stacey to Anastasia.

This was not a time of mystical princesses or foreign adventures. At twenty-two, I was very mentally unwell with chronic depression and anxiety, stuck in a world of psychiatrists, medications and the feeling this would be my life forever. My self-hatred knew no boundaries. I had ricocheted between different universities, cities, homes and breakdowns for years, always landing back in my childhood bedroom and unable to look after myself. Nothing ever seemed to help me. I became more unhinged as different therapies were added and dosages increased. In a desperate attempt to save myself, I decided to apply for my fourth degree course in a city I had never been to and change my name. I believed I needed to escape myself and my shitty circumstances so transformed from the weak and helpless Stacey into the new and improved Anastasia, a manifestation of the person I always thought I would be but who had become indefinitely lost in depression.

I can highly recommend creating an alter ego as the ultimate 'fake it till you make it' solution. Becoming a caricature of yourself in a new city with a new name felt enlivening and offered the fresh start I needed. Unfortunately, my master plan was foiled very early on when I realised Anastasia isn't a zippy name that easily trips off the tongue. 'What can we call you for short?' asked my new student pals. My new name was much nicer written in calligraphy than it was to keep repeating in a conversation. 'Umm . . . Stacey is short for Anastasia,' I offered up, wasting my opportunity and a few hundred pounds.

No one calls me Anastasia now, but it still reminds me of how important a name is. Whenever I introduce myself with my Russian princess name, I am treated differently. There are associations everyone brings to the table that have nothing to do with me – the name Anastasia is seen as exotic, romantic, artistic, rich, royal, poetic, impressive, noble. Stacey is associated with American teenagers, preppy mean girls in the 1980s and the TV programme *Gavin & Stacey*.

I love the name Anastasia but don't use it anymore because, even though it was entirely my choice to change my name, it doesn't sit comfortably with who I am. The decision was made in a hurricane and used like a shield to protect myself from the winds of life. Ultimately, the problem is – wherever you go, there you are. I was still the same person underneath.

Like my own pick 'n' mix bag of titles, there are names we choose and some that feel thrust upon us. In the many transitions during a woman's life, our titles are based on our relationship to others. Some can make us feel powerful and others weak. When Greg and I got married, I chose not to change my surname. The tradition of taking a man's name felt outdated and I hated the idea of having neither name I was born with. And what would happen when Greg died? It felt so much safer to have my own family's surname, anything other would feel like floating adrift in the aftermath.

Even if we keep our surname when married, it is assumed we will move from Miss to Mrs. A marriage transforms us from 'single' to 'married', but to take the spouse away through divorce or death gives us the consolation prize of 'widow' or 'divorcee'. Even if we become a mother, the parental relationship devoid of the father becomes 'single mother', a term laden with negative tropes. I'm unsure I've ever heard the term 'single father' used in any substantial way.

These terms might seem just part of day-to-day lives but they hold enormous weight in how we feel about ourselves and how others treat us. When we tick 'single' on a form, it doesn't necessarily mean we don't have a partner, only that we aren't legally married. The term 'single' has connotations of loneliness, of the perennial singleton Bridget Jones and, as a woman grows older, 'left on the shelf' – a term I would bet my life savings on you never having heard said about any man.

I went from 'wife' – a revered term by society, even compensated financially by the government – to 'widow' overnight. 'Widow' is a confusing word for me. It has terrible undertones but I'm also aware that in the aftermath of death and all the people it affects, I'm the only person crowned with a title, and for this reason, my grief is allowed to be visible. This might offer some allowances but the status holds conditions; there is a need to be a 'good' widow. Through the eyes of many, this can translate to abandoning yourself, idolising your past life and keeping yourself small with quiet reverence for your dead husband. It can also mean giving up the need to want, whether that be fun, sex, love, money or a better life.

The title of 'mother' is made from gilt gold. It is seen as a woman's ultimate accolade but, again, it comes with conditions. A 'good' mother is seen as self-sacrificing, endlessly accommodating and selfless – note these are not adjectives appropriate for the role of 'parent', only for the woman. It is the cultural expectation for women to construct the majority of their identity from their role as mothers.

Maybe it's just me who finds all the different names and titles so jarring, after experiencing so many changes to my own. I know how important a name can be while also being totally insignificant.

For today, I am Miss Stacey Heale, just as I started out forty-three years ago. Wherever I go, there I am.

The drowning

I was so scared I could have vomited all over the borrowed top I was wearing and the bubblegum-scented Vivienne Westwood shoes I'd bought especially for the occasion. In fact, the terror was so intense, I couldn't speak a word backstage. This is a pretty big issue if you're about to walk onstage to deliver a TED Talk.

In preparation for the day, my bedroom walls were covered in Post-it notes, diagrams and rudimental sketches, all trying to shoehorn the order of words into my head. I practised like a wind-up toy, in between looking after the girls and taking Greg to the hospital. My TED Talk was a vulnerable moment for me; its focus was the power of social media in a crisis and its ability to create real connections and community with those in hard times. Speaking about the details of mine and Greg's lives to an entire theatre instead of from behind a screen suddenly felt very exposing.

I have no memory of the talk itself. My mind blurred into static white noise the moment I walked onto the stage but there is video footage to prove I *did* manage to speak and mostly in the order I'd practised. What I *do* vividly remember is coming off stage to find a group of women crying in the green room. They had been listening to me speak and I assumed were upset because of the ultimate end my story would have.

'Please don't cry!' I begged, knowing these speakers were about to go on stage themselves soon and needed to be composed. 'Greg is currently really well.'

The women wiped their eyes and looked awkwardly at each other. 'Um, we weren't crying about that,' one of the speakers said. 'We just really resonated with what you said about not being able to do it all as women. It just described all of our lives.'

What I said was this:

'I was a full-time working mum, I was a fashion academic, and I suffered from harrowing morning sickness with my second pregnancy. I was also trying to run a degree course. I was a mother to a toddler and I was also trying to care for my partner, who was becoming mysteriously more and more ill. I struggled on with all of these things because I was a fully paid-up member of the strong, independent women club, doing it all, got it all going on – which was rubbish. Instead of talking to people about it, I would cry myself to sleep every night because I had no idea how I could spread myself any thinner. The post-natal depression I suffered from for five months, I did so in silence because I was so scared to be vulnerable and to say to people, "I'm not coping with this very well." It was a revelation to me, that you could just say, "This is a bit hard" or "I'm not doing so well today, I could do with some help with this." I realised I didn't want to be signed up to this gang, thinking, I can have it all, because I wanted to say, "I can't do it all." This was the most empowering thing I had ever said as a woman.'

We are a drowning generation of women; brought up in families where our mothers unquestioningly gave up work entirely when having a baby and landed in a domestic life. Maternity leave didn't exist and, despite growing up in the liberating sixties, it was still presumed you worked until you found someone to marry and have children with. When your children were old enough to look after themselves, you could re-enter the job market after a decade out of it. These women had issues of their own, returning to a new world where technology had grown and blocked opportunities for those who didn't engage.

Our generation were taught from a young age that as girls, we could be anything and everything we wanted – we outperformed our male friends in exams and more female CEOs were needed at the board tables. We were taught to aim high, to think and act like a Girl Boss in our Hustle Lives. We are encouraged to break the glass ceilings, just as long as we ask ahead of time if it's OK with everyone and immediately sweep up the broken shards on the floor, to make sure no one else gets hurt by our actions.

Something strange happens at a certain age – the messaging we've received doubles back on itself. From being an independent boss babe, breaking glass ceilings and leaning in, the narrative subtly changes to 'you can't pour from an empty cup' – a gear change from focusing on yourself to being all about serving others.

Now we are encouraged to abandon ourselves at the first hurdle we face – motherhood, career, as a carer to our children, our partners, our parents – in the name of selflessness, our new goddess to bow down to. These two polar opposite ideologies sit uncomfortably next to each other, yet we plough on, believing we can live both lives – the independent woman and the selfless carer of others – simultaneously.

There's another problem on the horizon. We hit the ages of long-term relationships and motherhood to find the boys we grew up with didn't get the same memos as us. We are met with male peers who haven't factored in the support they will need to provide while we are 'doing it all'. This gap in understanding means we are now destined to live our mothers' lives by still carrying the majority of physical and emotional domestic burdens but with the added bonus of living the feminist dream of being anything we want.

There is no doubt women *can* do and have it all; the question is at what cost? Basic maths can unravel this modern narrative in a heartbeat – there are just not enough hours in the day, energy in the tank or fucks left to give to fulfil all the roles in women's lives. In the continuous ticker tape flashing before our eyes from morning to night, we mentally prioritise a never-ending to-do list and find the cost is *us* – our health, our sleep, our sex drive, the quality of our relationships, the connection with our children and our effort at work.

We live within the cultural celebration of female burnout. The heaviest of weights on our shoulders becomes the medals we are told are the most coveted and desired. This is the patriarchy's most clever and insidious disguise – as modern feminism. It will whisper in the ear of the smart teenage girl who outranks the boys in her exam results, that she can be whatever she wants. She just needs to work harder to fulfil her potential through the years, through the exams, through the pay grades. The patriarchy fails to mention the exhaustion, the imposter syndrome, the internal pull of different voices and the self-flagellation when feeling like you are always ten steps behind.

We have been told we need to 'lean in' when in fact, we all just want to lean *on* something because we are exhausted. We are drowning in the middle. It's while we are busy drowning that we have taken our eyes off the ball. You can't focus on anything when you can't breathe, and are only trying to survive.

We just need to remember while you can do anything, you can't do everything.

Calling Dr Stacey

I applied for a PhD for the following reasons:

1. Because I thought I should.
2. Because I wanted to tick 'Dr' on forms.
3. Because I wanted to be referred to as 'the Doctor'.

While points two and three were truly motivating, it was the belief that as a senior academic I should study for a doctorate. It's important to note that no one pushed me to apply – this instinct full of ego and duty was fuelled purely by me and a lifetime of signals from the world telling me to move up the ladder and achieve more at every moment of the day.

I sat in the interview and watched as the professor looked over my credentials and artwork from the previous few years. I desperately wanted a place in the PhD school so badly; I was like an Olympic athlete, laser-focused on Getting In. I was disgruntled with the loud tick-tock of my burgeoning body clock, barely letting me formulate an application for the seven-year course, but I pushed these feelings aside to focus on the external validation I'd receive when phoning my parents with the great news – your daughter is going to be a doctor (of sorts)!

I wanted to call Greg and hear him scream down the phone. I couldn't wait to drop this delicious nugget of information into conversation and see how interested people would be. *Wow, a Doctor of Fashion, you say? How exciting!*

I sat watching as the team read my application, combed through my portfolio, and I thought about the first day of my new life. I thought about sitting alone in a library, formulating a research question to fill nearly a decade of study. The thought of actually *doing* a PhD left me cold. I didn't want to be a student again. If I sat quietly to ask myself what I wanted and really listened, I would have heard that I wanted a baby, a dog and *less* responsibility at work but I was addicted to a story of success. When did we forget what we wanted and why we wanted them in the first place?

Chapter Two

After Greg died, my life with the new title of 'widow' was often referred to in books, conversations and articles as now moving into 'Chapter Two'.

I was initially baffled by the mathematical errors of this phrase. I met Greg when I was twenty-six and he died when I was forty-one. While he had one steady girlfriend before we met, I'd had multiple boyfriends by this time and fallen in and out of love with abandon. In the book of my life, does that mean the twenty-six years before meeting him was just a very long prologue? If meeting Greg begins the first chapter, where is the fifteen-year-old girl who cried with laughter on the phone to her friends as she told them she'd just burnt off her hair by bleaching it on a whim? Where would I mention the boy, the one with feline blue eyes, mop of black curls and surly face, who I bumped into on a street corner as a ten-year-old, to move in with eleven years later? Where should I shoehorn in the twenty-two-year-old woman who reluctantly went to the local pool every day to teach herself how to swim when she suffered from crippling depression? I think the twenty-five-year-old woman who ate porridge for every meal in a bedroom of crumpled clothes and empty dishes to work on her final-year degree work probably deserves a mention too.

I'm left wondering if my new Chapter Two status will belong to me now, or if I am expected to wait for another man to arrive and claim the title. Why is the romantic relationship king in our story when we have been here all along playing all the other parts? I am the main character of my own book; I am who colours this story. I was here first and have put my flag in the sand too many times to let a new character arrive and be given their own volume.

I wonder if the Chapter Two narrative is ever levelled at divorced women and, if so, if it depends on who initiated the split. Is Chapter Two referring to the time after someone has left you single through either death or divorce or is it specifically directed at a significant person – your next relationship? If Chapter One is defined as your first significant relationship then Greg and I don't fit the criteria anyway. Greg and I met when worlds had already been created and exploded many times over before we'd even said hello. He'd had an eleven-year serious relationship and I had lived with my childhood sweetheart during my early twenties. Both relationships were critical for our development and understanding of what love is; they shaped who we are and, because neither ended in a spectacular blow-out, both Greg and I were still friends with our past significant people.

It also implies Greg's 'chapter' finished on the day he died. This is not the case; his pull, influence and love are still very present – in some ways even more so as his physical absence means I need to look harder for him in smaller spaces. To be together as a couple over multiple years means we leave traces of ourselves with each other: in the way we unconsciously pick up someone's language and idiosyncrasies; in how we view the world and what we introduce them to. Greg's chapter doesn't stop because he's not making tea in our kitchen; he is everywhere with me still. This idea doesn't apply only to those we have loved who have died; it's relevant to all those who have impacted us in both good and bad ways. For instance, I feel the influence of my favourite teachers as I give a lecture to my own students. The residue of past relationships still clings to me but this can seem inappropriate or degrading to 'the one', a title in itself given to indicate your life has now actually begun, or rather, your past life of just mucking around has no relevance anymore.

If we take other people out of the equation, it's impossible to ignore the encyclopaedias lining the walls of my life, filled with chapters where I'm front and centre with no supporting actors. There would be a chapter telling the bizarre story of my drama teacher's campaign to have me removed as Head Girl because I wore black nail varnish to school. A novella would be based on the mental breakdown of my late teens, probably in need of dramatisation for the screen to fully convey the bleak reality and the slow climb back to rejoin civilisation as a person who actually changed their underwear. Smaller vignettes would spin like a zoetrope of fleeting moments, conversations, songs, photographs, words which impacted my heart and mind, feather-light in touch. All the heavy tomes featuring the chapters up until a boy first entered the scene stage left would fill a library.

In Facebook's COO Cheryl Sandberg's second book, she refers to the life after her husband died of a heart attack as 'Option B'. As a fellow widow, I get it, I really do, but I have some problems with this phrase. Firstly, it infers your life situation is a choice – a fact I would contest alongside most of the world, as I'm sure Sandberg herself would agree. No one actively chooses disaster. Secondly, that anything afterwards is a consolation prize to be endured, as if the universe ran out of good things so you'll have to accept a substitution. To assume all future endeavours will be diluted feels dispiriting and just plain *bleak*. Thirdly, at what point do you begin counting what 'option' you're currently living in?

If this system is based on life not working out the way you wanted it to, I would have been on Option Z before I was ten years old. Our whole lives are built on hitting roadblocks and readjusting the compass; sometimes there is a newly built road to walk down, sometimes you will need to scramble in the dirt and pull nettles from the ground with your bare hands to forge a way through. Either may be of our own making or hit us like a surprise bus but each route is still a way forward.

Ultimately, Chapter Two and Option B are only phrases for those who love to categorise things, so who cares? They are just words, and they can't begin to define the complex twists in our tales. However, if we look around the library containing all the stories of our lives, it's easy to see how the words we choose have weight and can help define our realities in how we view ourselves.

Even as a lover of books, I would burn the library to the ground before I accept any consolation prize future for myself or my daughters.

The invisible maths of women

How many years will I be fertile?

How many years will we have together?

How long until I can start dating after my husband dies?

How many hours since I took my pill?

How long until I start needing to look after my parents?

How long until the school pick-up?

How long until bedtime?

How many months left of carrying this baby?

How many days until I'm ovulating?

How many years do I have left in a healthy body?

How many metres behind me is that man?

Love it, but are you having a midlife crisis?

'I love it, but are you having a midlife crisis???'

The message from an old friend after seeing a photograph of my new pink hair gave me a moment of pause. Fuck, *am I*? I could see why people might think I was having some kind of breakdown; I was forty-two and my husband was dead. Years earlier, my therapist had worried that when Greg eventually died, I would spectacularly lose the plot after keeping it together for so long. I was used to people eyeing me as a loaded gun, but this comment referred to age, not trauma.

'Am I having a midlife crisis?' I questioned myself while looking in the mirror at my pink bob. It was hard to think clearly about anything, but if I sat quietly to think about why I had changed my hair colour, a clear image appeared – my teenage self, sat on a stool in the kitchen of my parents' house, with music blaring and Madge and I chatting as she dyed my hair. I was twelve when I first dyed my hair a rich cherry red and, since then, there has never been a time I've had a full head of my natural colour. Thirty years of bright red, dark auburn, blue black, bleached blonde, bubblegum pink and lavender lilac. Changing the colour of my hair was nothing new; what had changed was my age.

When my best friend Clayton decided to learn to skateboard in his late thirties alongside his children, it was insinuated the slippery slope would lead to an inevitable sports car purchase, as if there is an invisible cut-off point in learning new skills. When my friend Emma left her marriage and successful career in music to move to London and become a full-time artist, some may have looked on with bated breath and waited for the crash because *surely* such brash decisions wouldn't work out?

Now I've reached the basecamp for Mount Midlife myself, I don't believe there is a crisis waiting at the summit; if anything, there is an awakening. In children, we know there are developmental milestones that don't end until well into adulthood, our brains not reaching maturity until twenty-five. Midlife is another milestone, an alarm clock of understanding that potentially half of your life is behind you and how time speeds up as we get older. There is a long, slow silence to losing yourself, no warning siren to alert you to the self you knew slipping away down the back of the sofa. How many years do we have left? How many of those will be healthy? That which is named a 'crisis' is something more nuanced; it can be a brutal, painful, messy yet beautiful and brilliant epiphany that must unravel before it can be woven back into something new.

There are lots of transitions to live through, with many gains to celebrate, but even when moving towards wanted, beautiful things, there is still loss. Every time you say yes to something, you must say no to something else. Each no carries a grief of its own and requires the mourning of a dead end or a change to navigate. It could be that the enormous loss of the self as a single entity when moving from 'single to married' or 'maiden to mother' fractures shards of us out into others while simultaneously asking us to grow and amalgamate. The identification of self also comes with transitions in loss: from loved to heartbroken, from married to divorced, married to widowed, fertile to infertile, employed to retired.

These transitions create a patchwork of new experiences, novelty, disappointment, experimentation and trauma. Often, we grow a thicker skin to protect what we have built as fact but, at some point in the middle years, these definitive truths no longer serve us. Their weight keeps us small and from being truly known by others as we grow. In this space, we have to unpick the versions of ourselves we have learnt, inherited or imagined over time. Finding yourself again, or creating a new identity, can look erratic, just like a teenager who ricochets between ideas. Maybe midlife is the acknowledgement of all the lives we had to say no to and a chance for nurturing reinvigorated energy to revisit the choices we cannot bear to never experience.

In the new emptiness of my house, I will catch glimpses of my pink hair and consider who I am now. There is still so much I want to do – big experiences that need to happen now rather than later because, if I have learnt one mistake, it is that we think we have time. I am still learning where I live within these four walls that used to contain four people. At times, I have lived purely on the well-trodden floor between kitchen counters and on the floor in the dark of a child's bedroom. I am trying to take up more space and live in this moment with eyes wide open. At forty-three, I might not be sure of exactly who I am yet, but I know for sure I am alive in the most ferocious way, electric yet broken with a mop of bubblegum hair.

Growth

Putting your own oxygen mask on

In February 2020, I gave myself the fortieth birthday gift of a solo trip to New York. Even though it was a special birthday, on paper this was certainly not the best time for a solo jaunt across the world to live out my bucket list. My four days away would coincide with the wait for Greg's latest scan results, but the unspoken truth was there was no other time *to* go. There would never be another time in the future where I could choose myself in this way when Greg wasn't here or when he became more ill in the future.

I felt guilt in every moment leading up to my holiday. I felt shame around choosing a solo trip instead of taking the girls away, for leaving Greg alone knowing he would never travel again, for putting pressure on both sets of grandparents to help with the day-to-day mechanics of our lives. I questioned myself in every moment until I stepped into the airport and felt a sense of myself that I hadn't experienced for years. I walked around Central Park in the winter's ice-blue light. I sat in cocktail bars, playing up my English accent to become the quintessential charming character Americans love. I trawled vintage stores and dawdled around art galleries, pleasing no one except myself.

I thought the trip was to tick a box on my bucket list in the tiny window I had available when, in fact, I needed to travel across the world just to exhale. The deep work of being a carer and mother in the trenches needs more than a long bath and a scented candle.

What does caring for yourself actually look like? We are told that to care for yourself, to actively choose you over others is selfish. Selflessness is the gold standard in parenting, especially as a mother. We have found a way to spin an alternative narrative in the self-care movement for women: 'You need to put your own oxygen mask on first in order to be able to help others', as if this isn't still laden with the same tired rhetoric – we can only consider our own needs when they are linked with giving back to everyone around us.

In the last few hours of my trip, I had wanted to visit the 9/11 museum but decided against it. I couldn't bear hearing the voice recordings of the passengers who knew they were about to die, especially as I was about to fly home alone. On the flight, I thought if the oxygen masks were to fall down, I would only have to look after myself and, as soon as I set foot in my house, the tables would turn and everyone else would become the priority again. I didn't want to show my daughters what it looks like to abandon yourself, not even for those you love most in the world. I wanted to show them I could choose myself AND Greg AND them. It *has* to be 'and', not 'or', because it is the women and the mothers who slowly fade into the background of their own lives.

As we touched down on the tarmac, I heard the news of a serious airborne virus in China. I'd had no idea how close I was to the gates closing on the rest of the world and in my own house.

Inspiration porn

'You are so strong.' 'You are an inspiration.' 'I don't know how you do it.'

In the worst time of my life, I began to receive compliments worthy of war heroes. I was falling apart in every way possible and losing my mind but just getting up in the morning gained a standing ovation. I realised I was going to need to fall apart very quietly on my own. I would need to create a new world of madness to break in because everyone needed me to be OK.

People love a happy ending – I know I do. We love a hero's journey, when good triumphs evil and true love wins. People are so afraid of the opposite, they will hold your nose and force you to drink the lemonade they've made from the lemons life has handed you.

I am not happy or grateful to have lived through the death of my husband. I didn't choose this life but it chose me. There is a crossover space of accepting the hand you've been dealt but also asking for the shuffle. What hard-won strength I have is more about my own desire to heal and not be engulfed by the shadows looking in from the sidelines. 'Making lemonade from lemons' might seem like a straightforward route through a treacherous terrain but it lacks all the nuance such experiences force upon us. We are programmed to resist the darkness and immediately throw glitter into the gloom. I never wanted Greg's death to be a life lesson but I'm aware that it very much is. That said, I am very mindful of not becoming the teacher of the hard life lessons in any conversation. No one wants to be *that* person but, so often, we need battle scars to provide visceral proof of our strength.

Women seem to be revered as strong when they have been

through trauma, but only in specific situations. If we find ourselves in roles we fear – caring for a disabled child or a terminally ill spouse, carrying on after a stillborn baby – we become an inspiration to others. This level of piety seems to only be available in relation to caring roles; the same cannot always be said for women whose strength comes in the form of asking for a pay rise, leaving their marriage, distancing themselves from toxic family members or reporting unwanted behaviour. It's also not extended to the daily grind of caring for children or domestic duties while working or the care of elderly parents; to spin those particular plates is considered just being a woman.

Strength in women is revered when in correlation with suffering but in the prevention of this happening in the first place, we are often seen as demanding, aggressive or troubled. In the situations where we have no choice in our circumstance, we are allowed to be bestowed with the crown of heroine but where there is any choice, we are branded as selfish and self-centred. The mother raising her disabled son is seen as an inspiration while the wife leaving her marriage of twenty years because it doesn't bring her joy anymore is deluded and having a breakdown.

In those situations, devoid of choice but rich in suffering, barely surviving is still classified as strength where the only other option is self-annihilation. My friend Ellie once spoke to me of the death of her daughter Matilda during birth and how she was constantly branded as strong in every situation, despite her ongoing breakdown. 'I wanted to shout at everyone, "My baby died and I didn't kill myself." Is that the only thing I could have done that would prove how I'm falling apart?' she told me. Measuring strength in ourselves and in others is subjective and seen differently through multiple lenses. Much like pain thresholds or how the colour red is experienced, we can't know the experience or capabilities of other people.

In circumstances where strength alleviates the burden of emotional labour from others, especially men, it is welcomed. This is particularly the case in managing pain, grief and big feelings that don't impose or ask anything of others. If our strength makes demands, it becomes an inconvenience that is unwelcome. Male perspectives of strength in women may focus on stoic behaviour, being less emotional and not crying, but we are expected to deal with and assimilate pain, whether emotional, mental or physical, more efficiently than them.

The phrase 'they never complained' is pinned on the lapels of those who stay quiet as a badge of dignity, as though not acknowledging pain or being dealt a shit hand in life is somehow more honourable. We love this imagery of the martyr, who takes everything life has to throw at her on the chin while doing it with grace and in silence. It allows others to sit back and avoid the emotions it brings up in themselves. Bizarrely, the phrase is often used for those who are either incredibly ill or dead. We applaud the cancer patients running marathons attached to chemo pumps while thinking those who want to stay home and watch reruns of *Sex in the City* during treatment should find a way to be a bit more positive.

Our obsession with strength and resilience seems personal but whose end does it actually benefit? It supports capitalism because we go back to work after three days of compassionate leave when someone we can't live without dies. Our strength suits the patriarchy because we go back to taking care of our homes, children and elderly. It certainly doesn't benefit us or our own healing; much like breaking your ankle and powering through instead of rest and recuperation, the bone will set in an odd angle and the pain will jar with every step you walk for the rest of your life. It is a false economy to carry on regardless. It is essential for us to ask of ourselves: what will I need to sacrifice of myself to meet this expectation and am I willing to do this?

I am strong, I know that, but I am also brittle, ready to break at the hint of any more bad news. I am not a superwoman. I cannot do everything and be everything for all people. To live through grief, to try to rebuild a life with no blueprint and with bills to pay means I will drop a lot of balls. My most pressing job is to recognise on any given day which are made of glass and will shatter if I drop them, and which are made from rubber and will bounce. All the while, I sit in the hurricane and wonder how to become a fully embodied version of myself after compartmentalising elements for so long? I want ease, delight, safety. I am so desperate to not have to be strong and to be looked after. I want to be soft like ice cream and melt.

A gift from Death

One of the most important conversations of my whole life happened within the first hour of meeting a new person for the first time.

Greg had a friend called Jilly, someone he had been to art school with as a teenager and who had disappeared into the ether of adult lives but appeared again when he became ill.

'I think you two would really get on,' Greg often suggested, as if he were playing matchmaker. On a day when Greg was sleeping off the chemotherapy pumping round his body, I met Jilly for a coffee on a blind date.

Greg had been correct – Jilly and I did get on. We had lots in common: the art scene in the city, our mutual friends, our own artistic practices and our love of textiles. Out of the blue, in between sips of coffee, Jilly asked me, 'What would you do if you had a million pounds?' I didn't think she meant it in the way we all like to mull over sometimes – I would probably buy 100 dogs and a vintage Christian Dior handbag – it was more about the concept. What if you didn't have to worry about bills, mortgage, childcare, pension – if you could do as you pleased every day, what would you be doing?

Immediately and from nowhere, I had a vision of myself, so clear it felt like a premonition. I was stood in a white shirt (have I ever even owned a white shirt?) next to a large wooden gate in the country. I was welcoming people arriving. I was in charge. I was the host. This was a community. I was a writer, hosting a writing retreat in the country.

This was a strange vision because I wasn't a writer and never had been. As a child, I had always wanted to be a writer but my dream was smashed to pieces by an English teacher, whose belief in me was so strong it boarded on grooming, and I used all my teenage defiance to kick back against him. At college, I had found all things photography and fashion, so dumped writing as a childhood idea. I stopped writing altogether until the day Greg was diagnosed, when I bought a notebook from the hospital shop to sit and write as if I were projectile vomiting.

It was there on the cold hard floors of the hospital corridors that Death gave me a gift, one I tried so hard to give back because I didn't want it. Death gave me the gift of seeing what was coming for me; not just the death of those I love but my own mortality. Like Ebenezer Scrooge after the night-time tour of his life, I woke up in the morning, alive and well, with a clear idea of what I still had, what I had to lose and what is important. I wanted to ingest all things like a hungry child.

Contrary to popular belief, living each day like it's your last is exhausting and often becomes meaningless when all your 'last days' pile up on top of each other. What doesn't kill you can make you weaker and break you down to a shadow of your former self, more frightened and paranoid, yet, at the same time, it can propel you into a supersonic, indestructible version of yourself. These two incarnations can exist at the same time and it is exhausting lurching between the two. I began to live in an emotional landscape full of colours and textures I'd never known, fear enhancing my ability to experience joy and elation in a way not available before. It became the night and day of what the human heart can experience – the terror and the sublime.

The headspace led me to question when we had learnt to drown out the voice of our own longing. Thinking back, I thought I should let Greg's career be the dominant lead in our lives as it was the most visible and prestigious. There is always compromise in relationships but I realised there were so many times I had given up what I had wanted, as if taking less and less is in direct correlation to how much we love someone.

From the moment Greg was diagnosed, there was never a moment of ease or normality again. All emotions were heightened, and my skin felt as though it had been peeled off to feel how terrifying life can be, how beautiful the sun is and to wonder why we aren't all bowing down to it as our own god, proclaiming we are already in heaven. In many ways, this left me craving so much less – I wanted to slow down and live more like I did as a kid, focusing on fun rather than productivity. I wanted to walk slower to think and absorb my surroundings with the curiosity of the beginner's mind. I didn't want to live with the manic panic of Armageddon; I longed for the slow awe, wonder and novelty of the first day on earth.

Why is there such deep personal growth in hard times? There is no bigger enemy to growth than certainty, so when there is chaos, boundaries become more fluid to open up new ways of thinking and feeling. Trauma leaves us hanging on for dear life to what we can know for sure. While the focus is elsewhere, our guard is lowered and what we've blocked out has the chance to bubble up and escape. With all the prisoners out of their cells, we can get a clearer lay of the land. Our thinking is streamlined and can hold multiple realities. Post-traumatic growth isn't an idealistic outcome though; the clue is in the name. Growth is painful and to get there through the gates of trauma isn't a free ticket to enlightenment. The residual memories still lie dormant.

All of this leaves me with the most complicated thought of

all – I wouldn't have done any of this if Greg hadn't become ill. That his demise was the fuel for me to set fire to the shrouds of doubt and imposter syndrome that had haunted me for years to become the most authentic version of myself. This was also true for Greg; the lifelong OCD he'd suffered from vanished overnight and he dumped his previous artistic style, moving on to what he had always wanted to do but felt he couldn't, trapped by what he thought others would think of him.

It is the ultimate case of holding multiple truths at once; I would have moved heaven and earth for Greg to not be ill or die, but in this space I found a part of myself I would never have witnessed. I'm not sure how to ever come to terms with that.

An unexpected place to find joy

When Dalí and Bay were very young, they were obsessed with dressing up in Disney princess costumes. As someone who had grown up being taught the societal implications of these characters, I was less than eager to indulge – a girl needing a prince to save her? No, girls, she saves HERSELF! I was convinced this was a perfect example of children being marketed to by capitalist wolves and wanted to resist these predetermined notions of what being a girl means. In between Belle and Elsa, I threw in Spider-Man and Batman to break the cycle and prove to *someone* that neither me nor my children would be kept down by gender stereotypes.

Pastimes associated with girls and women like chick-lit books and 'rom-com' films are often seen as lightweight and throwaway in nature; while the boys grow into men who still play hours of FIFA, girls are socialised to put the toys away because society is best served when women's attention is held elsewhere. A larger percentage of domestic and caring responsibilities means less available free time for fun or hobbies and what is left is encouraged to still be 'productive'.

My attempt to mix up the dressing-up box came from good intentions but I realised that by constantly diverting my daughters' attention away from what they were drawn to, I was teaching them not only were their interests not OK but they were false and not their own, just accidental attraction siphoned into their heads by brand executives. While there may be some truth to this, it is not the same messaging young boys receive. The trains, diggers, cars, spaceships and monsters marketed at them are believed to be their innate loves and passions.

Loving what you love will become even more important when my daughters enter their next decade. Teenage girls are given a short time frame to indulge their interests, often diluted as 'fluffy' or without substance whether that's fandom of a particular band or a love of horses. These are to be given up at a certain time to make way for adulthood but there are real consequences to not indulging your loves and interests.

What you love isn't necessarily what's at stake; it becomes an avatar for something else much deeper. An obsession reflects an eruption within ourselves looking for expression that has yet to materialise and can act as a conduit to realise feelings desperate to be felt. I wonder if this is what's at play when at the age of forty-two, I fall head over heels in love with K-Pop, specifically the band BTS.

One innocent morning, in the chaos of getting ready for school, Dalí said, 'Alexa, play the song "Butter" by BTS.' We danced along while shoehorning lunchboxes into bags and, on returning from the school run, I sat with a coffee and thought I would quickly look for the music video. It was here I fell down a rabbit hole and became absolutely obsessed.

Please know that when I say obsessed, I really do mean it in the truest sense of the word. Every moment of my days became filled with music videos, subtitled interviews and scouring the internet for new pictures. In those early days of discovery, the feeling was as close to love as it's possible to feel without a real person stood in front of you.

It was an abrupt turn. The CD collections and playlists of my life have always been full to the brim of dark, brooding, angry music from bands like the Cure, Smashing Pumpkins,

Bikini Kill and Sonic Youth. The sugary nature of K-Pop was confusing. To take the stance of an armchair psychologist, my fresh interest as a newly grieving woman made perfect sense. I had lost touch with what I wanted, felt or thought. I had no idea who I was anymore and no touchstone to start rebuilding from. I had become a gradual process of erosion, only existing as a living ghost who whispered memories in my own ears. I needed to focus on something totally different, something joyful, easy and as away from the shadows as possible.

The world of K-Pop was a perfect fit. Its music is simple and uncomplicated, using easy-to-digest chord structures used repeatedly across the genre that feel familiar and comfortable. Sparkly melodies that melt on your tongue were a novelty for me and the extreme opposite of anything Greg and I would reference. Most songs are sung in Korean, a language so inexorably different from English, it is impossible to understand most of what is going on, offering the chance to hide from the inevitable muse for most music – love and heartbreak. The bands are colourful and fun in a way modern Western groups have rarely been, playing with fashion, makeup and ideas of androgyny. Oh, and let's not forget the men in these bands are outrageously handsome. In fact, I cannot ignore the idea there is a sexual component to this – young, beautiful men living behind a screen become ultimate fantasy fodder for someone who is desperately starved of sex and emotion but terrified of what that looks like in the real world with a real man.

Maybe underneath the surface-level attraction of catchy songs and cool clothes was the more subconscious allure: I wanted to be a teenager again. I wanted to be in my bedroom listening to music, looking at the posters on my walls and fantasising about young men. When you are a teenager, there is a palpable feeling of being on the cusp of something great, that life is just beginning. I desperately wanted to feel that excitement again in a swamp of goodbyes and pain. I wanted something or someone *to think* about because I felt my life was over.

I'm unsure what to call this – an obsession? An outlet, fixation, fascination, preoccupation, addiction, passion, hobby, interest? The choice of words matters here as each of these comes laden with its own connotations and, crucially, their own affiliation with a gender bias. Any band adored by girls is often disregarded; female fans screaming at One Direction or even The Beatles have never been compared to air guitar or headbanging at Black Sabbath or Metallica. It's accepted that men will have their guitars, boxes of trainers with photos taped to the front, model trains and designated gaming rooms. I wonder what Virginia Woolf, who wrote a book all about the need for women to have space to grow in *A Room of One's Own*, would have thought about the modern 'man cave'. She would have questioned where the female equivalent was.

I didn't want to tell anyone what I was thinking about because forget dyeing my hair pink, this was *surely* grounds for a midlife crisis? I have a thirty-year-old Korean rapper called SUGA as my phone's wallpaper ('Why don't you have a picture of us on your phone like normal mums?' Bay asks one day. I smile a knowing smile and ignore the question). I didn't think it was appropriate to spend my time learning the choreography of BTS's music videos because if I could afford to spend time playing around, I most certainly had the time to mop floors and tick off more jobs on the endless to-do list. Play is not productive, except it absolutely is. It is needed to create vital energy to balance the monotonous slog of modern adult life. In play and enjoyment, we drop the roles and become our true selves, just as children do. There is a feeling of expansion. We have such little regard for daydreaming, reverie and just thinking in general, all seen as idle or that should instead be focused in ways that monetise our passions or assess them for productivity.

I believed this capitalist hype so wholeheartedly, I attempted to merge my preoccupation with BTS into just this – I wrote an article for a newspaper about them. This ticked a productive box in my head, but I wasn't prepared for the walls of the most unexpected place to find joy to expand even further. My now-public love of all things K-Pop and BTS drew the attention of others, in particular a renowned fashion editor. Jo Elvin had published an article on her love of the band on the same day and the internet sent our words back and forth like love letters through the ether. Immediately, we became daily pen pals and she soon introduced me to Sarah and Stef, two women also in love with the K-Pop bubble. This group of strangers living in different parts of the country began as sending funny memes but graduated to become deep connections. The K-Pop gang of me, Jo, Sarah and Stef was not one I could ever have anticipated; our daily chats are often funny, sometimes sad, but always fiercely supportive of each other. We talk every day about BTS together but have our own pockets of conversation; Jo is who I turn to for fashion advice and when I want to discuss something I hate because I know she will match my vitriol pound for pound. She is exceptionally funny and we send dog memes to each other all day, every day with no commentary. Sarah quickly became like a big sister, despite being five years younger than me. We talk endlessly about makeup, *RuPaul's Drag Race* and skincare. It is Sarah, who I have only met in person twice, who helps me understand my late ADHD diagnosis more than anyone. I have only met Stef in person once but our tight bond comes from our love of early eighties New Romantics. I go to her for career advice and her solid wisdom and life experiences.

Until knowing these women, I wouldn't have imagined I could make such real, solid connections through the internet. I also didn't realise you could love anything as much as you did as a teenager, as I found within the dopamine-heavy world of BTS and K-Pop. Building a new life can often feel like clothes shopping, trying things on for size to see how they fit. There is an undeniable excitement to this, in working out who you want to be next. I'm realising I can be an amalgamation of the new parts of myself and those I've not changed. I am still a daughter, a mother, a sister, a friend, a colleague. I am also a writer, an academic, a curator. But maybe most importantly of all, I am still silly and make stupid jokes, I still love Halloween, I can still create a perfect winged liquid eyeliner and will still beat anyone who dares to challenge me at Connect 4. I can dance in my bedroom to BTS with my girls and still listen to the Cure. I am still here underneath all this rubble.

How to be courageous

Long before Greg's diagnosis, I had very few experiences to test how courageous I was. In many ways, I had lived a life devoid of major crisis until one night, in the cold and barren flat Joe and I had shared in Nottingham, the entire metal fire escape staircase ripped itself from the building and collapsed while two men had climbed to the top. They had used the stairs to knock on the window of their friends' fourth-floor flat, who hadn't heard them ring the doorbell. The structure was decaying and flimsy but, as it ripped its frame from the bricks, you would have thought a plane had hit the building. We looked out the window and down to the concrete below to see a huge pile of broken metal and two bodies in the wreckage.

Everyone from the building immediately arrived to help. As we ran outside, the first man was laid directly outside the back entrance, unconscious with blood pouring from his nose, a sign of bleeding from the brain. I froze. The world went quiet despite the crunch of metal being pulled apart and distant shouting ringing in my ears. Someone pushed me towards the other man lying upside down on concrete steps. He spoke normally and asked me a question.

'I can't feel my legs,' he said. 'Why can't I move?'

I squinted to focus but in the dark I couldn't differentiate between the different textures – metal, concrete, the ripped denim of his jeans, the blood gushing from his leg and the white bone jutting out as if one of the railings. I was blank and listless, floating above the scene where I watched myself in my pyjamas just stand and stare. People shouted instructions at me that danced in front of my eyes.

My reaction shocked me. I had always been empathic and

325

a good leader but, in this crisis, I was utterly useless. There were lots of other people around to help – *real* adults, not the adult life I was pretending to live in my small, cold flat with my boyfriend.

Now, I *am* the real adult, with small faces looking to me to know what to do as the stairs fall away beneath our feet. Now, everyone says, 'You're so brave' to me on repeat. I wonder if I can use these on my CV or a future dating profile.

This was not always the case. No one said I was courageous in the first few months of Greg's diagnosis. To meet me, you would have concluded I was a shipwreck lost at sea. I stopped eating entirely. It felt like a reasonable act of resistance for my body to take. I rattled around the hospital alone for hours, passing other ghosts in the corridors on their own hunger strikes. Sitting in the hospital café, I force-fed myself a bowl of mushroom soup only to vomit it straight back into the bowl, mortified as the table next to me of handsome male doctors sat watching. I couldn't sleep so I started taking sedatives washed down with wine. I could only fall asleep with my mum next to me, stroking my head as she did when I was a child.

There was so much bad news. It showered down on us in torrential assaults; every phone call, email, scan result, blood test led to worse news. During a face-to-face meeting with a consultant, the news was so terrifying, I ran from the room before he had finished speaking, his words following me like an axe. I fell on the floor of the waiting room, at the feet of bald patients all silently saying their own prayers. In that moment on the floor, I gave up fully. I was not brave enough for what I needed to do. A nurse picked me up from the floor as routinely as if tidying up after a party and took me into a side room.

'You will do this,' she told me as she wiped my tears from my cheeks, her face only a few inches away from mine. 'I know you don't want to and you are scared, but you will do this because you have to.'

I learnt strength and resilience because it grows from being broken down and getting back up again on repeat. They are hard-won medals, ones I'm not sure I would choose to win. I would be much happier with the consolation rosettes of ease and comfort. I don't *want* to be the person people reach out to in hard times. I would much rather be the one who you ask for a great restaurant recommendation. But here I am, having walked through hell and now back to tell the tale.

We will be called in our lives to do something we will feel is categorically impossible in every way and yet, somehow, we will do it because of love.

A room of one's own

I had been staring at the ceiling for hours, ruminating on ugly thoughts making sleep an impossibility. In the dim light of my childhood bedroom, I could still see the edges of the drawing pin stuck in the plaster, a reminder of my impulsive past and a late-night decision to paint my bedroom without removing anything, just adding a new colour on top of or around what was already there. Whenever I stayed at my parents' house, which I did with increasing frequency, I would always look at this marker of time stuck on the badly painted ceiling and take great solace from it. Everything changes – people will die, others are born but, twenty years later, the drawing pin and my childhood bedroom are always there, the world revolving around its stasis.

As a child and teenager, I used this space to think, daydream and plot. I would use my bedroom to concoct extensive storylines, played out by dance moves to Madonna and Paula Abdul. This role play felt real to me; just as dreams can feel so realistic, they are as valid as any experience when awake. The fizz of flying over rooftops or the excruciating shame of finding yourself naked in a school corridor are feelings filed away in the same spaces as those experienced with eyes open.

My bedroom at my own house had become a living nightmare. I stayed out except to perch on the end of the bed to chat to Greg in between his endless sleep or to creep in after lying on the floor of the girls' dark room for hours while they fell asleep. I would quietly slip under the covers to sleep like an apology, curled up on the edge of the bed where there would be no real rest in this airless cocoon, its purpose now to hold Greg in his recuperation and then his demise.

There was so much trauma seeping from the walls; not just from illness but even down to the art we chose to decorate the space with. Above our bed hung a kitsch religious tapestry in a gaudy gilt-gold frame, the memento of a day shopping for second-hand trinkets that ended in a serious car crash, years before we had children. I hadn't understood the severity of the situation in the moment, even when a crew of fire engines were needed to cut me from the wreckage. As I was pulled out on a stretcher to a sea of mobile phones filming the scene, my only concern was my new art. 'GET THE TAPESTRY! GET THE TAPESTRY!' I screamed at an unscathed Greg or any of the passers-by, too busy uploading their videos to YouTube. By the time A&E had inspected my spine for breakages, Greg and I were delirious and hysterical. My back wasn't broken, in fact I was just bruised and shaken, so we thought it would be hilarious to share a photo of the wreckage on Facebook, my car surrounded by police and its roof torn off by an industrial chainsaw. From the onslaught of terrified phone calls, it turned out you needed to be there and as jacked up on hysteria as we were to find the joke funny.

In my bedroom, I can take the tapestry down from the wall, much like how my mangled car would have been towed away and the street cleaned of smashed glass and gnarled metal. The traffic would start flowing again and the moment would be forgotten. In this room, the memories of illness not so easy to remove.

One of the most important jobs for me was to take back my bedroom. Its design is a poetic love letter to myself, using soft, overtly feminine colours and textures to cocoon me in gentle rest. I buy myself fresh flowers and candles. Everything I choose for the space is to drown in colour, texture and beauty. A rug as soft as rabbits is at the side of my bed, ready to catch my feet at dawn and whisper in the dark, 'See, the world is still a delight.' There are big mirrors to reflect the life I am creating. I want to see its growth in real time and from all angles. It becomes an altar to my own existence; the walls and shelves are full of fashion photographs from my favourite eras, illustrations by an ex-boyfriend, drawings by the girls, magazines from my time at art school, collages made by my best friend and Prince vinyl records.

I need to peel back the layers of the recent years. They have protected me so well through the years of enduring pain, but their use is becoming redundant and I worry if I keep them as my armour, my exterior will become hardened and brittle. I don't need to dress as if I am ready for war anymore. I needed to mine the depths of myself to find the softness, curiosity and joy of this girl; not to hide in her or revert back to being a child but to tap into her reserves of energy and optimism.

In adulthood, we have so few spaces to explore who we were, who we are now and who we would like to become. There may be glimpses, small pockets of time or space to ringfence a thought – a scrawled observation in the corner of a notebook while the kids eat breakfast, a coffee break with a colleague or, if we are lucky, fifty minutes in a therapist's office.

This new space is for rest; not just sleep but gentle rest that feels so foreign to us – reading, listening to music, daydreaming, meditating and snoozing in the afternoon. It is also for playing, something we were encouraged to give up long ago; writing, drawing, playing games, makeup experimentation, dressing up, masturbation, dancing.

This is a space to find myself again, to go back to the

beginning of me. Death took parts of me along with Greg; my innate innocence and naïveté at the world are elements no amount of rest can replace, but I need to find the girl underneath those stolen facets. The girl who read *The Secret Garden* into the night, who wrote stories in her bed. So now I dance again and take up space in this room. The girls and I dance to songs of the past and the present in a playlist of my whole life. This is my resting place, a term for the dead, but here, I am alive. And it's here in the place where I am coming alive again that is the place where Greg rests, his ashes under my bed. Life and death, all in one design.

Epilogue:
Waiting for the Flowers to Bloom

We made the decision to leave the festival at 12.30 a.m., straight after the fireworks of the previous night. Torrential rain had been forecast and we would be stuck in a muddy field with 40,000 other people trying to leave on a single-track country road if we waited until morning. The heavens opened earlier than expected as we carried the last of our bags to the car. The girls whooped in delight with their friends, running in a pack with camping chairs under arms and hair slicked down to their faces. The silent camera in my head took a snapshot of this moment. Do you remember when we got soaked running to the car, with our best friends next to us and fireworks exploding above our heads? Is this what people mean when they talk of 'making memories'?

On the early-morning drive home, Dalí and Bay are cocooned in the back seat with a nest of pillows and duvets.

I could see their sleeping faces in the rear-view mirror, a sight that fills me with a level of contentment I have rarely felt in recent times. I vividly remember that feeling of exhaustion as a child – staying out late with your parents so a makeshift bed is made on a sofa with a coat as a blanket so the adults could carry on their night. I can still feel the drowsy walk to the car, the gentle hum of the engine lulling you back to sleep and the flashes of lights behind your eyelids on the drive home. Now, I am the adult. I am the parent driving us home and will be the one to gently remove their seatbelts and carry them into bed.

'Are we home?' Dalí asks drowsily as the car pulls up on the drive. 'I just want to go to bed.'

'Yes, we're home now,' I whisper as I gently remove Bay from her den of blankets and carry her limp body out of the car and into the warm glow of our house.

It's too late for teeth brushing or even getting into pyjamas. There are only soft sheets, a cool pillow and the joy of your own bed to think about. I remember that feeling too, when there is nothing left to do except let yourself drift into a delicious sleep.

I hope this is what dying feels like: a happy exhaustion after a lovely day, where you are taken home and tucked into your bed with clean sheets and no alarm clock, knowing you can now just rest.

It is now two years since Greg died and I'm sat alone in my garden, drinking coffee and thinking about the idea of soulmates. When I have told others I don't think they exist in a romantic sense, I am often met with the conclusion I must be clinical or unromantic when, in fact, I feel my romantic nature is the driving force in all I do. My life and how I've lived has always revolved around the idea of connection, of that spark and heartbeat around other people. I have been in love with different people, some of them delightful, some not so much in retrospect, but I take those individual loves forward with me, each one bringing different colours and textures to my life. There is one common denominator in all these relationships – the love I have felt was produced by me. Much like cancer is not a foreign body that infiltrates you like a virus; it is a part of you that morphs into something else.

Before I die, I want to be able to think back to all of the love I have given and received in my life, in all its different guises, and witness it all laid out in front of me like an exquisite bakery. Not just the romantic love but that between me and my family, my friends, my work colleagues, my dog.

When I had children, I met soulmates of a different kind, ones made from the deep connection between myself and Greg. These girls showed me love isn't finite, the heart is a muscle that wants to expand. In having multiple children, your ability to love hard and deep just magnifies; it doesn't need to be divided up and shared out when it is in abundance. Love can be battered and destroyed by our fallible human ways but, as a source, its indestructible energy is bigger than any of us can imagine.

But what of romantic love, the love of 'The One'? Does it become more special to be *chosen* as that person's soulmate? The person I chose and who chose me died but his love is still here, as is mine for him. I can also sense the feeling of love waiting for me in the future, an abstract sensation similar to the first colder breeze on a September morning to let you know autumn is on its way.

I have not had to let go of Greg because he died; in fact, I'm letting him in, just as I did when we met on that summer evening on the harbour, him wearing his lobster T-shirt and drinking tea. I let him, his love and our memories into me, deep into my cells and bones, mixing our essences together like a teenage blood pact. I could give Greg's things away, I could fall in love with multiple people, I could age another forty years and he will always be here because I have been changed irrevocably by his love and my time next to him.

This is why love and grief are ultimately the same, just opposite sides of the same coin. They are both so personal and unknowable and have a singular fingerprint. One hundred people could grieve the same person but each experience would be utterly unique. We will all need to understand and accept grief doesn't have one set path because if we are lucky and live a long life, we will grieve many different people we love. Each individual grief will expand and change with each new loss, as our hearts do with each new love.

To reflect on my relationship with Greg is akin to sailing across an ocean where I will encounter all weather fronts. There were times I could only describe as magical and transcendent but there were also the bleakest, darkest clouds that left me afraid of drowning. Like most couples, we didn't have a perfect relationship, far from it. Sometimes we had no idea how to reach each other when life fell off the tracks, when the sleep deprivation of becoming parents left us jangled or when illness and death forced a wedge between us, leaving us as strangers facing away from each other.

I have come to understand that love is a tricky beast; we think of it as pink bubbles fizzing from our hearts but we miss the rich texture of its form by skipping past its vastness.

336

To plumb those depths sometimes feels impossible – to keep eye contact and not look away when our lives are at their hardest – but real love means stepping forward to say, 'I'm choosing you again today, even though it's hard, I am here' in the dirt behind the Valentines cards. It's in this dirt that, over time, the flowers will bloom.

During Greg's final days, I asked him for some advice, any words of wisdom on life from the edge of the cliff where he held on by his fingertips and I stood above, waiting to watch him fall. I asked him the most obvious yet impossible question.

'What am I going to do without you?' I quietly asked, sat next to the hospice bed with my head lying on his legs, our fingers intertwined.

A pause.

'You'll be OK,' he whispered back.

At the time, his answer was frustrating in its simplicity when I craved some transcendent epiphany. But since Greg's death, I've pondered this advice many times and have come to understand I didn't need him to tell me what to do because the answers were always going to be inside me and had been there all along, sat patiently alongside all the different versions of myself, waiting to be asked the question. Their reply was the same as Greg's: I will be OK.

I will choose being OK because there is a life to live. There will also be times where being OK isn't even a choice on the table and I will be back on the floor. There will be so many more plot twists, newer ways for life to surprise me. Whether it's with a skip in our step or we are dragging our feet, we will need to move in the only direction available to us – onwards.

Acknowledgements

Thank you

To my agent, Carly Cook – for your support, truth telling and hardcore nature from the very beginning. Thank fuck you stalked me; you could obviously smell one of your own.

To my editor, Ciara Lloyd – for your long-term belief in my work, your nonchalance at my five-minute rambling voice notes and the space you've given me to find my own way with this book.

To all at Bonnier and Lagom – thank you for your energy and support.

To the Heale family – Madge, P Heale and Rich – to say I wouldn't have survived without your endless love and care is an understatement. You are literally everything.

To the Gilbert family – for demonstrating love again and again.

To the Cosmics – Chloe Adams, Clayton Burke, Jas Crockett, Maria Dimech, Florence Harvey and Emma Richardson – for your never-ending cheerleading, loud encouragement to always grow and the space to talk about the hardest, weirdest stuff with no shame or judgement. Thank fuck for us. As we always say, we are a lucky bunch. A particularly loud shout-out to CB, whose BFF energy and encouragement to live a big life blows my mind.

To Beth Ramshaw and Anna Driver – for being there since the beginning of time and keeping me in check.

To the conversations with my wise council of women whose words have shaped my own: Donna Lancaster, Clover Stroud, Caro Giles, Penny Wincer, Lotte Bowser, Stacey Duguid, Tanya Lynch at Ease Retreats, Sarah Standing, Nicola Washington and Holly Matthews.

To my K-gang – Jo Elvin, Sarah Siddell, Stef Jarman – for your daily support and showing me how deep friendship can grow in the most unusual places. But obviously, thank you more for the constant flow of imagery and TikTok videos.

To Josie Hughes – for appearing out of thin air and becoming my angel. I could not have walked through hell without you.

To Rachel Bown and Louise Blythe – for the endless chinwags about life and death.

ACKNOWLEDGEMENTS

To Jennifer Anyan – for many things but particularly the camaraderie in motherhood.
To Brendan Lea – for being the literary robot I so often need.

To Dana Miller – for the transatlantic conversations on what it is to be a woman but most importantly, all the glitter.

To Anna Lyons – for the talks on the edge of the cliff while wearing huge sunglasses.

To Eliza Tucker and Laura Flowers – for the hours (and hours and hours) of listening.

To Dalí and Bay Gilbert – for being my most important teachers. Just your existence in the world makes me glow.

To Greg Gilbert – for pushing me into creativity and walking the walk up ahead. I can hear your words ringing in my ears every day. I'll whisper a thank you to you forever. See you in the stars.